Underworld Gods in Anci
Greek Religion

This volume presents a case for how and why people in archaic and classical Greece worshipped Underworld gods.

These gods are often portrayed as malevolent and transgressive, giving an impression that ancient worshippers derived little or no benefit from developing ongoing relationships with them. In this book, the first book-length study that focuses on Underworld gods as an integral part of the religious landscape of the period, Mackin Roberts challenges this view and shows that Underworld gods are, in many cases, approached and 'befriended' in the same way as any other kind of god.

Underworld Gods in Ancient Greek Religion provides a fascinating insight into the worship of these deities, and will be of interest to anyone working on ancient Greek religion and cult.

Ellie Mackin Roberts is a Research Associate at the Institute of Classical Studies (School of Advanced Studies, University of London). Her PhD was awarded from King's College London, and she has also previously taught at the University of Leicester and Royal Holloway, University of London.

Routledge Monographs in Classical Studies

Titles include:

Homicide in the Attic Orators
Rhetoric, Ideology, and Context
Christine Plastow

Underworld Gods in Ancient Greek Religion
Ellie Mackin Roberts

Bride of Hades to Bride of Christ
The Virgin and the Otherwordly Bridegroom in Ancient Greece and Early
Christian Rome
Abbe Walker

Intertextuality in Seneca's Philosophical Writings
Edited by Myrto Garani, Andreas Michalopoulos, Sophia Papaioannou

Drama, Oratory and Thucydides in Fifth-Century Athens
Teaching Imperial Lessons
Sophie Mills

The Poetics in its Aristotelian Context
Edited by Pierre Destrée, Malcolm Heath and Dana L. Munteanu

Text and Intertext in Greek Epic and Drama
Essays in Honor of Margalit Finkelberg
Edited by Jonathan J. Price and Rachel Zelnick-Abramovitz

Frankness, Greek Culture, and the Roman Empire
Dana Fields

For more information on this series, visit: https://www.routledge.com/classicalstudies/
series/RMCS

Underworld Gods in Ancient Greek Religion

Death and Reciprocity

Ellie Mackin Roberts

Routledge
Taylor & Francis Group

LONDON AND NEW YORK

First published 2020 by Routledge

2 Park Square, Milton Park, Abingdon, Oxon OX14 4RN
605 Third Avenue, New York, NY 10017

Routledge is an imprint of the Taylor & Francis Group, an informa business

First issued in paperback 2022

Publisher's Note

The publisher has gone to great lengths to ensure the quality of this reprint but points out that some imperfections in the original copies may be apparent.

British Library Cataloguing-in-Publication Data
A catalogue record for this book is available from the British Library

Library of Congress Cataloging-in-Publication Data
Title: Underworld gods in ancient Greek religion : death and reciprocity / Ellie Mackin Roberts.
Description: Abingdon, Oxon ; New York, NY : Routledge, 2020. |
Series: Routledge monographs classical studies | Includes bibliographical references and index.
Identifiers: LCCN 2019046909 | ISBN 9781138574588 (hardcover) |
ISBN 9781351273725 (ebook)
Subjects: LCSH: Greece–Religion. | Death–Religious aspects. | Mythology, Greek. | Gods, Greek.
Classification: LCC BL795.D4 M33 2020 | DDC 292.2/11–dc23
LC record available at https://lccn.loc.gov/2019046909

ISBN: 978-1-138-57458-8 (hbk)
ISBN: 978-1-03-233688-6 (pbk)
DOI: 10.4324/9781351273725

Typeset in Times New Roman
by Swales & Willis, Exeter, Devon, UK

For Ainsley

Contents

Figures

Thanks

Hugh Bowden, Andrew J Roberts, Merryn and Lindsay Brown, Ainsley Mackin, Jessica Brown, Tomasz Rustowski, Sofia Rustowski, and Catherine Rustowski.

Emma Bridges, Becky Littlechilds, Viv McGlashan, Lucy Shipley, Liz Gloyn, Mary Harlow, Andy Merills, Emma Stafford, Chris Carey, Esther Eidinow, Greg Woolf, Aimee Hinds, Jack Lennon, Neville Morely, Katherine McDonald, Kate Cook, Emma Cole, Muneera.

Kylie Radford, Laura Wood, Robin Taylor, Diane Verrochi, Hanna Silverblank, Jennifer Wells, Charlotte Matheison, Toph Marshall, Aidan Budd.

The bulk of this research was conducted at and funded by King's College London, and writing was finished while I was a research associate at the Institute of Classical Studies.

Preface

Before I get into this study about Underworld gods, we should perhaps try to pin down what the Underworld itself actually *is*. This is a tricky question because, like many questions, it entirely depends who, and when, you ask. At the most basic level, the Underworld is a place where the dead and the gods who look after them live. No, not live, but *reside*, because, of course, none of them really live in the way that mortal people live. The dead are, well, dead and the gods are, by their very nature, deathless. Mortal people cannot reside in the Underworld unless they have died, but they can gain access to the Underworld on special occasions. Let me explain …

You are in a small sanctuary, near the banks of the river Acheron, in the Western Peloponnese. A priest comes to fetch you. 'It is time', he says, leading you through the darkness. Stop. Breathe in deeply. What can you smell? The fertile soil, wet and black. The moss that covers the stone temple. You think you can just hear the river, gurgling away in the background – leading the souls of the dead down, down, down into the Underworld. That is why you are here.

As you enter the temple, feel your body getting heavier. Relax your head, and neck, relax your shoulders. Feel a fog of tiredness wash over your mind.

You are about to commune with the dead.

You do not know how long you will spend living in the darkness of the temple, but you know it will be at least a week. You enter a long corridor. On your left, three arched doorways lead to the three small rooms you will live in. Here, in the impenetrable darkness, you will prepare. You find your first meal in the room through the first arched doorway. Pork, broad beans, barley bread, shellfish. These are the foods of funerary banquets. You lift a cup to your lips – expecting wine, you start back as the sweetness of honeyed milk fills your mouth. This is a banquet for the dead – and you begin to realise the seriousness of where you are and what you are doing. You are putting yourself in a state between the worlds.

Days pass. You don't know how many. You are disoriented. The mild toxicity of the broad beans begins to affect you. Slowly at first, but then one night – or day, you don't know which, it's all night right now – you feel your brother's strong arms around you, in a cold, dead embrace. You start to believe that you have died, and you are at your own funeral. The banquet truly is yours.

Breathe in, deeply. Smell the dank, wet stone. Smell your own sweat and tears and mud and excrement.

A man enters? Is it the priest? He brings a sheep, presses some smooth stones into your hands. He guides you down a deep passage that seems to never end. He tells you to throw one of the stones in a pile and then takes you into a room to wash your hands.

You take the sheep. The man tells you to dig a hole and hands you a knife. You are disoriented, but suddenly you snap back as the sharp metallic scent of blood fills you. You have slaughtered the sheep. Your hands are covered in blood and as you cut the sheep up the smell of half-digested sludge and offal overwhelms you. Now there is smoke, you don't remember setting the fire – it must have been the priest. In this small passageway, the smell and the smoke and the bile in the back of your throat have nowhere to go. They linger, settling on you, surrounding you, obscuring the way out and the way forward.

The man pulls you to your feet and directs you into a winding, twisting series of passages. You turn the wrong way and hit a wall. You stop and weep.

Breathe in. What can you smell, in the darkness? The metallic taste of blood clings to your hands. The smoke is still billowing up behind you. Your own panic begins to rise in your throat. You hear someone – or something – coming up behind you. You move on.

Finally, you enter a great hall, the air is clearer in here. Before you enter, you remember – somehow – to throw the barley in your hand onto the ground. You throw the final stone into the room and tentatively walk in.

As you sink to your knees, a figure appears in front of you. You can't quite see it properly. You blink, hard, several times. The figure moves towards you. Who is it? You can't tell. You try to speak – but the words don't quite come out the way you imagine. Your brain spins. You breathe in. Blood. Smoke. Sweat. Shit.

Whispers in the dark that you cannot make out. The figure moves, shifts, swaps, slowly levitates. A different figure comes out. You are disoriented.

You think you ask the questions you came to ask. You think you get an answer. You're not really sure. You fall into some kind of black oblivion.

Some time later, a man – the priest – enters the room and helps you up. He asks if you got the answers you wanted. Confidently, you say yes – and that feels like it's true. In your sleep you had a vision of the future and you know what you must do.

The priest helps you out through a different door and leads you to a room – bright, clean – and lays you on a bed. He helps you wash, gives you clean clothes. He lays you down and tells you that you're back from the other side. You must stay here to cleanse that miasma of the dead away from your skin.

Breathe in. Sweet, bright flowers. You hear the river in the background, gurgling the dead into the Underworld ...

A note about periodisation

Throughout this book I use the terms 'archaic' and 'classical' period to discuss broad-stroke themes that roughly apply to the period(s) I am looking at – which roughly equate to 800(ish) to 500(ish) BCE. The names we use to discuss the 'periods' of the ancient world are art historical terms that describe innovations in, predominantly, sculpture (cf. Waugh 2012: 18). I use these terms for ease, to discuss broad time-frames, and not because I think they represent periods of great difference. Arguably there is more similarity between the 'late archaic period' and the 'early classical period', than between the 'early' and the 'late' classical period(s). I have not set myself a firm chronology here, though I do not move beyond the 4th century BCE.

1 The religious landscape of archaic and classical Greece[1]

Jan Bremmer opened his 1994 study *Greek Religion* by posing the question 'was there ever such a thing as Greek religion?'[2] He does not commit to proving an answer, but sixteen years later, Emily Kearns goes some way when she comments that '[al]though we may speak of a Greek religious system, it is a system which is never consciously defined as such (at least until the end of pagan antiquity), and remained extraordinarily fluid and inclusive'.[3] But, before all this, in a 1985 essay titled 'On Making Sense of Greek Religion', John Gould noted that:

> To talk meaningfully about the religion of another culture is not easy and requires of us some degree of tact and imagination. We need to be aware of the pitfalls. To begin with, it will seem all too clear that what we are dealing with is a human intervention, a 'fiction' constructed by men [sic] for their own purposes – an interpretation which we can never quite give to the religion of our own culture, even if we have rejected it. To make that assumption will not help us to understand though it may boost our sense of superiority. And secondly, there is the difficulty, if not the impossibility, of avoiding thinking about someone else's religion as a kind of exercise of 'decoding', in translating myth and ritual into a 'natural' language (our own, of course) in which these things can be made to yield their true sense, which may be hidden from those who carry out of the rituals and who recount the myths.[4]

The gods of ancient Greece may well be a fiction to us.[5] From cinema to books and graphic novels, from near fantasy worlds to attempts to realistically represent religion in the classical world, our prevailing view of the Greek (and Roman) gods is through the lens of fiction. Even much of our ancient evidence fits this category – drama and comedy, historiography and poetry. The Greek gods are, in many senses a fictionalised 'other'. Perhaps this is also because the idea of the 'real divinities' that we are predominantly familiar with from modern 'mainstream' religion do not exhibit the same kind of moral flexibility that we know of the Greek gods and their tales of transformation, rape, adultery, murder, and more.

Reading through this lens, it is easy to understand why the Underworld gods of the Greco-Roman worlds have been cast at the 'wrong' end of the good–evil dichotomy, especially in popular culture representations of them. This has, often, leaked into scholarship about these gods. After all, many of these gods are shifty and slippery and they are almost impossible to define as a coherent group. So, the question then is: who counts? Hades and Persephone, yes obviously. Demeter and Hermes? Hekate? The Erinyes and Moirai? All these divinities will be addressed in this book in varying ways. In this opening chapter I will put these gods into some kind of context, looking at the religious landscape generally, and presenting thoughts on the 'chthonic', a term I do not frequently use in this book, but which demands addressing early on. Finally, I will present some methodological considerations.

In the last few decades, scholars of Greek religion have recognised that referring to a religious system with a single 'creed', or even with a minimally consistent set of beliefs, is erroneous. It has become customary to approach religion with more caution, with an attempt to understand what makes different religious experiences unique from one another. By and large, 'uniqueness' can be delineated by place, person, and space. That is, variation from sanctuary to sanctuary or *polis* to *polis*, and differences in experience based on personal circumstance: a wealthy citizen male, an enslaved person, a farmer, a youth, a woman, a priest, and so forth.[6] Space is perhaps more difficult to define, because 'space' is also dependant on things we cannot measure, like personal expectations and experiences, atmosphere, and sensorial expressiveness. A *place* can be a ritual space at one point in time and a mundane space at another. And thus, we run into the sacred–profane nexus.

Despite this recognition of the place of individuality in the religious landscape, we still must talk about the ubiquitous influence of Homer and Hesiod and their effect on an increasing systematisation of religious practices throughout the Greek world. This is enhanced by the generalisations of travelling scholars, such as Herodotos,[7] who himself alludes to the 'connectedness' of the 'Hellenes'. In this oft-cited passage, the historiographer records the indignant response the Athenians make to a Spartan suggestion they would desert the Greek collective and make an alliance with the Persians, following Alexander I of Macedon's advice. Herodotos's Athenians say:

> αὖτις δὲ τὸ Ἑλληνικὸν ἐὸν ὅμαιμόν τε καὶ ὁμόγλωσσον καὶ θεῶν ἰδρύματά τε κοινὰ καὶ θυσίαι ἤθεά τε ὁμότροπα, τῶν προδότας γενέσθαι Ἀθηναίους οὐκ ἂν εὖ ἔχοι.

> and next the kinship of all Greeks with common blood and speech, and shared sanctuaries and sacrifices, and similar customs to all of which it would not become the Athenians to be false.[8]

Although Herodotos mentions ὅμαιμόν (common blood), ὁμόγλωσσον (common language), θεῶν ἰδρύματά τε κοινὰ καὶ θυσίαι (shared sanctuaries and sacrifices), and ἤθεά τε ὁμότροπα (similar customs), this phrasing refers to the context of a specific military alliance. It is not a philosophical espousal of what it meant 'to be Greek'. Jonathan Hall has argued that the rarity of statements of 'shared Greekness' in the extant literature shows that 'ultimately, [the Athenian's] primary concern is with avenging their sacked temples, suggesting that the Athenian community of cult outranked any broader Hellenic affiliation'.[9] He suggests it is simply not Herodotos's style to explicitly point something out that would otherwise have been obvious to his audience. What we have here, then, is not an appeal to the panhellenic nature of religion, and we know that religious practice between *poleis* varied significantly when we start looking at local context. This is not to say, of course, that there was no coherence between *poleis* at all. An Athenian would recognise Zeus at Olympia, as an Elian would recognise Athena in Athens. There are many ritual types that transcend political boundaries, broadly including some of the most common ritual activities like sacrifice and *epiclesis* ('calling down' or invocation).

It is also worth noting here that the term 'panhellenic' was, as Michael Scott says,

> imposed on the Greek world by its Roman masters in order to assert the unity of the province through a focus on its common ancestry and historical kinship, rather than a term often used by the Greeks themselves to describe their unity.[10]

I have a certain uneasiness about the broad strokes that 'panhellenic' connotes and tend to use the term 'universal' to denote something that is relatively understood by or common to Greek speakers and their associated allies.

Universalism is forged though by the wholesale adoption and adaptation of local divinities – who may or may not have shared a name in the first place – who then become intercultural and interstate and who have aspects that can be understood as 'commonly Greek'. This, in large part, occurs when individuals, who are members of variously sized *polis* and non-*polis* related religious communities, encounter one another and exchange ideas. It does not follow that these universally recognised traits were utilised in religious practices in any other parts of the Greek world, and localised variations of each divinity retained their own attributes, honours, and rituals within their local contexts. Local divine identities still made up most worship in the Greek-speaking world, and local variation still coloured gods who had been 'universalised'. The universal names given to these local identities – Athena, Zeus, Poseidon, and so forth – become a shorthand for simplifying a much more complex and nuanced system of worship. There are some areas of religious life where we can find a complete lack of regard for creating harmony in cultic practices from *polis* to *polis*. *Poleis*, for example, maintained their own ritual calendars without any form of coordination.

What we can deduce is that there are interlinking and overlapping aspects that become common to various independent but complementary 'religions', through an assortment of communities of various sizes – from one individual inscribing and burying a *katadesmos* to all the participants at the Olympic games – and which operated in both public and private spheres. In reality there was no overarching 'Greek religion'; there was local variant practices which influenced, and were influenced by, other local variant practices of the same of similar divinities, who became amalgamated over time.

Greek religion

All Herodotos's talk of 'shared sanctuaries and sacrifices' only serves to highlight that there is no Greek word for 'religion', which is nowadays a commonplace observation to make. But what Herodotos shows in this passage – and others – is that there were ideas about religious practices, and ideas about θεραπεία τῶν θεῶν (service to the gods).[11] On top of this there is a large and very specific vocabulary to articulate all different kinds of religious actions and ideas. The lack of one word for 'religion' does not mean that there was no concept of 'religion' or 'religious practice'. In fact, there is significant evidence that there was a strict religious system in place. More accurately, there is a series of independent, but overlapping, systems. It is not necessarily the acknowledgement of the complex and chaotic nature of the study of 'Greek religion' where one may fall, but the application (or lack thereof) of a frame of understanding that ensures we do not resort to the easy habit of generalisation. How, then, should we map local beliefs and religious structures without falling into the trap of reducing the local subtleties and variations to unexplained or unimportant points in the schema of general 'beliefs'? One of the ways scholars have attempted to do this is through the application of the *polis* religion model, initially formulated by Christiane Sourvinou-Inwood.[12] This theorises that all religion in the ancient Greek world was mediated through the *polis*, and this mediation operated in both directions – that is, from the *polis* up to the universal level and down through the smaller political municipalities, households, families, and (finally) to the individual. *Polis*-religion has been criticised because it inadequately describes personal and individual religion,[13] which is perhaps the integral component of building reciprocal relationships with the gods.

I do not want to suggest that there are no common elements in religious practices around the Greek-speaking world. There are structural similarities, with local variations that more or less conform to type, with some outlying exceptions. At least this is the picture that the relatively limited evidence suggests. Mythology is one aspect of religious life that does indeed appear to be relatively ubiquitous throughout the Greek-speaking world, and though myth may have limited direct influence on ritual, it would have had significant influence over the way that people think about the gods. This is where the influence of Homer, Hesiod, and other early poets comes to the fore. Myths can be told and retold, changed and manipulated, through song or in poetry or on the stage or on vases. There perhaps might become a stable version of a given myth in a local cult setting. But, as Robert Parker comments, 'the idea of an Attic priest or priestess recounting myths to the faithful is just as unfamiliar as the idea of their using books in the conduct of ritual'.[14] So, people have a stable idea of a local god's identity, but the background to that identity is not (usually) overtly referenced in religious practices. Added to this, different myths are told about the same god at different cult centres based on local context and needs. At Delos, the story of Apollo's birth is of prime importance, but at Delphi his victory over the Python and the appropriation of the site is more important. At the universal level, the Homeric *Hymn to Apollo* includes both events. And the events are not necessarily incongruous, but they place emphasis, and therefore importance, on different aspects of the myth. We must also account for Delians travelling to Delphi to consult the oracle or to participate in the Pythian Games. There they would find some other Apollo (that is, it is a recognisable Apollo, but not *their exact* Apollo), but with the same, or at least a very similar, mythic background to theirs. But this is, again, as always, not an argument that there is a shared, universal system in which these myths operate, merely that there is a system of overlapping and inter-compatible myths that is 'thinly compatible' (rather than any kind of thick or 'universal' compatibility),[15] which I discuss below.

A common assumption is that mythology works together with ritual to make a 'whole' in religious practice, which cannot be complete if one of these elements is removed. That is, as Lisbeth Christensen says: 'traditionally, religion is characterised as consisting of myths and rituals ... myth represents "the things said" and ritual represents "the things done"'.[16] But a lot of what constitutes religious practice is personal: 'things said' and 'things done' are concepts external to personal belief that, in and of themselves, have little or no meaning without meaning ascribed to them in the mind of an individual. In this way the same ritual activity can mean different things to each participant of that ritual, as the words of a hymn might be interpreted slightly differently. This is where the nexus of religious education, mythic knowledge, community engagement, and ritual worship collide to form 'individual belief', but this belief is not something we can map. Externally, rituals may appear meaningless without the attached aetiology, but the act of participating in the ritual activity is not meaningless. Rather, it is meaningful evidence for the forging of relationships between the mortal practitioners and the divine. Active participation is evidence for belief, in some individuals and in some religious frameworks. The idea of ascribing 'belief' to the Greeks seems at odds with current scholarship,[17] and there has been a tendency to study either myth or cult activity, or the interplay between the two without an examination of how these fit into actual beliefs of the ancient Greeks themselves. What follows is the notion that, as Parker comments, 'myths imply certain conceptions of the gods' capacities and attitudes, what we might be tempted to term "beliefs" about the gods, were "belief" not a term that has often been declared inapplicable to ritual-centre religions'.[18]

The difficulties in reconciling the gods of myth and the gods of cult have resulted in a recent tendency to overlook the role that the gods themselves played in ritual activity.[19] But it was precisely these gods who were the focus of ritual activity and, ultimately, of the religious life of the Greeks. As Albert Henrichs comments: 'from a Greek point of view, the gods not only existed prior to the rituals practised in their honour but were regarded as the ultimate *raison d'être* for these rituals'.[20] Giving the gods importance over ritual practice does one other thing: it makes a place for mythology in religious practice. This is not to say that myth and ritual have a mutually exclusive relationship. But thinking about mythology is important when looking at how and why people formed relationships with the gods, because this was one of the biggest avenues that allowed people to *know* the gods on a 'personal' level, which both facilitates and was facilitated by the physical act of worship. Gods also reflect their worshippers, and the society that produces them, and this is predominantly noticeable in physical and literary remnants of that culture. This is to say that the portrayal and understanding of gods includes an understanding of the changing concerns of those self-same divinities. Alongside this, both mythology and ritual give participants (or audiences) the opportunity to undergo experiences normally forbidden to them.[21] These often involve dangerous transitions, and where the ritual presents a symbolic version of the experience, myth can allow its protagonist to undergo the experience. Symbolic death and rebirth, for instance, occurs in several ritual types, including almost all initiatory rituals. But in myth *actual* death and rebirth can be described and experienced. When these experiences are enacted in a ritual setting, they become falsified, symbolic, and reversible, whereas these same experiences in myth are realistic, actual, and irreversible.[22] Theseus and Herakles could travel into the Underworld while still alive and return unharmed, whereas the initiates at Eleusis could only play at such a journey by wandering the sanctuary looking for Persephone in the dark (if, indeed, this is what they were – or thought they were – doing).

A complex system of gods, and people, and their relationships with one another requires an equally complex system of aetiological and explanatory material, both mythic and cultic. To this end, and perhaps paradoxically, my references herein to 'myth' shall not be complex or theoretical. While recognising that there is no knowable 'traditional' or 'original' version of a story I refer mainly to mythic narratives. That is, retellings of well-known stories which may or may not have some form of aetiological connection to ritual (though the majority of those which are discussed in the context of this book will be viewed as being at least somewhat aetiological in nature). Each individual myth which we have extant, in whatever form they may have come down to us, as Calame says, can 'only be read in the particular version in which it reaches its audience and it is also important to avoid setting "myths" up as new universals'.[23] What I am interested in is not the 'right' version of a myth or ritual, but the version that informed people's lives and religious practices and beliefs. This does not need to be a static idea in each person's mind; what is 'right' will be dependent also on context, as we shall see.

The same is true for the 'nature' of the gods, and for the way they are depicted in art. In many ways the gods who populate the friezes, pediments, statues, and other votives and small personal offerings, are the same as the gods who stride across the landscape in Homer and Hesiod. They are like people. Stronger, smarter, and faster than people, but enough like people to be familiar. And, superficially, they are familiar across the Greek-speaking world. They have enough consistent attributes and personalities, with the same set of iconographic indicators in visual culture to be nearly universally recognisable. From cult to cult images of the gods display the same semiotic vocabulary for their worshippers. Broadly, each god is depicted in roughly the same form over disparate places and media. By the inclusion of specific iconographic attributes, epithets, the description of recognised traits or simply using a common cult name, worshippers may have come to recognise their local god as an instantiation of a major universal god, or more likely that their (local) god was *the* version of that particular god who is worshipped elsewhere (or, indeed, else*when* or else*why* by the same individual or group) in different ways. There are some circumstances that naturally deviate from this. For instance, a god may appear in different representations as both aged and youthful, sometimes even within the same sanctuary. In the sanctuary at Kato Syme on Krete, for example, Hermes appears on terracotta *pinakes* as both a youth and an adult, as I discuss in Chapter 5. His double guise at this temple is significant in the context of his cultic role as a leader across liminal boundaries – that is, his ability to guide worshippers through metaphysical liminal crossings, which are, in Kato Syme as elsewhere, explicit age barriers. There are also specific cases in which a visual representation of a god deviates more significantly from the 'normal' anthropomorphised form: Zeus Meilichios, for instance, usually appears as a snake and embodies very few, or none, of the attributes normally associated with Zeus(es) under other epithets. Regardless of these few inconsistencies, it may be easy to conclude that the mostly consistent 'universal' representations of the gods colour local interpretations and, therefore, influence cult practice. This also does not consider personal relationships with the gods, where an individual might still recognise an outlier like Zeus Melichios as related to *their* Zeus, which is something personal and special.

Even as different local areas are influenced by new or different versions or retellings of myths and iconographical representations of the individual gods, there is still not a single universal identity of each god. The connection between 'mythic' gods (those found in literature, material evidence, and oral culture) and 'cultic' gods (with whom local people maintain personal relationships and who are greater in number and variation than those commonly found in myth) would not necessarily be the first connection which came into the minds of the ancient Greeks.[24] When the Greeks approached the (cult) gods with whom they shared intimate relationships, they did not direct their petition to the abstract gods depicted in myth or on the stage, but to 'specific gods of specific places'.[25] On the other hand, however, the Greeks would no doubt have been influenced by representations of the gods they saw around them and heard about in stories. As Parker comments, 'it is scarcely plausible to dismiss this [mythological, poetic, and iconographic tradition], the main source of Greek imaginings of the divine world, as a delusive façade'.[26] If you were to watch *The Hunger Games* movie before reading the book, you will probably imagine Katniss Everdeen as Jennifer Lawrence. If you read the book before seeing the film, you will have your own mental image of Katniss, and find it disconcerting to see Jennifer Lawrence in the role.

Homer, Hesiod, Pindar, Archilochus, the classical tragedians, and all the other writers and poets, did not invent the gods with whom they worked. And, by and large, they did not introduce new gods into a socio-religious context in which they did not already exist. The influence they exerted over the religious landscape was in helping to cement associations between pre-existing local divinities and the more broadly defined universal gods who appeared in their works. Alongside this, these works helped to consolidate narratives of the relationships the gods maintained with one another and encouraged the wholesale alignment of more generalised attributes, behaviours, and epithets by which each god may be identified. It is this aspect that Herodotos refers to when he credits Homer and Hesiod with having ποιήσαντες θεογονίην Ἕλλησι ('made a theogony for the Greeks').[27] Their greater influence was, perhaps, on the following generations, who were consciously looking to create a unified Hellenic identity[28] and were more open and accepting of 'truly' universal practices and identities both for themselves and in 'reading back' these identities to earlier religious practice. For example, the west pediment at Olympia (installed in c. 460 BCE) depicts the fight between Lapithae and the Centaurs, showing Peirithous at the centre. Pausanias, writing in the second century CE, comments that the sculptor, Alkamenes, depicted this scene because Πειρίθουν τε εἶναι Διὸς ἐν ἔπεσι τοῖς Ὁμήρου δεδιδαγμένος ('he learned from Homer's poem that Peirithous was Zeus' son').[29] This is obviously not proof that Alkamenes had actually referenced Homer's version of the story when designing the pediment, but it does show that when Pausanias viewed the sculpture several hundred years later *he* recalled the Homeric tale, and that whomever Pausanias had heard the story from was also reminded of the Homeric poem. The two stories – from Homer and the pediment – have had their backgrounds amalgamated to make a harmonious whole, by Pausanias at the very least and by the (post-classical) Elian community member(s) who Pausanias spoke with.

The obvious problem here is the question of how widely disseminated Homer and Hesiod's works were, particularly in the late archaic and early classical periods. And then, to what extent different literary opinions on the gods were, or could have been, concurrently assimilated into well-established religious beliefs and practices, which were cemented in custom. And then the question arises about where influences comes from and how they come about. Homer gives us different versions of the gods than those Pindar presents. This is partly because of the nature of 'universal' gods and their actual local manifestations. The presentations of the gods in Homer and Hesiod are the poets' own ideas about divinity mediated through their work, with some need for internal consistency. Pindar, on the other hand, notes Irene Polinskaya,

> could make abstract statements about gods in general, and they would indeed have the same and equal relevance to any Greek; but he had to call upon specific gods, i.e. gods of specific cities and sites, to shower benevolence upon the victors and their communities, and hence the bipolar tension of his poetry, at once panhellenic and epichoric in scope.[30]

Homer and Hesiod's works were, arguably, more widely disseminated than Pindar's, which shows that when utilising these literary sources as evidence for the common perception of the gods we must keep in mind not only a probable pattern of dissemination but also to what extent the author's views could have been smoothly integrated into common, well-established practices. Pindar may present an image of the gods different from those we find elsewhere, but that does not necessarily indicate that anyone accepted his images.

The anthropomorphic appearance of the gods that is used in both literature and iconography – even in cult iconography – tells us that this is the main way that the Greeks imagined their gods. But the Greeks, in general, also considered the gods to be much more than just an anthropomorphised version of *a something*. In the same way that Zeus could simultaneously be 'Soter' and 'Chthonios' with no disparity, he could simultaneously be the father of the gods, with a human-like form, who lives atop Mount Olympos, and be the sky or the flashing thunderbolt. The Greeks accepted that each of the Zeuses were one and the same, and there was no contradiction in the idea that Zeus could be meaningfully represented as both the anthropomorphised father of the gods and an elemental force, and that these were two aspects of the same individual divinity, albeit with different titles. As Xenophon points out, καὶ γὰρ Ζεὺς ὁ αὐτὸς δοκῶν εἶναι πολλὰς ἐπωνυμίας ἔχει ('for Zeus, though thought to be the same, has many names').[31] Elsewhere Xenophon delineates between different Zeuses after being told that his financial worries are the result of neglecting Zeus Meilichios, even though he is a regular worshiper of Zeus Basileus.[32] This is a difficult case given that Zeus Meilichios is often considered to be different to other Zeuses. Nevertheless, it reinforces the idea that only in very specific circumstances should the dedication to one conception of Zeus be removed from any other variation of Zeus. Neither Zeus nor Xenophon are remarkable here.

The identity of singular gods in universal mythological narratives and in local cultic practices may derive aspects from one another, and the two disparate entities can be considered simultaneously as the same god without either incarnation encroaching into the sphere of the other as the *individual* deems necessary. The Athena to whom the local Attic man makes offerings during the Panathenaia does not need to be informed by the Athena who assists Odysseus in Homer's epic and vice versa. However, they can comfortably co-exist in his conception of the goddess as the same divinity with various aspects to be called upon at the appropriate time: Athena Polias during the Panathenaia and Odyssean Athena during recitation of Homer.

For the study of archaic and early classical Greek religious practice it is much more apposite to talk about variety of local representations and how they embody the various inter-regional, but not necessarily universal, 'Greek' gods. Because of the process of associating local gods with universal identities there are some characteristics that are commonly shared throughout the Greek-speaking world and, although not every representation of each god conforms to these, they become universally recognisable attributes. One of the ways that this occurs is through the increased adoption of epithets, of both locality-derived names and more generic cult names. The simple fact that localised variations of the divine exist, sometimes even in multiple versions of the 'same god' in a single *polis*, indicates that the distinction of divine 'guises' between these identities was important to the communities that worshipped them.

Alongside the influence of well-known and widely disseminated literature, universal attributes may also develop, and eventually be ascribed to local divinities, through syncretic relationships between different public and private macro- and micro-communities, and particularly those with relationships forged at shared Hellenic festivals and sanctuaries like Delphi and Olympia. There are two main variants of the common shared Hellenic sanctuary: those that are 'local' (or mono-variant) and those that are multi-variant. These multi-variant sanctuaries might, for instance, serve several small *poleis*, which are culturally, politically, or socially connected, and thereby fulfil much the same purpose as more closed-off mono-variant, or single *polis* cults[33], to form a shared community identity. The federal meeting sanctuary of the Phokian κοινόν, the Phokikon, is an example of such a local sanctuary. The Phokikon represents the creation of a shared identity for the cities who were members of the federation,[34] and in doing so also creates a space from which the 'other' is excluded. The Greekness of the excluded 'other' in this case reinforces the earlier assertion that shared Greek identity was a sporadically used tool rather than a permanent label.

In contrast to the closed nature of mono-variant and multi-variant cults and sanctuaries, universal (so-called 'panhellenic' or, in my taxonomy, maxi-variant) sanctuaries were, theoretically, open to all Greeks (and potentially to non-Greeks), although there is significant evidence suggesting that exclusions could and did take place. For example, the Elians prevented the Spartans from entering or sacrificing at the sanctuary of Zeus at Olympia, thereby effectively banning them from participation in the Olympic Games of 420 – and this ban may have been upheld until 400.[35] Nevertheless, these important sanctuaries – most notably at Delphi and Olympia, but also Isthmia, Nemea, Delos, and others – provided a location for the promulgation and development of a 'common Hellenic' identity, and all the interstate politicking and sharing of local customs that thrived in such an environment. This would occur both formally and informally and would have served to reinforce some of the shared religious and social ideologies;[36] though it may have also served to highlight significant differences. It is through this environment of sharing that we can account for some of the various cultic similarities from *polis* to *polis*, particularly in cases where the *poleis* with 'shared' or similar customs were not geographically close to one another. It was in these locations that the individuals of various communities – big and small, public and private – interacted with one another, mingling ideas that they would later take away, and potentially alter slightly to suit their own local practices.

Although the emphasis may be on the cultivation and celebration of a common Greek heritage, participating at universal sanctuaries would still have meant different things to different communities of people,[37] particularly within the context of the quest for their own civic, social, community, and individual identities. The various communities of the Greeks did not, themselves, consider that each of their gods were the same, although they may have approached 'universal gods' – that is, gods at universal sanctuaries – with a similar amount of reverence that they paid to the gods of their own local communities. Universal sanctuaries initially emerged as important interstate sanctuaries in the archaic period due largely to their location: being on the (social, cultural, or geographical) periphery of the Hellenic world in the early archaic period, and not directly controlled by any single powerful state, they would have been relatively insulated from the political and social rivalries of the dominant *poleis* of the period.[38] Participation at universal sanctuaries most likely began sometime during the eighth century, but was cemented into a formalised framework of worship, including the institution of the quadrennial and biennial games oscillation between Olympia, Delphi, Isthmia, and Nemea, during the early sixth century.[39] Thereafter these major sanctuaries functioned as centres of religious, social, cultural, and artistic sharing and learning. They were, at least in part, responsible for the propagation of a shared religious ideology and activity, and a staging ground for advancements in artistic and architectural styles.

We can assume that the 'universal' identity of the gods mirrored that of widely disseminated works of literature and large-scale visual representations at major, universally used, sites. So, universal sanctuaries presented images of individual gods that conformed to these 'Greece-wide conceptions'. In this way the universal image of the gods was self-replicating and self-reinforcing. However, even in these great universal sanctuaries we can also find evidence of local 'variations' or aspects of the gods appearing alongside the universal divine image. Often these local variants have little or no discernible relationship to the image of the universal deity. For instance, in his description of the sanctuary of Olympia, Pausanias mentions forty-four different images of Zeus, including the famous chryselephantine statue of Zeus Olympia made by Phidias.[40] One example, a group of statues dedicated by the people of the island of Aegina clearly shows the Zeus of their local foundation story,[41] but several others appear either with universal attributes (like the thunderbolt), or Pausanias offers no description at all, indicating they were probably not sufficiently 'different' to warrant singling them out.

Thin coherence and the Underworld

Religion was an integral component of civic life in the ancient world. It was embedded. That is, as Julia Kindt comments: it 'was structured alongside the socio-political structures of the *polis*'.[42] Communities formed around religious practice in the Greek world could exist in a number of overlapping ways, and individuals would necessarily belong to multiple different religious communities. These communities broadly consist of public and private religious bodies. Generally, 'the public' is bounded by the *polis*, although some public communities exist at phratry and deme level.[43] A larger community was formed through participation at 'universal' sanctuaries, in festivals such as the Olympian or Pythian games, and membership of other kinds of federation, such as *Amphiktyonies*, confederated states with shared sanctuaries. For the most part, however, participation in communities larger than the *polis* were still bounded by an individual's political identity. That is to say, individuals would not normally participate in religious activity at a universal level without reference to their *polis* identity, and membership to a Hellenic *polis* played a large role in the ability to participate in some universal sanctuaries.[44]

Christiane Sourvinou-Inwood's model of *polis*-religion can help us to conceptualise religious identity and the way that it helped to shape the 'universal' religious landscape,[45] but it has some limitations. The role of the individual is severely underplayed, although individuals are the key component in establishing ideas about the gods and ensuring their longevity. Religious concepts, like any culturally specific concept, are not created in isolation from one another, and are not sent out into the world fully formed.[46] Instead, concepts are subtly modified by each person who takes them up, before they are either passed on or discarded. They may be internalised and deliberated on for long periods of time before either scenario occurs. Alongside this, we have to remember that religious ideas held by individuals within a community do not need to be exactly the same, and most likely are not. Ideas may be similar from person to person, without being identical, and their similarities may be shared among various, overlapping, or even completely unconnected groups. Pascal Boyer's explanation makes this very clear:

> knowing that culture is a similarity between people is helpful because it forces you to remember that two objects are similar only *from a certain point of view*. My blue eyes may make me similar to some people, but then my short-sightedness makes me similar to others.[47]

What Boyer is articulating is something we might most easily imagine as a Venn diagram, where 'blue eyes' or 'believes in god' and 'short-sightedness' or 'believes in reincarnation' might overlap to a greater or lesser extent without overshadowing the idea that they are two fundamentally unconnected concepts.

What occurs when scholars downplay the idiosyncrasies of religious practice in favour of a more congruent model of religion is that certain ideas and practices become marginalised. That is, as Esther Eidinow says, 'while *polis* religion offers a useful schema for understanding some aspects of ancient Greek religious activity, it cannot provide a comprehensive account of ritual practice across and within ancient Greek communities'.[48] Although Sourvinou-Inwood acknowledges the individual as the 'basic cult unit',[49] the only possible framework for the individual to work within is the *polis*. But the individual does not just make up a part of a distinct 'community', they are an essential part of those communities, each one a stand-alone, distinct building block, with their own ideas, experiences, and thoughts about religious practice, the gods, ritual, and mythology. And religious communities can only be constructed using these individual building blocks. What that means is that non-*polis*-bounded religion was operating not only on the level above the *polis*, but also below it. To give an example of the very smallest possible practice we could take an individual inscribing a *katadesmos* and burying it in a grave, in secret, without having involved anyone else.[50]

This is not to say that the practices of different religious communities operated in different spheres of religion, that there was '*polis* religion' and 'personal religion' and 'universal (or maxi-variant) religion' or some other similar categorisation, or even a dichotomy between 'public' and 'personal' religion. Not only would there have been interaction between these different forms of religion in strictly theological terms,[51] but there would have been large amounts of interaction, and co-mingling of ideas, at the level of every engaged individual (and, in many regards, even some who are not engaged in practical religious thinking). These people would have undertaken religious practices within the confines of multiple different communities, without considering that there may be incompatibility between the ideas presented in each of those spheres. Our person burying their *katadesmos* to curse their business rival might do so the night before they travel to the Delphic Oracle as a *theoros*. A woman might participate in her deme's Thesmophoria, be initiated into the Mysteries at Eleusis, and march in the Panathenaic procession. Here, she participates in three different kinds of community religion: her local community, a wider 'private' cult, and the cult of her entire *polis*. This does not even begin to touch on the innumerable ways she might participate in family or individual practices, or other civic religion she might be involved in. As a matter of course, a person's religious life involves participation in all different kinds of overlapping communities which may be public, private, or those that cannot be easily categorised as either.

Each of these communities operates with the same kind of framework and uses similar semiotic vocabulary. This shared vocabulary enables people to speak with one another across community divides, and – probably more importantly in their own thoughts – with the gods they are trying to connect with. This language is formed by a complex structure of signs, which facilitates communication between participants, and also enables others to properly decode and interpret the messages being put across.[52] Communities that have a semiotic logic that is shared must, in some ways, be coherent with one another. However, we do not have to overestimate this coherence. Signs and symbols may have subtle differences in meaning without being incoherent through wider culture; they may have an 'overall' meaning that has small, albeit fundamentally important, differences within smaller cultural components; or smaller communities within or overlapping with larger ones (we can call these smaller units 'micro-communities', because they occur only within the context of another community but do not include all the larger community's members). However, as William Sewell points out:

> This conception actually implies quite minimal cultural coherence – one might call it a thin-coherence. The fact that members of a semiotic community recognise a given set of symbolic oppositions does not determine what sort of statements or actions they will construct on the basis of their semiotic competence. Nor does it mean that they form a community in any fuller sense. They need not agree in their moral or emotional evaluations of given symbols. The semiotic field they share may be recognised and used by groups and individuals locked in fierce enmity rather than bound by solidarity, or by people who feel relative indifference toward each other. The posited existence of cultural coherence says nothing about whether semiotic fields are big or small, shallow or deep, encompassing or specialised. It simply requires that if meaning is to exist at all, there must be systematic relations among signs and a group of people.[53]

That non-congruent communities might live harmoniously with one another, and that a person might belong to multiple communities with no particular issue, is reflected in the makeup of the religious landscape itself. The gods appear in contradictory guises with no cognitive inconsistency. As we will see, Persephone can easily be thought of as a virginal maiden or as wife of Hades with no contradiction because these two ideas of the goddess occur in different micro-communities. Even though the semiotic language that indicates 'Persephone' occurs in each micro-community – indicating a level of coherence – there are subtle differences that create incongruent characteristics unique to each cultic or mythic setting. These non-congruent ideas about single divinities can co-exist in society without raising alarm because they are ideas that individuals do not directly consider as incongruous: they belong in different spheres and are called upon in different cultic settings. This is more obvious when we recognise that it is the person, rather than any real or imagined divine being, who is responsible for the incongruity. So, as Henk Versnel points out, 'it is not the gods who decide where they are from or where they arrive. It is the mortal manipulator, who may even claim the authority to decide who is god and who is not'.[54]

Imagined differences: 'chthonic' and 'Olympic' gods

The idea of 'chthonic' has garnered a lot of scholarly attention over the last few decades,[55] though it did not have a very wide significance in ancient Greece.

Although popular in late nineteenth- and early twentieth-century scholarship, more recently ancient historians and archaeologists have actively questioned whether it is a valid label for either gods or cultic practices.[56] The use of the term 'chthonic' as something which deviates in a set way from 'normal' practices is not accurate. There is no way to delineate what 'normal' religious ritual practice is in the ancient Greek world, and so therefore, by definition, nothing can deviate from that 'normal'. Although there are several ritual markers – that is, individual components of a ritual – that might indicate that the god being worshipped is a 'chthonic' or 'Underworld' god, there is no tidy description and no ritual markers that occur in all 'chthonic' worship and also *only* occurs in 'chthonic' worship. I will not attempt to provide a definition of 'chthonic' to be used in this book, but rather show what some ancient Greeks said about the 'chthonic' and explain why I do not use the term in the more scholarly sense of 'Underworld'.

The history of scholarship on the Olympic/chthonic dichotomy has been thoroughly set out by Renate Schleiser in her 1991/2 article 'Olympian versus Chthonian Religion'.[57] She concluded that scholarship has moved away from a strict division between the two poles of practice and now, more rightly, focus on the shades of meaning that we find in both real-world cult practice and in literature focused on the nature of gods. She goes on to stress the importance of understanding each specific context, while continuing to take the wider landscape into account. As Robert Parker points out: 'Greek religion was not dualist, and all gods were potentially sources of harm as well as of benefit, of benefit as well as of harm'.[58] What we must take away from this recent scholarship on the nature of chthonism is that the distinction between the chthonic and Olympic is not absolute.[59]

Having said that, the distinction between the Olympic and the 'other' (though notably not explicitly the 'chthonic') were also relevant and discussed in the ancient world. For example, Isokrates, in the late fifth century, comments on this:

ἀλλὰ καὶ τῶν θεῶν τοὺς μὲν τῶν ἀγαθῶν αἰτίους ἡμῖν ὄντας Ὀλυμπίους προσαγορευομένους, τοὺς δ᾽ ἐπὶ ταῖς συμφοραῖς καὶ ταῖς τιμωρίαις τεταγμένους δυσχερεστέρας τὰς ἐπωνυμίας ἔχοντας, καὶ τῶν μὲν καὶ τοὺς ἰδιώτας καὶ τὰς πόλεις καὶ νεὼς καὶ βωμοὺς ἱδρυμένους, τοὺς δ᾽ οὔτ᾽ ἐν ταῖς εὐχαῖς οὔτ᾽ ἐν ταῖς θυσίαις τιμωμένους, ἀλλ᾽ ἀποπομπὰς αὐτῶν ἡμᾶς ποιουμένους.

In the case of gods too I observe that those who bring men blessings are called Olympians, while those responsible for calamities and punishment have less pleasant names; private individuals and cities have founded temples and altars of the one group, while the other is honoured neither in sacrifices nor in prayers, but we perform rites of expulsion against them.[60]

The passage does not necessarily tell us anything about Isokrates's personal beliefs, and it does not chime with the contemporary religious landscape. Here,

Isokrates is attempting to persuade Philip to treat the Greeks with kindness and humility, rather than harshness.[61] Harsh treatment, he says, equally affects both the one exercising harshness and its recipients, and so too with the gods. Greeks offer worship to 'Olympian' gods and attempt to expel the negative forces from the city. It is not clear that the gods with 'less pleasant names' are the Underworld gods. George Norlin's Loeb Classical Library edition of the text suggests that 'the contrast here is between Zeus, Apollo, Athena, etc., and the under-world deities Hades, Persephone, the Furies etc.', although the strict delineation is less than clear from Isokrates's own words. 'Less pleasant names' do not, for instance, automatically bring 'Persephone' to mind and she is not a divinity to whom 'expulsion' rights are performed against. Arthur Darby Nock suggests that the group 'probably' refers to the Erinyes, Hades, Thanatos, Hekate and her entourage, the *alastores*, the *keres*, the *strinx*, 'or something like Envy or the evil eye',[62] which makes more sense in the context of the actual cult landscape at the time, which was not really like the black and white distinction presented by Isokrates, and which Parker rightly comments is exaggerated 'to make a particular rhetorical point that has nothing to do with religion'.[63]

Roughly contemporary to Isokrates, Plato also distinguishes between Olympic and 'other' gods, though we should always keep in mind that Plato is commenting on how he thinks religion *should* be performed, not how it actually was performed.[64] The picture we get here is of a system in which Olympic gods are honoured above chthonic ones, and suggests that people should not worship 'nether gods' and Olympic gods together. At one point, Plato aligns the 'Olympic' with odd numbers and the right-hand side. Both, according to Pythagorean doctrine of opposites, are superior to their counter.[65] Again, however, he does not name the 'chthonic' nor give definition to the gods who should be defined as 'chthonic'. Rather, he speaks about 'the opposite' of the Olympic. Later, he does address an Underworld god with specificity:

ὁ μὲν γὰρ δὴ νόμος ἐρεῖ δώδεκα μὲν ἑορτὰς εἶναι τοῖς δώδεκα θεοῖς, ὧν ἂν ἡ φυλὴ ἑκάστη ἐπώνυμος ᾖ, θύοντας τούτων ἑκάστοις ἔμμηνα ἱερά, χορούς τε καὶ ἀγῶνας μουσικούς, τοὺς δὲ γυμνικούς, κατὰ τὸ πρέπον προσνέμοντας τοῖς θεοῖς τε αὐτοῖς ἅμα καὶ ταῖς ὥραις ἑκάσταις, γυναικείας τε ἑορτάς, ὅσαις χωρὶς ἀνδρῶν προσήκει καὶ ὅσαις μή, διανέμοντας. ἔτι δὲ καὶ τὸ τῶν χθονίων καὶ ὅσους αὖ θεοὺς οὐρανίους ἐπονομαστέον καὶ τὸ τῶν τούτοις ἑπομένων οὐ συμμεικτέον ἀλλὰ χωριστέον, ἐν τῷ τοῦ Πλούτωνος μηνὶ τῷ δωδεκάτῳ κατὰ τὸν νόμον ἀποδιδόντας, καὶ οὐ δυσχεραντέον πολεμικοῖς ἀνθρώποις τὸν τοιοῦτον θεόν, ἀλλὰ τιμητέον ὡς ὄντα ἀεὶ τῷ τῶν ἀνθρώπων γένει ἄριστον.

For the law will state that there are twelve feasts to the twelve gods who give their names to the several tribes: to each of these they shall perform monthly sacrifices and assign choirs and musical contests, and also gymnastic contests, as is suitable both to the gods themselves and to the several

seasons of the year; and they shall ordain also women's festivals, prescrib-
ing how many of these shall be for women only, and how many open also
to men. Further, they must determine, in conformity with the law, the rites
proper to the nether gods, and how many of the celestial gods should be
invoked, and what of the rites connected with them should not be mingled
but kept apart, and put them in the twelfth month, which is sacred to
Pluton; and this god should not be disliked by men who are warriors, but
honoured as one who is always most good to the human race.[66]

He does not say that the Olympic gods should be celebrated and the 'nether
gods' deprived of celebration, but rather that it is most appropriate to worship
Underworld gods in the month sacred to Plouton – that is, Hades. As with
Isokrates we cannot take Plato as evidence for the actual religious practice
when so much other evidence gives a contrasting picture of the religious
landscape of the classical period.

Perhaps a better way of getting at what the Greeks thought of as a 'chthonic' god
is to look at the use of 'chthonic' as a cult epithet. Epithets are a common and
consistent feature of Greek religion during the archaic and classical period. Parker
describes two distinct ways that cult epithets work: 'one looks upwards, to the
heavens: it differentiates and selects among the powers of the gods. One looks
downwards: it gives names to the sanctuaries of the gods here on earth'.[67]
Underworld epithets, including the obvious 'Chthonios' and 'Chthonia', serve the
same purpose as any other cult epithet yet they do not neatly fit into either of
Parker's categories. In a very real sense, they are toponymic. They refer to a specific
place, namely beneath the ground. But they also function as a way to recall a divine
function, namely being 'of the place under the ground' (i.e. in the soil, denoting the
possible agrarian nature of the 'chthonic') or 'of the Underworld'. And, of course,
these two things are intricately interlinked – the function exists for and around the
place, and the place exists for and around the function of Underworld and other
death-related and agrarian gods. We find a plethora of examples of 'Chthonios/a' in
literature,[68] of which Hermes is the most frequent. In religious practice we find
examples of Demeter Chthonia,[69] Ge Chthonia,[70] Hermes Chthonios,[71] Persephone
Chthonia,[72] Zeus Chthonios,[73] and Hekate Chthonia.[74] Mentions of *Chthoniai Theai*
more generally refer to Demeter and Persephone.[75] For non-'Chthonios/a' epithets
we find, for example, Hermes Pompaios ('guide') and Psychopompaios ('guide of
souls'),[76] and Demeter and Ge Anesidora ('sender up of gifts').[77] The inscriptional
evidence also shows that the epithet Chthonios/a was widely applied to various
divinities, over a large time frame. However, as Irene Polinskaya notes, use of the
word as an epithet was not at all evenly distributed across the Greek world.[78] Most
instances occur in Magna Graecia, with significant numbers also found in Asia
Minor and Attica, but much smaller numbers elsewhere.

While in religious practices 'chthonic' epithets usually indicate a god has
some kind of Underworld or under-ground (that is, agrarian) function, in
literature these epithets are usually used to indicate that a god should be
conceptualised, by the audience rather than by the other characters, as a specific

type of character. So, they are presented as either an agrarian or Underworld god in a single-faceted way, rather than having multifaceted traits that are ritually significant. Gods in literature often appear, as J Given comments regarding Dionysos in Aristophanes's *Frogs*, 'disconcertingly human',[79] and are very different to the way they are rendered in artefacts of religious practice. This is shown in the way other (predominantly mortal) characters interact with them, from their corporeal physicality (and therefore physical interaction), to the ways they are manipulated by other characters to advance the storylines. For instance, in 'real life' people tend to credit the gods for positive outcomes in their lives, but lay blame for bad at the feet of fortune, fate, or a daemon; in literature, blame for the negative is usually laid squarely with the gods, either generally or with a specific god.[80] This does not always reflect the intricate, multi-directional relationship that people build with gods over time, though. Most instances in tragedy that involve the epithet Chthonios/a are, however, an indirect invocation to an absent divinity. So, what we often find in literary uses of the epithet is an attempt to say something about the direction of the narrative, rather than the ritual nature of the god being called upon.

It is easy to see the universal aspect of Underworld gods without looking at the local versions of these divinities that people build relationships with. Is that because it intuitively feels wrong for a 'normal', 'good' person to want to build a relationship with an Underworld god? What I will lay out over the course of this study is that they should be viewed as all other major gods in the Greek world – as complex, multi-dimensional, predominantly localised gods with whom people go to lengths to build and maintain relationships.

Notes

1   To declare my own biases and prejudices upfront: I identify as a 'soft' atheist, have an enduring fascination with religion, and rebelled against my parents as a teenager by getting confirmed in the Church of England.
2   Bremmer, 1994: 1.
3   Kearns, 2010: 2.
4   Gould, 1985: 1.
5   This is not necessarily true, there are a great many contemporary pagans who worship the traditional Greek gods, identifying by and large as practitioners of Hellenismos.
6   For a fuller discussion of this see Parker, 2011: 224–264.
7   Bowden, 2007: 77.
8   Hdt. 8.144.2.
9   Hall, 2001: 90.
10   Scott, 2010: 261.
11   Mikalson, 2010: 29.
12   Sourvinou-Inwood, 2000a, 2000b.
13   Bremmer, 2010b; Eidinow, 2011; Kindt, 2009, 2012: 12–35.
14   Parker, 2011: 21.
15   Cf. Larson, 2016: 31–40.
16   Christensen, 2009: 13–14.

17 This will be discussed below but see also Kearns, 2010: 88–89; Kindt, 2012: 30–32, 42; Versnel, 2011: 539–559. On Versnel's definition of belief see 548–549; on the belief in divinity of human rulers but dealing with many aspects of what belief is and means see 465–471, 476–477. On this Mair (2012: 451) says 'the irrelevance of belief in understanding religion has been so well attested that it has become something of an anthropological truism'. In the introductory books that deal with 'Greek Religion' we often find the idea of belief left out completely, authors will discuss ritual and sacrificial practice, but the concept of belief is unaddressed; for example, Bremmer, 1994; Burkert, 1985; Mikalson, 2010. That is not to say that all such books have left out discussions on belief – although he does not discuss cognitive approaches to belief, Parker (2011) titles one of the chapters in *On Greek Religion* as 'Why Believe Without Revelation', and Price (1999: 3) addresses belief as a concept in *Religions of the Ancient Greeks*, dismissing it summarily by saying: 'practice, not belief is the key, and to start from questions of faith or personal piety is to impose alien values on ancient Greece'.

18 Parker, 2011: 2.

19 Bremmer, 2010a: 15; Henrichs, 2010: 25.

20 Henrichs, 2010: 26.

21 Versnel, 1993: 3.

22 Bremmer, 2007b: 43.

23 Calame, 2009: 38.

24 Kearns, 2010: 5, 32.

25 Polinskaya, 2010: 61.

26 Parker, 2011: 95.

27 Hdt. 2.53.2.

28 Schachter, 2000: 11.

29 Paus. 5.10.8; cf. Hom. *Il.* 14.317–318.

30 Polinskaya, 2010: 68.

31 Xen. *Symp.* 8.9.

32 Xen. *Anab.* 7.8.4.

33 I use the term '*polis*-centred' to avoid the discussion on what constitutes 'state' cult activity. For more on state cults see Aleshire, 1994: 9–16.

34 McInerney, 1999: 157.

35 Thuc. 5.49; Xen. *Hell.* 3.2.21.

36 Morgan, 1993: 18.

37 Morgan, 1993: 22.

38 Kearns, 2010: 276; Schachter, 2000: 10; Snodgrass, 1980: 55.

39 Morgan, 1993: 36.

40 Paus. 5.21.1–25.1. The chryselephantine statue of Zeus here, perhaps the most enduringly famous visual representation of the god today, lacked the god's most distinctive attribute – the thunderbolt – and yet was universally recognisable. We cannot imagine that a single 'attribute' of a divinity can be added or taken away to aid visual identification, because in reality a more intricate web of attributes makes up the visual vocabulary of each god.

41 Paus. 5.22.6.

42 Kindt, 2012: 16.

43 For more on categories of division, see Sourvinou-Inwood, 2000b: 28–31.

44 Sourvinou-Inwood, 2000b: 15–16.

45 Sourvinou-Inwood, 2000a, 2000b.

46 Cf. Boyer (2002: 37) who comments that 'all scenarios that describe people sitting around and inventing religion are dubious. Even the ones that see religious as slowly coming out of confused thoughts have this problem'.

47 Boyer, 2002: 41.
48 Eidinow, 2011.
49 Sourvinou-Inwood, 2000a: 47. The examples are of: individual sacrifice being treated in sacred laws as akin to polis or group sacrifices; categorisation of individuals in a cult setting by age, gender or profession; individuals participating in certain polis-centred festivals; and the incurrence of religious restrictions on the individual for various reasons.
50 See Chapter 6 for further discussion.
51 Cf. Kindt, 2012: 23–24.
52 Gould, 1985: 4.
53 Sewell, 1999: 50–51; cf. Kindt, 2012: 22; Ober, 2003: 235–255, 2005: 69–91.
54 Versnel, 2011: 94.
55 As a brief guide see Henrichs, 1991; Mikalson, 2010: 36–39; Parker, 2011: 80–84, 283–286; Polinskaya, 2013: 63–64; Schleiser, 1991; Scullion, 1994, 2000; Versnel, 2011: 144–145, and in the collection of Hägg and Alroth 2005.
56 See, for instance Schleiser, 1991; van Straten, 1995.
57 Schleiser, 1991.
58 Parker, 2011: 80.
59 Cf. Polinskaya, 2013: 63–64; Scullion, 1994: 90.
60 Isok. 5.117; trans. Parker.
61 Isok. 5.116.
62 Nock, 1986: 600.
63 Parker, 2011: 80.
64 Pl. *Leg.* 717a-b, 828c-d.
65 Arist. *Metaph.* 986a; cf. Lloyd, 1962.
66 Pl. *Leg.* 828b-d; trans. R. G. Bury.
67 Parker, 2003: 117. The examples Parker uses to illustrate this point are Zeus Meilichios and Artemis of Brauron. Zeus Meilichios was not tied to a geographic location but the epithet gives a sense of the aspect of the god who is being offered worship, whereas when one was at the sanctuary Brauron it might be just as likely to refer to 'Artemis' without her topographic epithet because that was implied by the location, the sanctuary and the religious occasion. This is necessarily a simplified reading of Parker's views.
68 By way of brief example; Hes. *Th.* 465, 697; Aisch. *Ag.* 88–91, *Cho.* 1, 124b, 354–359, 399, 476, 727, *Pers.* 628, 640–642, *Supp.* 24–25, *fr.* 273a. 8–10. (Sommerstein); Eur. *IT.* 1272–1273, *Hek.* 78, *Pho.* 1320–1321, *Alk.* 744–745, *fr.* 868 (Collard and Cropp); Soph. *El.* 110–112, *OC.* 1568, 1606, *Aj.* 832; Aristoph. *Th.* 101–103, *Fr.* 1126, 1138, 1145; Hdt. 6.134, 7.153.2.
69 See Chapter 3, and Appendix 2, for detailed discussion of cults of Demeter Chthonia.
70 For example, *IG* III Ap. 99; *IG* Bulg I² 398; Audollent, 1904: no. 79.
71 See Chapter 4 for discussion of Hermes; Hermes Chthonios is the most prevalent chthonic-epitheted god in epigraphical texts.
72 *AA* (1907) 126; see Jordan, 1985: no. 170.
73 Zeus Chthonios is mentioned, along with Ge Chthonia, on the festival calendar from Mykonos, *SIG* 615; Paus. 2.2.8, 5.14.8; cf. Cook, 1914: 668 and n. 3.
74 For example, *IG* III Ap. 104, 105, 106, 107, 108; *SEG* 30:326.
75 Schleiser, 1997: 1187.
76 See Chapter 4 for discussion of Hermes.
77 Demeter: Paus. 1.31.4; Ge: *MDAI(A)* 37 (1912) 288.19.
78 Polinskaya, 2013: 79.
79 Given, 2009: 115.
80 Mikalson, 1991: 18.

2 Landscapes of the Underworld

Is Thanatos an Underworld god? Is Thanatos a god at all? In name, at least, Thanatos is D/death. In the Homeric epics, Thanatos is only anthropomorphised on a few occasions, usually in his absence.[1] The Homeric non-proper-noun θάνατος occurs frequently and just means 'death'; a non-personified concept that has no agency of its own. Every time θάνατος appears in the Homeric poems and is *not* actively personified, it represents the 'veil of mist' that descends over the dead to take their life-force away and is more usually used to explain the actions of other divine death-agents, or the activity of a person inflicting 'θάνατος' in battle. Thanatos only *appears* 'in person' once, when he and brother Hypnos ('Sleep') appear to carry Sarpedon's body:

καὶ τότ᾽ Ἀπόλλωνα προσέφη νεφεληγερέτα Ζεύς·
εἰ δ᾽ ἄγε νῦν φίλε Φοῖβε, κελαινεφὲς αἷμα κάθηρον
ἐλθὼν ἐκ βελέων Σαρπηδόνα, καί μιν ἔπειτα
πολλὸν ἀποπρὸ φέρων λοῦσον ποταμοῖο ῥοῇσι
χρῖσόν τ᾽ ἀμβροσίῃ, περὶ δ᾽ ἄμβροτα εἵματα ἕσσον·
πέμπε δέ μιν πομποῖσιν ἅμα κραιπνοῖσι φέρεσθαι
ὕπνῳ καὶ θανάτῳ διδυμάοσιν, οἵ ῥά μιν ὦκα
θήσουσ᾽ ἐν Λυκίης εὐρείης πίονι δήμῳ,
ἔνθά ἑ ταρχύσουσι κασίγνητοί τε ἔται τε
τύμβῳ τε στήλῃ τε· τὸ γὰρ γέρας ἐστὶ θανόντων.
ὣς ἔφατ᾽, οὐδ᾽ ἄρα πατρὸς ἀνηκούστησεν Ἀπόλλων.
βῆ δὲ κατ᾽ Ἰδαίων ὀρέων ἐς φύλοπιν αἰνήν,
αὐτίκα δ᾽ ἐκ βελέων Σαρπηδόνα δῖον ἀείρας
πολλὸν ἀποπρὸ φέρων λοῦσεν ποταμοῖο ῥοῇσι
χρῖσέν τ᾽ ἀμβροσίῃ, περὶ δ᾽ ἄμβροτα εἵματα ἕσσε·
πέμπε δέ μιν πομποῖσιν ἅμα κραιπνοῖσι φέρεσθαι,
ὕπνῳ καὶ θανάτῳ διδυμάοσιν, οἵ ῥά μιν ὦκα
κάτθεσαν ἐν Λυκίης εὐρείης πίονι δήμῳ.

And now Zeus who gathers the clouds spoke a word to Apollo:
'Go if you will, beloved Phoibos, and rescue Sarpedon

from under the weapons, wash the dark suffusion of blood from him,
then carry him far away and wash him in a running river,
anoint him in ambrosia, put ambrosial clothing upon him;
then give him into the charge of swift messengers to carry him,
of Hypnos and Thanatos, who are twin brothers, and these two shall lay him
down presently within the rich countryside of broad Lykia
where his brothers and countrymen shall give him due burial
with tomb and gravestone. Such is the privilege of those who have perished.'
He spoke so, and Apollo, not disregarding his father,
went down along the mountains of Ida, into the grim fight,
and lifting brilliant Sarpedon out from under the weapons
carried him far away, and washed him in a running river,
and anointed him in ambrosia, put ambrosial clothing upon him,
then gave him into the charge of swift messengers to carry him,
of Hypnos and Thanatos, who are twin brothers, and these two presently
laid him down within the rich countryside of broad Lykia.[2]

Thanatos as an anthropomorphised god becomes increasingly fixed iconographically in the late sixth and early fifth centuries,[3] and he is usually accompanied by Hypnos. He begins appearing on Attic red-figure vases around 515 BCE, in images depicting the removal of Sarpedon's body from the battlefield.[4] Thanatos and Hypnos are usually depicted as warriors, indistinguishable from those around them except for their wings and, later, winged sandals. They often appear on white-ground *lekythoi* (oil flasks), but these do not only show the twins bearing heroes to the Underworld, but also ordinary men and, by the end of the fifth century, women as well (see, for example, Figure 2.3).[5] Figure 2.1 is a rather beautiful example of such a scene, where we can see a winged Thanatos (or Hypnos) grasping a youth, who slumps backwards but does not appear completely limp, under the armpits. There is a tenderness in the god's face, looking downward upon his charge. Such pots are usually found in funerary context, and the iconography they depict is obviously death and Underworld related. But Thanatos is not usually such a strongly psychopompic god. In Homer, Thanatos and Hypnos neither collect Sarpedon's body from the battlefield nor take it to the Underworld. It is Apollo – a god of youths, who has form in dealing with dramatic stories of young men's liminal experiences[6]– who retrieves Sarpedon's body from the battlefield, washing and purifying him, embalming him with ambrosia and only then delivering the body to Thanatos and Hypnos. In turn, they only take him *home to Lykia* so that his body can be buried.

In Euripides' *Alkestis*, Apollo describes Thanatos as hateful to mankind and loathed by the gods (ἐχθροὺς γε θνητοῖς καὶ θεοῖς στυγουμένους).[7] He carries a sword, but he does not use it as a weapon, but simply to cut locks of hair off those he has taken charge of.[8] Hair is a presumably innocuous offering in the landscape of death. It was sometimes dedicated to the dead,[9] and was also important in some rites-of-passage, including age transitions where, mythologically, the young person often 'dies' and is reborn into their new status as 'adult'.[10] But it is not innocuous when Thanatos takes your hair, as he does to Alkestis. It signals that he is taking her

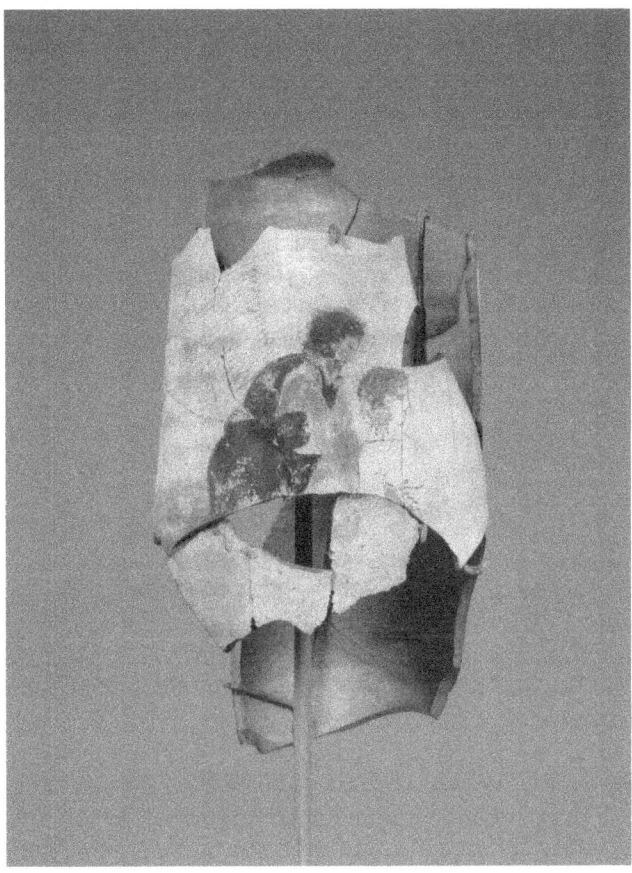

Figure 2.1 Attic terracotta white-ground lekythos showing a winged Thanatos (and Hypnos?) carrying a young man. Attributed to the Painter of the New York Hypnos. c. 440–430 BCE. Metropolitan Museum of Art (Rogers Fund, 1923), 23.160.43

to the Underworld. Thanatos himself points out that he has rights and honours proportionate to the youth of his victim,[11] but that his duty is to take whoever needs killing,[12] and that he cannot act independently. The *Alkestis* shows that being taken by Thanatos is dying. But Thanatos does not swoop in and take Alkestis's soul away. He takes her *body*, leading her – willingly – into the Underworld.[13] Thanatos is a death god, but he is not a god that kills. Rather, he receives the dead for a time before passing them on again. As we have just seen in the Homeric context, this does not even entail taking the dead into the Underworld, but rather the time the deceased spends with Thanatos is part of their liminal journey into death as a state of being for the *physical*, rather than the metaphysical, body. So, although linguistically *thanatos* represents death in all its forms, Thanatos-personified does not embody all these forms.

Moving the dead into the Underworld is normally reserved for gods known as the *psychopompoi* – or 'soul guides'. Charon is perhaps the most well-known example, as the ferryman who literally shipped the dead from the mortal world into the Underworld. But the *psychopompos par-excellence* in the archaic and early classical periods was undoubtedly Hermes. And Hermes is not an Underworld god. Or perhaps he is, but only as a very specific sub-section of his traditional role as a boundary crosser.[14] Hermes's name derives from stone *hermai*[15] that were originally boundary demarcations, which evolved into guardian figures as well.[16] In addition, they were also used to mark out the physical and metaphysical space of 'death', including in the form of grave markers,[17] and they are depicted in the relief carvings of gravestones.[18] So, Hermes comes to represent, as Marinatos comments, 'the idea of boundary-crossing in all its ritualised forms, which entails both territorial and symbolic transitions'.[19]

In the final book of the *Odyssey*, Hermes rouses the souls of the dead and leads them, gibbering, past the streams of Okeanos and into the Underworld.[20] He features as *psychopompos* on Athenian white-ground *lekythoi*, controlling the movements of souls between the worlds.[21] He sometimes appears with Charon,[22] leading the dead person to the boat by the hand, wrist, or upper arm as in Figures 2.2a and b.[23] This gesture is reminiscent of a groom leading his young bride to the marriage bed, which also has a strong link to death.[24] Sometimes he waits by the tomb to take the dead person from Thanatos, who appears with or without Hypnos, as in Figure 2.3.[25]

In his role as *psychopompos*, Hermes has a direct and, more importantly, physical relationship with the dead, further emphasised by his role in the Athenian ritual activity. Here, there was an annual festival called the Anthesteria (which I discuss in detail in below), which was dedicated to Dionysos. During the festival the *psychai* ('souls') of the dead were believed to roam freely around the city at night, and on the last day, sacrifices were made to Hermes to ensure that he got the souls back into the Underworld at the end.[26] This fits with another of Hermes's Underworldly aspects: as someone who not only leads souls from one place to another but also acts as a kind of guard, ensuring souls only return to the mortal world as the proper time, like during the Anthesteria, or during necromantic rites. As a messenger – the only messenger to Hades (the place or the god, it makes no difference), as we are told in the Homeric *Hymn to Hermes*[27]– he is partly responsible for ensuring that messages between the worlds are received, and so he has a rather large presence on *katadesmoi*.[28] Being the 'sole messenger' to Hades not only connects Hermes to the Underworld, but in a subtle, and decidedly more important, way it gives him the singular ability to *pass through the Underworld*. This is keenly utilised in the most notable story of traversing the Underworld in classical mythology: Persephone's abduction, which I will discuss in detail in Chapter 4.

Where early depictions show Hermes leading the dead, past the streams of Okeanos, into the Underworld itself, by the middle of the fifth century, we find

Figures 2.2 Attic terracotta white-ground lekythos showing Hermes leading a youth to Charon, who stands in his boat wearing the typical rustic hat. Attributed to the Sabouroff Painter. c. 450 BCE

Metropolitan Museum of Art (Rogers Fund, 1923), 21.88.17

Figure 2.3 Attic red-figure calyx-krater showing Hermes standing watch as Thanatos and Hypnos move the bleeding body of Sarpedon. Attributed to Euphronios (painter) and Euxitheos (potter). Formerly in the Metropolitan Museum of Art, New York (L.2006.10); Returned to Italy and exhibited in Rome as of January 2008

Photograph Jaime Ardiles-Arce via Wikimedia Commons

Hermes collecting the dead and leading them to the river, where Charon takes them into the Underworld.[29] An inscription from Phokis, dated from around 500 BCE,[30] is the first extant textual reference to Charon:[31]

χαῖρε, Χάρōν· | οὐδὶς τὺ κακὸς| λέγει οὐδὲ θα|νόντα,
πολὸς | ἀνθρōπōν λυ|σάμενος | καμάτο.

Hail, Charon. No one speaks ill of you even in death,
for you freed many men from pain.[32]

But Charon does not become a popular figure, particularly in visual representations, until around halfway through the fifth century.

In myth, Charon expected payment of one or two obols, as first depicted in Aristophanes's *Frogs*.[33] The first time the payment is mentioned in the play Herakles tells Dionysos that he must use them to pay to get passage across the lake, and that the custom was introduced by Theseus. In the second, Charon (now named) throws Dionysos out of his boat and demands the two-obol fare, which Dionysos pays. The fare may have been considered a way of distinguishing those who really belonged in the Underworld from those who did not. In literature this works because it allows us, the audience, to know who 'belongs' and who is 'other' to the Underworld. Even though Dionysos pays the fare, we see Herakles explain how the fare works in practice. We know that he does not belong, because he does not have the requisite knowledge to gain entrance on his own. In reality coins did not make up a significant part of grave goods, either on the person or elsewhere in the tomb, before the Hellenistic period,[34] so this did not represent actual burial practices or eschatological belief in the archaic and classical periods. Charon appears on funerary *lekythoi* more than in any other context. There are around ninety extant examples, including the vase shown in Figure 2.2. In the earliest known iconographic representation, a sixth-century black-figure vase from Attica, he is shown as an old man surrounded by a swarm of child-sized *eidola*, one of which is trying to gain passage onto his boat, which is already full.[35] He is usually shown as a middle-aged, bearded man, wearing a rustic hat.[36] Classical literature sometimes uses Charon as a motif of impending death, represented, as John Oakley comments, as an 'impatient, demanding workman, intent on carrying out his duty'.[37] Contrary to the image of Hermes as the 'helpful' *psychopompos*, Charon is at best uncaring and at worst callous. In most visual representations, however, he is calm and patient and even when he appears stern, he does not exude callousness.

Whether connected to Charon and his boat or not, water plays a prominent role in Greek eschatology,[38] and mythologised symbolic death often involves a journey over, into, or under water. The Underworld has always been characterised by its proximity to water – Odysseus, for example, is directed by Kirke to cross the ocean to find the Underworld,[39] and the Orphic gold tablets advise the deceased not to drink from any spring that they encounter in the Underworld until they reach the Lake of Memory.[40] Water had a deeper connection to death in general. This is a long-recognised connection and there are many examples of death being visualised as a leap into the ocean or lake.[41] Death or burial at sea were not considered to be ritually adequate for entering the Underworld, unless a physical tomb was also built on land and the dead was given funerary rites as normal. This liminality is represented in questions regarding whether the dead or the living are greater in number, found prominently in Diogenes Laertius. The response comes: τοὺς οὖν πλέοντας ποῦ τίθης; ('where, then, do you place the sailors?').[42] There was an idea that those lost at sea would find it more difficult to find their loved ones in the Underworld.[43] Crossing the water represented crossing a boundary between life and death, one state of being and another, so the increasing popularity of the ferryman figure becoming the dominant psychopompic figure makes sense. By crossing the water, the dead were integrated into the Underworld, coming under Hades's control.

'Death' is not something represented by any divinity, and even the most hardened of Underworld gods have very little to do with an individual *actually dying*. This is even true for Thanatos, Charon, and Hermes, who have direct contact with the deceased through their prominent roles as *psychopompoi*. So, we cannot simply take ritual or artistic context to tell us which gods are Underworld gods because some gods are sometimes and are not at other times. When Hermes is Hermes Chthonios he is 'An Underworld God', and when he is Hermes Psychopompos he is a 'liminal' god who is 'an Underworld god' because he has direct contact with the dead; but, when he is Hermes Agoraios ('of the marketplace') he is not at all an Underworld god because the marketplace is not a place distinctly associated with the Underworld. We may be able to conceive of a circumstance in which Hermes Agoraios might be called upon in a *katadesmos*,[44] if a merchant wanted to curse a rival merchant, for example. In that circumstance, would Hermes *Agoraios* become an Underworld god? Even this is doubtful, as the purpose for invocation would be related to this Hermes's rule over the marketplace, rather than anything more sinister.

For this purpose, then, an Underworld god is a god who functions in a context of or guise related to the Underworld or the dead, in the thoughts, beliefs, ideas, stories, and myths of communities who conceive of those gods. The individuals in these communities do not need to be 'worshippers' of the divinity (which presupposes active engagement that is just not present for some Underworld gods). The circularity of this definition is intentional both on my part and, I believe, in the way that the Greek individual appears to approach their Underworld-related gods in literature, art, ritual practice, and the intersection thereof. A god does not need to be 'an Underworld god' all the time. Gods, like people, have shifting identities and it is the identity that an individual chooses to engage with that either aligns a god to the Underworld or does not.

The Anthesteria

The Anthesteria is a strange festival of Dionysos and wine-drinking, but with individual ritual sections dealing with death and pollution (for example, it has associations with Orestes's pollution for the murder of Klytaimestra). As a festival with a specific rite of passage, the first time a child religiously becomes a part of the *polis*-at-large, it becomes particularly important during the Peloponnesian War, as the number of healthy and strong Athenian citizens (read, of course, men) dwindles. Hermes plays a large role, even though it is primarily a festival of wine and celebrating Dionsysos. The red-figure *lekythos* in Figures 2.4a and b show several aspects of the festival; almost every aspect *except* Dionysos. A woman pushes a young girl on a swing, a young man sits on an altar holding a strigil, Hermes stands in a temple precinct (denoted by the column he stands next to). Yet, this is not an Athenian vase, but from southern Italy,[45] perhaps indicating that this strange festival of life and death and wine had been migrated to other parts of the Greek world.

Figures 2.4 South Italian (Apulian) red-figure terracotta lekythos showing a woman pushing a girl on a swing, with a youth sitting on an altar, and Hermes standing. Associated in style with the Lecce Painter. c. 375–350 BCE

Metropolitan Museum of Art (Rogers Fund, 1913), 13.232.3

The most apposite place to start is with the girl being pushed on a swing. As part of this festival Athenian girls would swing on what looks and is very similar to a modern child's swing. Aetiologically, this is because these young women had been cursed by Erigone, daughter of Ikarios – one of the mythical kings of Athens. He was dismembered by a group of cowherds after Dionysos gave him the gift of wine and he shared it with them. Being drunk for the first time, they believed themselves bewitched or poisoned and killed him. In grief, Erigone hanged herself. It is unusual for an unwed young woman to hang herself. Often, mythical and tragic female suicides actively subvert the character's sexualisation, rather than reinforce it. So we find Phaedra hanged after making a false accusation of rape against her son-in-law,[46] and Jokasta hanged after the discovery of her incestuous marriage to Oidipous.[47] They hang themselves because they want to deny their sexual experiences – Phaedra's fantastical rape and Jokasta's incestuous marriage – thus the constriction of the throat is a metaphorical constriction of the vagina.[48] This is not a universal trope, and in tragedy is found primarily in cases of sexual deviance, but it seems particularly pertinent here because it is so out of place. Erigone has no such deviant experience in her past, and her father's death – though brutal – was not due to sexual deviance. By hanging herself, Erigone closes herself off to all sexual experience, not just deviant experience. She is now, in death, a perpetual maiden. There is a connection between suicide completed by hanging and virginity in real life.[49] Often, as I discuss in Chapter 4, the families of unwed girls who die dress them up for weddings instead of funerals so at least in death they can accomplish what good Athenian women should want to accomplish, namely, becoming a wife. But Erigone here specifically denies herself that, and the constriction of her throat plays into this desire. She is choking off the supply of new Athenians.

Not content with this performance of her own grief, as she died she prayed that other Athenian girls should meet the same end as she was suffering for as long as the Athenians did not investigate, and ultimately avenge, the death of her father. Following this, there was a spate of Athenian girls commiting suicide by hanging. The Athenians took to Delphi and were advised to set up the rite of Aiora, or 'swinging', during which, as I briefly mentioned above, girls fulfilled Erigone's curse by a technicality, that of swinging from trees using chairs suspended by ropes.[50] This took place on the last day of the Anthesteria, a festival dedicated to Dionysos, which had the un-natural feature of shade-return. That is, shades of the dead were thought to return to the living world during the festival.[51] They were kept out of the houses by people spreading a mix of buckthorn and pitch on their doorways,[52] and they were taken back into the Underworld on the final night by Hermes. This is, as we will see in Chapter 5, entirely in keeping with Hermes's character, both as a general boundary crosser and as a god who has the relatively unique ability to cross between the worlds of the living and the dead without hesitation.

There is one final, albeit tentative, association to an Underworld divinity in the Anthesteria. The second-century CE scholar, Zenobius, makes a general comment about the Anthesteria: θυράζε Κᾶρες, οὐκ ἔτ' Ἀνθεστήρια ('to the door, Kares, [it's] no longer Anthesteria').[53] There is some debate about whether this statement refers to the Keres or to Karian slaves.[54] The argument for this follows that Κᾶρες may be substituted with Κῆρες, and it appears to have been that way in some versions.[55] The confusion may have arisen because Hesychius glosses κήρ and κῆρες with ψυχή and ψυχαί.[56] This would make the statement something more similar to 'Get out, evil spirits!' Ker is not equivalent to a shade, particularly the ghost of a normal person, and there is no other indication (in our period at any rate) that this might have something to do with Ker. There is no evidence to suggest that Zenobius means to imply that the pseudo-divine Keres should be aligned with the ghosts of the dead. The Keres are never characterised as such elsewhere, and there is nothing to suggest that should be the case here, nor that (even if it were the case) it would apply to the beliefs surrounding the Anthesteria in fifth-century Athens.

The third element seen in Figure 2.4 is the boy, casually sitting on an altar. The Anthesteria was the first real religious festival that Athenian children took part in on their own behalf, it was their enrolment into the religious life of the *polis*, celebrated on Choes – the middle day of the festival. For boys this was one of the stops on their journey to becoming citizens, and the beginning of their transition out of women's areas of the house.[57] The day of the festival is so named because of a connection to *choes* – the jugs – and it is the small (13 cm and under) *choes* that are particularly interesting. These were predominantly produced in the last quarter of the fifth century and the first quarter of the fourth century. That is, during a time of great civic unease where population replenishment, particularly of strong citizen men, was of vital importance. Thus, we can see this part of the festival, at this particularly chronographic juncture, as the physical representation of the Athenian's desire to reaffirm that the next generation of citizens was, in fact, coming. What we get is a set of jugs that 'depict a highly conventionalised and unique iconography of boys apparently participating in ritual activity'.[58] These smaller jugs are a direct response to the depletion of citizen-soldiers in Athens because of the Peloponnesian War.

The Keres: when is an underworld god not an underworld god?

Ker – the 'Doom of Death' – represents the Homeric hero's desire for fame and everlasting glory. Although this is not explicitly stated anywhere, it is obvious from Ker's ability to snuff out the hero's glory. She does this by simultaneously embodying the potential oblivion of death and the absence of personal victories on the battlefield. A man's Ker represents his own specific fate of death and, in this way, she is a different kind of fate than Μοῖρα or Αἶσα. Ker is the enforcer of Moira's will, or Zeus's will. She is not a 'fate creator'. Ker does not relate to the context of the life that leads to death but refers specifically to the mode and timing of death itself. It appears that most soldiers have a single Ker appointed to them (although it is relatively clear that a single Ker could be the performer of many different men's deaths).

Famously, Achilleus has two death-fates, which he comments on when hosting a small group of Greeks for dinner:

μήτηρ γάρ τέ μέ φησι θεὰ Θέτις ἀργυρόπεζα
διχθαδίας κῆρας φερέμεν θανάτοιο τέλοσδε.
εἰ μέν κ' αὖθι μένων Τρώων πόλιν ἀμφιμάχωμαι,
ὤλετο μέν μοι νόστος, ἀτὰρ κλέος ἄφθιτον ἔσται:
εἰ δέ κεν οἴκαδ' ἴκωμι φίλην ἐς πατρίδα γαῖαν,
ὤλετό μοι κλέος ἐσθλόν, ἐπὶ δηρὸν δέ μοι αἰὼν
ἔσσεται, οὐδέ κέ μ' ὦκα τέλος θανάτοιο κιχείη.

For my mother Thetis the goddess of the silver feet tells me
I carry two sorts of destiny toward the day of my death. Either, if I stay here
    and fight beside the city of the Trojans,
my return home is gone, but my glory shall be everlasting;
but if I return home to the beloved land of my fathers,
the excellence of my glory is gone, but there will be a long life left for me,
    and my end in death will not come to me quickly.[59]

He describes having two Keres between which he can choose, giving him an unprecedented amount of power over his own fate (although to what extent he actually has the power to choose between them is something that is not within my remit here). All this means is that there are two potential points in his life when Achilleus could die, giving him two possible courses of life – staying in Troy to die or going home to live – and he must choose between them. Both these Keres, then, represent the snuffing out of Achilleus's potential for future glories. One by the obscurity of death and one by the oblivion of old age. One – dying on the battlefield – allows a partial redemption: the longevity of his name.

For 'ordinary' men who are fated to die in battle the way *their* Ker reaches out for them has far-reaching implications. A battlefield death wrought by a Ker means, in all likeliness, that the dead man will not have a perfectly preserved body, a grand funeral, or a beautiful and well-kept tomb at home (although funerary requirements would still be carried out without access to a body, this is clearly not ideal). In this way Ker, as a divinity, is monstrous. This is not because of who she is or what she does, but because of the presage of her presence.[60] So there is very little difference between the personified and non-personified instances of *ker* in the *Iliad*: because it does not matter whether an instance is personified or abstract, the mythical meaning is implicit in the non-mythical use, and vice versa. This is certainly not true of all gods who are personifications of concepts: there are, for instance, many cases in which abstract *moira* means 'lot' or 'portion' of a tangible product. But Ker as a goddess is still death's doom and *ker* as death's doom still introduces the idea of Ker as a direct harbinger of death.[61]

The intersection occurs in the language used of ker. Abstract *ker*, the doom or fate of death, can become pseudo-personified by active verbs to describe her.

An example of this occurs when Patroklos's ghost visits the mourning Achilleus to reproach him for failing to carry out the things necessary for Patroklos's entry to the Underworld. The ghost addresses Achilleus: οὐ μὲν γὰρ ζωοί γε φίλων ἀπάνευθεν ἑταίρων βουλὰς ἑζόμενοι βουλεύσομεν, ἀλλ' ἐμὲ μὲν κὴρ ἀμφέχανε στυγερή, ἥ περ λάχε γεινόμενόν περ ('No longer shall you and I, alive, sit apart from our other beloved companions and make our plans, since the bitter doom that was given me when I was born has opened its jaws to take me').[62] There is a resonance of agency in Patroklos's doom. What drives this agency is the use of the verb ἀμφέχανω – rare, even in Homer – that suggests that *ker*, doom, is yawning around Patroklos. This kind of action endows this Ker with personality, even though she does not appear as an anthropomorphised divinity. The yawning or gaping suggests a physical presence. So her personality is not found in the noun of her name – and the concept associated with it – but in the verbs used to drive her actions.[63] Here, the act of gaping open indicates, as Jean-Pierre Vernant describes, 'that when Ker opens her mouth to swallow you, she sends you back to the original abyss'.[64] This transforms Ker from a simple agent of fate and death into a kind of bloodthirsty monster. And she shares many attributes with other, more traditional, monsters and monster-like animals – particularly in the act of gaping open. Michael Clarke, connecting the act of yawning open to monstrousness, comments that 'by ἀμφέχανε, "yawned", "gaped", [Homer] must mean that Ker opened her mouth to seize him like some monstrous beast'.[65] In the *Choephoroi*, Aischylos has Orestes used the same term – ἀμφέχανω – to describe the snake-child opening its mouth to suck at Klytaimestra's breast, her milk mixing with thickly clotted blood, the liquid of life being drowned out by thick and sticky death.[66]

Ker's monstrosity is reflected in the physical descriptions of her that Homer and Hesiod supply. In her only verifiable personification in the *Iliad*, Ker appears during the description of battle on Achilleus's shield:

ἐν δ' Ἔρις ἐν δὲ Κυδοιμὸς ὁμίλεον, ἐν δ' ὀλοὴ Κήρ,
ἄλλον ζωὸν ἔχουσα νεούτατον, ἄλλον ἄουτον,
ἄλλον τεθνηῶτα κατὰ μόθον ἕλκε ποδοῖϊν·
εἷμα δ' ἔχ' ἀμφ' ὤμοισι δαφοινεὸν αἵματι φωτῶν.

And Hate was there with Confusion among them, and Ker the destructive;
She was holding a live man with a new wound, and another
one unhurt, and dragged a dead man by the heel through the carnage.
The clothing upon her shoulders showed strong red with the blood of men.[67]

Here, along with other children of Nux (Night), she grabs men, dragging them around the battleground. She wears their blood, and the description names the colour – strong red – even though the physical shield would have been uncoloured.[68] She appears to be in a kind of unthinking frenzy – not caring whether the men she grabs at are wounded or not. This description is closely echoed in Hesiod's depiction of her on Herakles's shield:

ἐν δὲ Προΐωξίς τε Παλίωξίς τε τέτυκτο,
ἐν δ' Ὅμαδός τε Φόνος τ' Ἀνδροκτασίη τε δεδήει,
ἐν δ' Ἔρις, ἐν δὲ Κυδοιμὸς ἐθύνεον, ἐν δ' ὀλοὴ Κὴρ
ἄλλον ζωὸν ἔχουσα νεούτατον, ἄλλον ἄουτον,
ἄλλον τεθνηῶτα κατὰ μόθον ἕλκε ποδοῖϊν·
εἷμα δ' ἔχ' ἀμφ' ὤμοισι δαφοινεὸν αἵματι φωτῶν,
δεινὸν δερκομένη καναχῇσί τε βεβρυχυῖα.

On it Pursuit and Retreat were fashioned.
On it Tumult and Murder and Slaughter of men blazed.
On it Discord, on it Din of battle darted, and on it baneful Fate
holding one alive just wounded, another unwounded,
another, dead, she dragged into the fight by the feet.
She had about her shoulders a garment red with blood of men,
glaring terribly and roaring with sharp sounds.[69]

Again, she appears with her terrifying siblings, children of Nux, the counterparts of Zeus's shining children. Her treatment of men's bodies is the same. She does not just take the dead and wounded, but indiscriminately snatches men up in all states from unwounded to almost putrefying. But, Hesiod goes further still:

αἳ δὲ μετ' αὐτοὺς
Κῆρες κυάνεαι, λευκοὺς ἀραβεῦσαι ὀδόντας,
δεινωποὶ βλοσυροί τε δαφοινοί τ' ἄπλητοί τε
δῆριν ἔχον περὶ πιπτόντων· πᾶσαι δ' ἄρ' ἵεντο
αἷμα μέλαν πιέειν· ὃν δὲ πρῶτον μεμάποιεν
κείμενον ἢ πίπτοντα νεούτατον, ἀμφὶ μὲν αὐτῷ
βάλλον ὁμῶς] ὄνυχας μεγάλους, ψυχὴ δὲ [Ἀϊδόσδε]
κατῆεν
Τάρταρον ἐς κρυόενθ'· αἳ δὲ φρένας εὖτ' ἀρέσαντο
αἵματος ἀνδρομέου, τὸν μὲν ῥίπτασκον ὀπίσσω,
ἂψ δ' ὅμαδον καὶ μῶλον ἐθύνεον αὖτις ἰοῦσαι.

Behind them
the dark Keres, gnashing white teeth,
fierce-eyed, shaggy, blood-red, and unapproachable,
were having a fight over those falling, and all were eager
to drink their black blood. One they caught first,
lying dead or falling just wounded, they cast alike
great claws about him and his soul went down to Hades
into chilling Tartarus. Then when they'd sated hearts
with human blood, they'd throw that one behind them,
head back, and rush again to drudgery and tumult.[70]

Here the Keres appear and act monstrously. In both action and physicality, they embody, and become, the violent destruction of death: a type of destruction where life is ripped out or stolen away rather than given over. She leaves the body distorted and broken in death, and as the treatment of the body after death is highly important to the Greeks, any kind of action that compromises the integrity of the body is terrible. By sucking the blood out of her victims, casting them aside, or tossing them to and fro, Ker is taking away a chance for the families of her victims to complete the proper, required rituals of burial. Proper burial is a key aspect of funerary rites and a body that has been violently torn apart by Ker would prove significantly more difficult to honour appropriately than one that has been taken more gently. In the *Iliad*, we see proper burial and celebration being carried out, for τὸ γὰρ γέρας ἐστι θανόντων ('such is the privilege of the dead'),[71] and this is made clear regarding Sarpedon's death and the gentleness with which he is transported to the Underworld by Thanatos and Hypnos.[72] The gods preserve Hektor's body despite Achilleus's attempts to destroy it,[73] showing how seriously they (and therefore men) take the integrity of the body at burial. But when Ker takes ownership of the deceased a perversion of the body takes place, the man is immediately turned into a corpse, and the corpse is turned into rotting flesh before any chance for burial.

Ker's gaping mouth is a passage between the upper world and the netherworld, a passage between life and death that leads to a shady abyss. The Ker inhabit the mortal world, controlled by the Olympic gods but she serves a primordial and chaotic function. Vernant concludes that Ker represents 'death proper, that domain beyond-the-threshold, the gaping aperture of the other side that no gaze can penetrate and no discourse can express ... nothing but the horror of unspeakable Night'.[74] As the herald of destructive, violent death, Ker drags men across boundaries; not only the boundary between life and death, but that border between the potential glory that awaits the heroic warrior in life and the obscurity and anonymity of death; a state which directly contravenes the hero's desire for himself in death. Men want to be celebrated and remembered, but Ker destroys the man and flings his body into unknowable territory, without the promise of a glorious burial.

Clarke warns, in *Flesh and Spirit in the Songs of Homer*, that we must be vigilant not to ascribe a complete personification where there is no need to do so. He points out two things in particular. First, the names of agents alternate freely in the epics, without distinction, and sometimes from line to line, including abstract nouns which are never given any kind of anthropomorphisation, πότμος for μοῖρα, for example. Second, there are some instances when uses of Ker (and Thanatos) are incompatible with her characterisation and the doom of death. He says, by way of example, that:

> Death must be something abstract or intangible when a man scheming against another is said to plan or establish his death. Likewise, when one brings about another's death it has been made or wrought ... and a killer can boast to his victim that he will 'forge' or 'fashion' the ker of his death'.[75]

However, what these instances show is not that Ker is incompatible with the personified doom of death that we have seen but one that extends and casts a hand over the actions of men. After all, in another form Ker is simply the fate of death that is assigned to a man at the beginning of his life, and that death may well be at the hands of another man. We do not question the ability of other gods to influence man's will, and the question of man's free will has always been, and continues to be to this day, about whether man only assumes that he has free will. We must, of course, heed Clarke's advice not to ascribe a wholesale personification to Ker – or any of the other shadowy figures we encounter in Homer – but the non-mythic uses, enhanced by the active verbs that push death upon us – that is, 'us' the dying man and 'us' the reader or listener – needs to be taken seriously as a death-agent and Underworld god. In her personified form, Ker stands for the sickness or accident or weapon that kills her victim. Unlike Thanatos, who is a generalised Death, Ker is a specific, fated, individual malicious agent that is assigned – as Patroklos tells Achilleus – to each person at birth. She is not just any monster; rather she is each man's personal monster, waiting on the boundary with gaping mouth to suck the life out of him.[76] There is also the threat the Ker will swallow you, but the implication seems to be a more uneasy sense of the oblivion that awaits the you on the other side. She swallows you into a black hole where no glory can be won, and no memory can be retained. But, as a divinity she is not ever fully anthropomorphised, and does not appear in cult, and did not receive attention outside the early literature of Homer and Hesiod. It is more likely that Ker was used in a very specific literary sense to convey the horrors of war and wartime death, and therefore appeared in a very different context to the 'major' Underworld gods. Minor gods more often are used to say something meaningful about the state of death or dying. This is particularly true of the Keres, who represent a 'monstrous' death on battlefields that rely on the reputation of heroics and heroic deaths.

This slightly roundabout interlude into Homeric death has a purpose. Because there is no doubt that the Keres are related to the death and the Underworld, they are divine agents of death and that makes them 'Underworld gods'. But the Keres are never given cult worship. People simply do not propagate them. Why not? Why do some Underworld gods get cult and others do not? Very simply it comes back to this: people form *multi-directional relationships* with gods. They form relationships with gods who they can get something from, in return for their worship (though this is not as simple as presented in the 'I give that you might give' model of Greek religious practice). The Keres are ruthless, propitiating them for mercy would make no difference to their actions.

Concluding note

In this chapter I have looked at the landscape that enables that worship to take place and looked at an example of an Underworld god who is not really a divinity in any meaningful sense outside literature, and who does not receive cult practices, including notably, sacrifice. As we shall see in the following chapters, the act of sacrifice was central to the religious experience of the Greeks, and most other ritual activity was associated with, or performed alongside, sacrifice in some way.[77] The Greeks who undertook sacrifices to Underworld gods were cultivating a relationship between themselves and Underworld gods in the very same way that they cultivated relationships with any other gods. Building a relationship with the gods was one of the – if not the – most important aspects of Greek religious life. These relationships were built on the idea of mutual benefit, so the worshipper perceived that the god received adoration and gifts (in the form of sacrifices and other offerings), and the worshipper gained the favour of the god. This is not the kind of relationship that is predicated on equal and direct exchange of gifts or 'favours owed' (that it, 'I will give you x, in direct exchange for y'), but it is reciprocal in the sense of creating good will and predisposition (that is, 'I will give you x, in the hope that you will think kindly of me and bring about good things for me, because we have formed a relationship').[78]

The primary method of communication was ritual, and we see this reinforced by the literature and in material finds. In Homer's *Iliad*, the gods are shown receiving (and sometimes denying) the smoke of sacrifices,[79] and there is mythic heritage to the idea that the gods claimed certain parts of the sacrificial animals.[80] Myth interacts with ritual, and in turn myth itself is shaped by ritual. Because we find evidence for the Underworld gods being worshipped – including being sacrificed to – then we must treat this the same way as any other god being worshipped, so the Underworld gods fit into the same religious landscape as these other gods. Even the very limited (unambiguous) physical worship offered to Hades, this still must be considered – why is Hades offered this cult? The presence of Underworld gods in the religious landscape, no matter how small, is an important consideration if we are to grasp the full picture of Greek religion.

Notes

1 Hom. *Il.* 14.231, 16.672, 16.682.
2 Hom. *Il.* 16.666–683.
3 Vermeule, 1979: 148.
4 *LIMC* s.v. Thanatos 14, 15, 16, 18. This motif was more or less fixed by Euphronios's red-figure krater, the '*Sarpedon Vase*', see Spivey, 2018: 46–75.
5 Vermeule, 1979: 150.
6 See Chapter 4.
7 Eur. *Alk.* 62.
8 Eur. *Alk.* 74–75.
9 For example, at Aisch. *Ag.* 6–7.
10 Leitao, 2003; cf. Parker, 2005b: 210; Versnel, 1993: 314, 17.
11 Eur. *Alk.* 55.
12 Eur. *Alk.* 49.
13 Though, of course, this is in part so that Herakles can rescue her and is a feature of the tragic motif of death-and-rebirth.

14 See further discussion in Chapter 4.
15 Baudy, 1997: 426; Beekes, 2010: 462; Furley, 1996: 18–19; Larson, 2007: 144. This etymology is generally accepted.
16 2007: 146.
17 Burkert, 1985: 158.
18 See *LIMC* s.v. Hermes 89–91; cf. Sourvinou-Inwood, 1995: 219.
19 Marinatos, 2003: 141–142.
20 Hom. *Od.* 24.1–14.
21 *LIMC* s.v. Hermes 598, 606, 611c; Fairbanks, 1907: 306; Kurtz, 1975: xxi; Oakley, 2004: figs 100, 02, 03; Shapiro, 1993: 83, 91; Vermeule, 1979: fig 19.
22 Oakley, 2004: 139. *LIMC* s.v. Charon 6, 5, 7a, 7b, 10, 12, 22; Fairbanks, 1907: 190, 91, plate VII .
23 *LIMC* s.v. Hermes 606, 1907: 284; Oakley, 2004: fig. 103. Literary examples including Soph. *Aj.* 831–834; Eur. *Alk.* 743–744.
24 For discussion on this see Chapter 5.
25 *LIMC*. s.v. Hermes 593; Kurtz, 1975: plate 50.52.
26 Deubner, 1966: 111–14; Parke, 1977: 119; Simon, 1983: 93.
27 h.Hom. *Herm.* 572–573.
28 Eidinow, 2007a: 148–149; Parker, 2005b: 296. Examples include Audollent, 1904: Nos. 50, 52, 67, 68, 72, 73, 85, 86, 88, 105; Jordan, 1985: Nos. 18, 42, 44, 75, 109, 18, 19, 20, 21, 70; Wünsch, 1897: Nos. 79, 81, 84, 87, 88, 89, 93, 100, 02, 05, 06.
29 For example, *LIMC* s.v. Charon I.1, I.2, I.3, I.5, I.7a, I.7b, I.10, I.11, I.12, I.13, I.19, I.24, I.27, I.30, I.32, I.33a, I.36, I.37, I.40, I.41, I.42, I.43.
30 Alexiou, Yatromanolakis and Roilos, 2002: 138; Garland, 1985: 55.
31 Charon is also called the 'old ferryman' in the epic poem *Minyas*, possibly of fifth-century date; see Kinkel 1877: 215. See also Paus. 10.28.2; Eur. *Alk.* 554; cf. Huxley, 1969: 119.
32 Peek, 1955: no. 1384; trans. Alexiou.
33 Aristoph. *Fr.* 139–140, 269–270.
34 Stevens, 1991: 215, 23.
35 Cf. Oakley, 2004: 113.
36 See fig. 2.2.1 above and *LIMC* s.v. Charon I.1, I.3, I.5, I.7a, I.7b, I.10, I.11, I.13, I.19; cf. 2004: 113.
37 2004: 125.
38 See discussion in Chapter 5.
39 Hom. *Od.* 11.639, 24.11.
40 See discussion in Chapter 6, and cf.Bernabé and Jiménez San Cristóbal 2008: 29–35; Janko, 1984: 91.
41 Vermeule, 1979: 179.
42 Diog. Laert. 1.8.104.
43 1979: 184–185, 88.
44 I discuss *katadesmoi* in detail in Chapter 6.
45 Many of these vases may have been originally intended for single ritual use and resale on the secondary market in Italy.
46 Eur. *Hipp.* 373–430.
47 Soph. *OT.* 1289.
48 Loraux, 1987: 9–10.
49 See, for example, Johnston, 1999: 216.
50 Ps-Hyg. *Poet. Astr.* 2.2.
51 Hsch. s.v. μυσαχνή (*polluted days*).
52 Phot. s.v. μιαρά ἡμέρα (*polluted day;* Hamilton, 1992: T24); ράμνος (*buckthorn;* Hamilton, 1992: T26).
53 Zenob. *Cent.* 4.33 (Campbell).

54 Hamilton, 1992: 50–51.
55 Campbell's Loeb edition mentions this, and also see Robertson, 1993: 203–204.
56 Hsch. s.v. κήρ, κῆρες.
57 Ham, 1999: 201.
58 Ham, 1999: 201.
59 Hom. *Il.* 9.410–416.
60 Cf. Atherton, 2002: VI.
61 See Clarke, 1999: 231–239.
62 Hom. *Il.* 23.77–79 (trans. Lattimore, with amendment).
63 Clarke, 1999: 244; cf. Burkert, 2005: 4; Stafford, 2000: 10.
64 Vernant, 1991: 98; cf. Clarke, 1999: 249.
65 Clarke, 1999: 249.
66 Aisch. *Cho.* 527–533; cf. Vermeule, 1979: 40.
67 Hom. *Il.* 18.535–538; trans. Lattimore.
68 The shield is wrought from bronze, tin, gold, and silver (*Il.* 18.475–476). I think the addition of colour in the description of the shield is meant to enhance the audiences' ability to imagine the physical object, and here specifically adds to the horror of the characterisation; cf. Becker, 1990.
69 Hes. *Sh.* 154–160; trans. Huddleston.
70 Hes. *Sh.* 248–257; trans. Huddleston.
71 Hom. *Il.* 16.457.
72 Hom. *Il.* 16.453–457.
73 Hom. *Il.* 23.184–191.
74 Vernant, 1991: 75.
75 Clarke, 1999: 254.
76 Cf. Dietrich, 1965: 240.
77 Georgoudi, 2010: 92.
78 Cf. Parker, 1998; Pulleyn, 1997: 12–13.
79 For example, Hom. *Il.* 1.434–456 (receiving), *Od.* 9.551–555 (denying).
80 Hes. *Th.* 445–541, which relates the story of Prometheus tricking the gods into accepting the fat and bones of a sacrificial animal.

3 Hades as god and place

Is Hades a god or a place? Or both? Hades-the-god was the shadowy figure who ruled over Hades-the-place – a dim world for the dead. Either way, as Euripides describes, Ἅιδης χωρὶς ᾤκισται θεῶν ('Hades dwells apart from the gods').[1] In Homer, Hades – Ἀΐδης – as an individual god is barely distinguished from the Underworld as a locality, and sometimes it is near impossible to differentiate between the god and the place even by context. For example, the 'gates of Hades' could refer to either gates belonging to the god, or gates that lead into the Underworld.[2] Every time this ambiguous phrase is used in the Homeric corpus, Hades's name appears in the Homeric genitive: Ἀΐδαο – which is, as Michael Clarke comments, is

> odd but not unparalleled in our author: compare Διὸς ἔνδον ...[3] for "inside the house of Zeus," εἰς Αἰγύπτιοι, διιπετέος ποταμοῖο ...[4] for "into the river ...," and ἐς πατρός ...[5] for "to the father's house".[6]

This ambiguous description is not limited to epic but appears in grave epigrams as well, for instance where one might find Ἀΐδα δῶμα μέλαν ('the dark house of Hades').[7] Of the forty-six mentions of Ἀΐδης in the *Iliad*, only sixteen unambiguously describe either the god or the Underworld. Unambiguous references to the god may include epithets, like where he is Hades 'of the famed horses',[8] or instances where he undertake substantive actions, such as where he draws governorship over the ζόφον ἠερόεντα ('gloomy darkness') when he, Poseidon, and Zeus balloted for parts of the world to govern.[9] Although predominantly called Ἀΐδης,[10] he is also called Ἀϊδωνεύς (Aidoneus) twice in Homer's *Iliad*,[11] four times in the Homeric *Hymn to Demeter*,[12] once in Hesiod's *Theogony*,[13] and twice in the extant works of Aischylos.[14] The only clear difference between 'Hades' and 'Aidoneus' is the completely unambiguous characterisation of the latter. Aidoneus is always the god, and there is no obfuscation in his presence. This is not to say that 'Hades', or other names, are not contextually unambiguous, but it is clear that 'Aidoneus' is meant to signal to us 'This is Absolutely Hades the God, and Not Hades the Underworld' is clear by its repeated use in the Homeric *Hymn to Demeter*, where the storyline requires strong characterisation of both the god of the Underworld and the Underworld itself. Sometimes, Hades is also called the 'underground Zeus' or the 'other Zeus'.[15]

There is one place, in Homer, where Hades becomes viscerally real, almost human-like. Poseidon shakes the earth, the Underworld also shakes, and Hades gets scared:[16]

> ἔδδεισεν δ' ὑπένερθεν ἄναξ ἐνέρων Ἀϊδωνεύς,
> δείσας δ' ἐκ θρόνου ἆλτο καὶ ἴαχε, μή οἱ ὕπερθε
> γαῖαν ἀναρρήξειε Ποσειδάων ἐνοσίχθων,
> οἰκία δὲ θνητοῖσι καὶ ἀθανάτοισι φανείη
> σμερδαλέ' εὐρώεντα, τά τε στυγέουσι θεοί περ

> Aïdoneus, lord of the dead below, was in terror
> and sprang from his throne and screamed aloud, for fear that above him
> he who circles the land, Poseidon, might break the earth open
> and the houses of the dead lie open to men and immortals,
> ghastly and mouldering, so the very gods shudder before them.

This short episode is one of the most complete personifications of Hades, showing his emotional reaction and the vulnerability that goes along with such response – familiar, and relatable, to the mortal audience. In this one brief passage, Homer makes Hades like us: scared of the gods. Fear of the gods, and their actions, is not unusual in the ancient literature, but it is people who fear gods. And, indeed, Poseidon's shaking is not aimed at evoking Hades's fear: it is about gripping the mortal men who fight atop the shuddering earth to know, and feel, that the gods have entered the battle and to fear for their lives. But Hades fears too. He fears that his world will be exposed, the earth cracked open and the land of the dead laid bare for all to see. Fear that Poseidon's power was stronger than his own. Fear that his valuable charges could rush back into the living world at the wrong time. Gods have no normal need to fear death or the destruction of their lands and property. The fact that Hades fears exposure says more about him, and the world that bears his name, than any other passage in the epic poem.

Exposure is particularly problematic for Hades – both the god and the place – because they are both meant to be invisible or unseen.[17] Hades's name probably means something like 'unseen one'[18] or 'the invisible',[19] so the god was unseeable. This was also true in cult: the only real example of a cult of Hades that we have evidence for did not admit the general public to the temple, making Hades invisible to everyone except the priest.[20] Other gods also appeared, at one time or another, invisible to some or all the people present,[21] and were sometimes unseeable in cult,[22] the difference was in the intent. All other times when gods appear invisible they do so because it will aid their purpose in some way, but Hades is always invisible to (living) people. But this does not mean that Hades, as a god, is imperceptible. Rather, that under certain conditions (namely, being alive), he is withdrawn from sight or concealed from the worshipper. A person may see Hades clearly, but only after that condition has been lifted; that is, after the worshipper has died and journeyed into the Underworld. Hades remains in the Underworld, and his realm cannot easily be accessed by people or gods who have no direct business being there. If Poseidon cracked the earth open, and the Underworld *was* perceptible to living people and gods then Hades's largest asset, his invisibility, would be stripped away. The Underworld would become open, and he would no longer be able to maintain the border between the living and the dead.

Hades's reputation as 'unseeable' may have been further perpetuated by his mythic 'cap of invisibility', first attested in Homer when Athena uses it to hide herself from Ares.[23] According to pseudo-Apollodoros, the Cyclopes gave the cap to Plouton, the name used in *Bibliotheka* for the god of the Underworld,[24] when they gave Zeus the thunderbolt and Poseidon the trident. Hesiod also mentions the cap, but rather than bestowing invisibility, it cloaks him with the νυκτὸς ζόφον αἰνὸν ('awful gloom of night').[25] Darkness and night are also associated with death in Homer's work, where dying heroes are described as having night or darkness descend upon them or cover their eyes,[26] and this description is enough to indicate that the hero had died.[27] The contrast between dark and light can be rendered as juxtaposition between living and death; the living man sees the light whereas the dead are shrouded in darkness. Darkness itself forms a natural attribute of invisibility.[28] The Underworld, and by association the god who governs it, is also shrouded in darkness, and the dead are, similarly, rendered invisible to the living until they are brought out into the light. The absence of light and seeing can be directly linked to the invisible, and so these two caps – Homer and Hesiod's – are the same.

The hazy rendering Hades receives elsewhere, as Christiane Sourvinou-Inwood comments, 'befits the god who rules over the unseeable',[29] and who is, himself, unseen. His ambiguous characterisation in the *Iliad* is complemented by near absence in the *Odyssey*. Here, Persephone takes the leading role in governing the dead.[30] References to Ἀίδαο δόμος (the 'house of Hades') might imply Hades's presence, as is the case in references to Ἀΐδαο δόμους καὶ ἐπαινῆς Περσεφονείης (the 'house of Hades and dread Persephone').[31] In the *Odyssey*, Hades is never called Aidoneus, which reinforces the idea that this is the primary corporeal god, and 'Hades' is the ambiguous place-god.

On the other hand, Hesiod explicitly refers to ἴφθιμόν τ' Ἀίδην, ὃς ὑπὸ χθονὶ δώματα ναίει νηλεὲς ἦτορ ἔχων ('mighty Hades, who resides in palaces beneath the earth and has a pitiless heart'),[32] and elsewhere Hesiod describes Hades as ἐνέροισι καταφθιμένοισιν ἀνάσσων ('lord over the dead below').[33] So, in Hesiod's cosmology Hades is not ambiguously related to the Underworld, he is its indisputable ruler. That Homer and Hesiod present quite different versions of the rulership of the Underworld is not insignificant, though these differences are enhanced by differences in genre. Their description of the realm and its guardians demonstrates that there was not a fixed way that the Underworld was conceived of poetically. This may also show shifting ideas about the Underworld in people's ideation and beliefs. Could this be because people just did not want to think about the Underworld and its gods? This is doubtful, based on other evidence, particularly the artistic evidence, of both the main and subsidiary Underworld gods.

The way Hades is represented in art changes our ideas about him as a god, and as an Underworld ruler. Visual representations show several versions of the same god, and these bleed into cult practices. In both spaces we find several gods who appear to be the same, or who have a critical mass of overlapping aspects of the same: notably Hades and Plouton (later 'Pluto'), but also, in the specific context of the Eleusinian Mysteries, Theos. In earlier visual representations, it can be easy to distinguish between Hades and Plouton, although they are both mature, bearded, and often have white hair. Each sometimes carries a sceptre, but Hades's is more like the one Hermes carries in his role as *psychopompos*[34]– but in art Hermes is more likely to be seen with the *kerykeion*. Either Plouton or Hades can be represented carrying a horn, but Hades's is a drinking horn, and Plouton's an overflowing cornucopia.[35] Plouton is usually standing, and fully clothed, and can appear with either (or both) Demeter or Kore.[36] Hades can be standing, seated, or lying, and is normally bare-chested, and predominantly appears with a Persephone-like figure.[37]

But the apparently clear delineation between the two does not mean that identification is simple, particularly in circumstances where there are only fragments of artefacts remains. This is particularly true in the case of cult items. In these cases, recipients are often unidentifiable and can only be ascertained through context of deposition or by inscriptional evidence, which may not be present. In addition, there are obvious exceptions to these rules, as in the example shown in Figure 3.1, in which a half-clothed figure holding a cornucopia lies on a couch with Persephone (labelled, appropriately, Pherephatta, on which see more in Chapter 4). The male figure could easily be Hades or Plouton from the description of attributes given above but is labelled Plouton. The context is not clear enough and although there may be more iconographical links to 'A Hades', the labelling of the figure as Pluton leaves us with no doubt that the *kylix*'s painter intended the figure to be read, literally, as Plouton. So clearly Hades and Plouton have overlapping attributes and appear to shift between clear and obfuscated representations. While such representations may appear confusing to a modern reader it is most likely the ancient audience would have understood the images. This is true even in cases, as in the example above, where they are indistinguishable from one another without taking wider context into account. There are, however, several clear distinctions in artistic representations, both in literature and in art, and this is generally enough to identify which god is being depicted. Therefore, even though they are practically amalgamated in later literature and art and may be closely associated in the archaic and classical periods, we should not read them as two faces of one divinity in archaic or classical period religious activity. Rather, because they represent related aspects (that is, because there is a strong link between the Underworld and agriculture), have very similar iconographic attributes, and are each paired with a Persephonean figure, they were often

Figure 3.1 Attic red-figure kylix (interior) showing Plouton (labelled ΠΛΟΥΤΩΝ) and
Persephone (labelled ΦΕΡΡΕΦΑΤΤΑ) seated on a dining couch. Attributed to
The Codrus Painter. c. 430 BCE. British Museum, 1847,0909.6

associated with one another. Originally – but decreasingly throughout the
archaic and early classical periods – they were two separate gods and did not
become fully amalgamated until later. We can, however, see the seed of that
amalgam in some of these early works.

It may appear superficially that Hades and Plouton were being seen as two
faces of the same god, but that they do retain local and authorial variation. In
other words, at this stage Plouton and Hades may be the same god, or at the
very least interchangeable, in literary (and artistic) contexts. In local cults,
however, there was still some clear differentiation. This indicates that sites
described by later authors as dedicated to Plouton may have originally been
cults of Hades – and indeed may still have been. Clearly there were originally
two separate characterisations: one an agrarian god who was called Plouton,
and the other an Underworld ruler who was called Hades. Over time, the two
may have been conflated in name but their major aspects remained separate.

Gradually, during the sixth and fifth centuries, Hades became increasingly
associated with ideas of plenty, related both to his close tie to Plouton (whose
name literally means 'Wealth'),[38] and to the inevitable link between the
Underworld and 'under-ground' and agrarian concerns. This may have been

related to his marriage to Persephone, and his increasingly close relationship with Demeter (from brother to son-in-law). Homeric Persephone has none of the agrarian or fertility aspects that she has in religious practice. Even so, the association in both cult and literature with Demeter makes her agrarian characteristics more prominent. For example, one of the most prominent aspects of her abduction myth is that she is out with the nymphs picking flowers.[39] This was a connection both to the fertility of soil – and thus, 'under-ground' – and to her own budding sexual maturity. Hades becomes associated with the fertilisation of the ground, the burial of seeds, and care for the parts of plants that stay under the earth – those parts that transgress the border between his world and Demeter's.

The act of burying seeds in the earth has a relatively obvious link to death and the Underworld, as they were buried the same way that bodies were interred into the ground. Farmers bury their seeds to create life; both the life of the crop itself and the lives those crops sustain. Although there is insufficient evidence to say this is a widespread connection, it is referenced directly in the Homeric *Hymn to Demeter*, where, we are told, men σπέρμ᾽ ὑπὸ γῆς κρύπτουσα ('hide seeds beneath the earth').[40] The harvest provides wealth and is a sign of public fertility. There is, therefore, a link between death – more specifically burial – and agrarian plenty. There is also a change in vocabulary describing the dead. They are no longer the weak and feeble beings portrayed in Homer, but are instead 'blessed'.[41] For example, the *Odyssey* describes Odysseus entreating the νεκύων ἀμενηνὰ κάρηνα ('feeble heads of the dead'),[42] but by 405 BCE, in the first showing of Aristophanes' *Frogs*, the dead, or at least the initiates of the Mysteries who are depicted in the comedy, are described as being a θιάσους εὐδαίμονας ('happy chorus').[43] Similarly, attitudes towards the dead changed as the 'familiar, hateful rather than frightening'[44] death of "Homeric" mentality – something akin to Airès's 'Tamed Death' – gave way to a conception of death that was categorised by avoidance. Sourvinou-Inwood comments, on this change, that:

> Clearly, an eternity as a witless senseless ghost was not, to an early Greek, a more frightening prospect, likely to generate more anxiety, than an eternity as a lively shade. After all, the former belief is a way of visualising and articulating the notions 'cessation of life' and 'continuing survival' in a peaceful image of the unseeable existence after death akin to 'they are sleeping'.[45]

This change, from the peaceful but witless dead found in Homer to active and 'lively' shades found in visual representations and later poetry and drama, also signals a change in attitude towards Hades, particularly as a location, and this is played out in the association of Hades with Plouton and agrarian concerns.

The god of the Underworld in Eleusinian cult is called Theos.[46] This (unnamed) god is not the consort of Kore, which is Plouton, but is rather the partner of Thea. Plouton and Theos appear together in iconographic representations at Eleusis, the most striking example being the 'Lakrateides Relief' of around 100 BCE.[47] Theos has, generally, a closer iconographic resemblance to Hades than to Plouton, but this does not designate the gods as the same. Theos and Thea were originally identified as Hades and Persephone by Martin Nilsson in 1935.[48]

Hades and mortals

With the literary and iconographical differences between Hades and Plouton it may seem that any worship directed at Hades is directed towards Plouton, and that Ἅιδης is solely a god of mythology – and even then, barely so – and does not exist in religious undertakings in the world. After all, he is a god who has no cult: ἐν οὐδεμιᾷ πόλει Ἅιδου βωμός ἐστιν ('in no city is there an altar to Hades').[49] Funerary rituals, grave markers and goods, or calls for magical assistance to the Underworld rarely – if ever – include references to him, and there is no epigraphical record of Hades until the fourth century.[50] Likewise, no temples or altars dedicated to the god have been found. It does not necessarily follow, however, that (per Robert Garland) 'Hades had no generally recognised cult'.[51] Although there are a number of cults in which Hades plays a direct role, it may be that most of Hades' long-lasting cultic participation occurs only through his relationship to other divinities, usually those associated in some way with the Underworld.

There are several sanctuaries of other gods that contain dedications to the god of the Underworld, including, as Pausanias tells us: an image of the god, along with those of other Underworld deities, in the sanctuary of the Semnai Theai at Athens;[52] a temple dedicated to Artemis Soteira in Troezen which contains altars to the gods who rule under the earth (it was said that this was the location of Semele's return to the upper world after her rescue by Dionysos, and also where Herakles dragged Kerberos up from the Underworld);[53] an image of the Underworld god appears alongside Demeter, Kore, and the Moirai, in a temple of Apollo at Amyklai in Lakedaimonia;[54] and at the temple of Athena in Phokis, Hades was in some way involved in dedications presented to the goddess.[55] Hades is only mentioned by name in reference to the cult at Elis and the temple of Athena at Phokis; in most other circumstances, the named god is Plouton. These only provide an indication of the long-lasting cultic dedications which may have been made to Hades. There is much reason to think that most cultic worship of Hades – in fact of any 'Underworld' deity – may have been much less enduring, and this will be elucidated below.

The most well-known cult in which Hades is the main recipient of honours is in the western Peloponnesian city of Elis. Pausanias notes that the temple here was only opened once each year and that, even then, only the priest was permitted to enter.[56] This restriction was due to the axiom that each man may only enter the realm of Hades once, upon his death, and by so entering the temple here he would be, in effect, dying.[57] Pausanias tells us that:

ὁ δὲ ἱερὸς τοῦ Ἅιδου περίβολός τε καὶ ναός – ἔστι γὰρ δὴ Ἠλείοις καὶ Ἅιδου περίβολός τε καὶ ναός – ἀνοίγνυται μὲν ἅπαξ κατὰ ἔτος ἕκαστον, ἐσελθεῖν δὲ οὐδὲ τότε ἐφεῖται πέρα γε τοῦ ἱερωμένου. ἀνθρώπων δὲ ὧν ἴσμεν μόνοι τιμῶσιν Ἅιδην Ἠλεῖοι κατὰ αἰτίαν τήνδε. Ἡρακλεῖ στρατιὰν ἄγοντι ἐπὶ Πύλον τὴν ἐν τῇ Ἤλιδι, παρεῖναί οἱ καὶ Ἀθηνᾶν συνεργὸν λέγουσιν· ἀφικέσθαι οὖν καὶ Πυλίοις τὸν Ἅιδην συμμαχήσοντα τῇ ἀπεχθείᾳ τοῦ Ἡρακλέους, ἔχοντα ἐν τῇ Πύλῳ τιμάς.

The sacred enclosure of Hades and its temple (for the Elians have these among their possessions) are opened once every year, but not even on this occasion is anybody permitted to enter except the priest. The following is the reason why the Elians worship Hades; they are the only men we know of to do so. It is said that, when Heracles was leading an expedition against Pylos in Elis, Athena was one of his allies. Now among those who came to fight on the side of the Pylians was Hades, who was the foe of Heracles but was worshipped at Pylos.[58]

Pausanias links the sanctuary at Elis to the war between the local Pylians and Herakles' forces during which time Hades fought for the Elians. This was not because of any particular affinity the god had with the local population, but due to his intense hatred of Herakles.[59] This animosity is explained by Pausanias using the Homeric story of Herakles shooting and wounding Hades with an arrow.[60] Pausanias claims that the Elians dedicated the sanctuary to Hades as their ally in battle, not as lord of the Underworld. The proximity of the sanctuary to the temple of Demeter and Persephone, however, creates a clear juxtaposition between the agrarian fertility and the death-related infertility of the Underworld god. This, coupled with the closeness to the river Acheron, indicates that this may have been, if not originally, then after some time, related to the god in his Underworld context. Even the name of the city in which this occurs can give us a clue to this cult, according to Harrison:[61] Pylos comes from the Greek πύλος, meaning 'in the gateway' and sometimes explained as the entrance to the gates of Hades,[62] and it is at the western point of the Greek mainland, that is, the direction of the setting sun. Less that 16 kilometers to the east of Elis, Pausanias records another instance of Hades worship. And, around 55 kilometers to the south, at Triphylia, Strabo mentions that a *temenos* that was dedicated to Hades, that was situated near to a river named Acheron by virtue of its close association with the god. Strabo says that Hades's cult maintained a close relationship to nearby cults of Demeter and Persephone because the locals may have[63] believed that the land would produce either a plentiful harvest or no harvest at all:[64]

πρὸς ἄρκτον δ' ὅμορα ἦν τῷ Πύλῳ δύο πολείδια Τριφυλιακὰ Ὕπανα καὶ Τυμπανέαι, ὧν τὸ μὲν εἰς Ἦλιν συνῳκίσθη τὸ δ' ἔμεινε. καὶ ποταμοὶ δὲ δύο ἐγγὺς ῥέουσιν ὅ τε Δαλίων καὶ ὁ Ἀχέρων, ἐμβάλλοντες εἰς τὸν Ἀλφειόν. ὁ δὲ Ἀχέρων κατὰ τὴν πρὸς τὸν Ἅιδην οἰκειότητα ὠνόμασται·

ἐκτετίμηται γὰρ δὴ σφόδρα τά τε τῆς Δήμητρος καὶ τῆς κόρης ἱερὰ ἐνταῦθα
καὶ τὰ τοῦ Ἅιδου, τάχα διὰ τὰς ὑπεναντιότητας, ὥς φησιν ὁ Σκήψιος Δημή-
τριος. καὶ γὰρ εὔκαρπός ἐστι καὶ ἐρυσίβην γεννᾷ καὶ θρύον ἡ Τριφυλία:
διόπερ ἀντὶ μεγάλης φορᾶς πυκνὰς ἀφορίας γίνεσθαι συμβαίνει κατὰ τοὺς
τόπους.

Towards the north, on the borders of Pylos, were two little Triphylian
cities, Hypana and Tympaneai … And further, two rivers flow near these
places, the Dalion and the Akheron [named after the famous River of
Hades], both of them emptying into the Alpheios. The Akheron has been
so named by virtue of its close relation to Hades; for, as we know, not only
the temples of Demeter and Kore [Persephone] have been held in very high
honor there, but also those of Hades, perhaps because of 'the contrariness
of the soil,' to use the phrase of Demetrios of Skepsis. For while Triphylia
brings forth good fruit, it breeds red-rust and produces rush; and therefore
in this region it is often the case that instead of a large crop there is no
crop at all.[65]

This shows that the cult was both not the same as Pausanias's Elian cult,
despite the closeness of the two, and that the cult was most likely agrarian in
nature, given the proximity and connection to Demetrian cults in the vicinity.
However, this cult also shows the interrelationship between death and
agriculture – the ground is not only fertile is it also capable of producing death.

Concluding note

Like most other Underworld gods, Hades does not feature in physical death-
related ritual activity. He is not invoked in funerary or burial rites, nor is he the
subject of prayers or offering during festivals that honour the dead. He does not
have an immediately apparent eschatological function. He does not (usually)
judge the dead, with the only extant occasion he is assigned this role appearing
in plays by Aischylos. The chorus of the *Eumenides* says: μέγας γὰρ Ἅιδης
ἐστὶν εὔθυνος βροτῶν ἔνερθε χθονός, δελτογράφῳ δὲ ἐπωπᾷ φρενί ('For mighty
Hades is the judge of mortals beneath the earth, and he observes all things and
records them in his mind').[66] But even in Aischylos his primary function is as
the near-absent custodian of the dead.[67] The job involves ensuring that
everyone stays where they should be. That is, that the dead remain in the
Underworld and the living stay out of it. This is not a job he personally does,
though. Kerberos, for instance, guards the entrance to the Underworld. Hades
does not have any control over when people die, nor does he collect their souls
from the earth and bring them into the Underworld. So, although he rules over
the dead, Hades himself does not have any direct control over death or the fate
of men's deaths.[68] From this position we can see that Hades's role in the
landscape of Greek religion was somewhat different to that of other gods.

Gods exist so that people can worship them. This is their primary function, as the comfort (and other benefits, tangible and intangible) that religion provides is performed by worship. Therefore, worship reinforces comfort by providing an opportunity for a worshipper to feel like they are building a relationship with the god in question. Gods are constructed to be worshipped and so they must satisfy something within the worshipper themselves and whether the god does or does not *actually* exist is irrelevant to this. If the worshipper believes that the god exists then in that time and place they do, for that specific person. This creates issues for gods like Hades though: living people do not, for the most part, need to worship Hades because he cannot reciprocate their sacrificial gifts in any meaningful or tangible way. Hades cannot ensure a better afterlife, a kinder death, or a more plentiful harvest. Similarly, there is no idea that the dead worship Hades as they have no need to ask favour of the god who (perhaps) rules over them; they have completed their assigned life and died at the fated time,[69] at this stage the god either cannot or is not willing to change the condition of their death.

Early representations of the dead show them as witless shades who did not have the ability to act as they did while alive.[70] The dead in Homer, then, not only would not need the comfort provided by religious activity, they may very well have been unable to actually participate in ritual activity. The dead are subjects of Hades in the way that citizens are subject to kings and lords, and they maintain a certain amount of individual autonomy (at least, in iterations in which they have the mental faculties to exhibit individual autonomy). Thus, Hades truly is the 'Lord' of the dead, rather than a god of death. Even if we consider that the sole purpose of Mystery initiation is to bring about blessings in the afterlife,[71] this does not entail any kind of religious devotion in the afterlife – there is no mention of continued religious practice and scenes of the dead certainly do not show them taking part in such ritual practice.

Notes

1 Eur. *Hec.* 2.
2 Hom. *Il.* 5.646, 9.312, 23.71; *Od.* 14.156. See also Hom. *Il.* 6.487, 7.330, 11.55, 16.856, 22.213, 22.362, 23.76, 23.244.
3 Hom. *Il.* 10.13.
4 Hom. *Od.* 4.581.
5 Hom. *Od.* 2.195.
6 Clarke, 1999: 157 n.51; Janda, 2000: 69–70.
7 *SEG* 41.540A; 44.463[3]; cf. *IG* 12.4.3 1241.
8 Hom. *Il.* 5.654
9 Hom. *Il.* 15.187–191 (quoted 191); cf. h.Hom. *Dem.* 84–87; Pl. *Gorg.* 523a.
10 Including ambiguous references, forty-six times in the *Iliad*, thirty-five in the *Odyssey*, nine in Hesiod's works, and six in the Homeric *Hymns*.
11 Hom. *Il.* 5.190, 20.61.
12 h.Hom. *Dem.* 2, 84, 358, 377.
13 Hes. *Th.* 913.
14 Aisch. *Pers.* 650. *Emp. fr.* 6.3.

15 For example, Hom. *Il.* 9.457 (underground Zeus – Ζεύς καταχθόνιος); Aisch. *Ag.* 1386–1397 (Underground Zeus, protector of the dead – κατὰ χθονὸς Διὸς νεκρῶν σωρῆρος); Aisch. *Supp* 231 (the other Zeus – Ζεύς ἄλλος). There are some guises of Zeus that have Underworld aspects, including Zeus Chthonios (although this is an agrarian characterisation). 'Chthonic Zeus' is a well-established epithet for Hades, just as 'sea-dwelling Zeus' is an adjectival name for Poseidon. 'Zeus Chthonios' is not always a name for Hades, but it is relatively easy to distinguish the name of the Underworld god with an agrarian Zeus though context.

16 Hom. *Il.* 20.57–65.

17 This is not clear etymologically, although it is a connotation given over to Hades repeatedly, and obviously something that exists in contemporary popular imagination; Beekes, 1998: 18; 2010: 34; Bremmer, 2002: 4; Farnell, 1907: 282.

18 Bremmer, 2002: 4; Farnell, 1907: 282.

19 Beekes, 1998: 18; 2010: 34.

20 It should also be noted that it is possible that, rather than being 'the invisible' or 'the unseeable', Ἀΐδης may instead refer to the god being the lord of the unseen. Cf. Clarke, 1999: 167 n. 18.

21 For example, Athena appears to Achilleus alone in the opening of the *Iliad* (1.198), although many others are gathered around.

22 For instance, Pausanias (2.4.6–7) says that the cult statue of Demeter and Kore and the Akrokorinth was 'unseeable' to worshippers, cf. Bookidis and Stroud, 1997: 3–4.

23 Hom. *Il.* 5.8.44–845.

24 [Apollod]. *Bibl.* 1.2.1. Showing that, by this late stage, the two had, at least in some circumstances, become interchangeable.

25 Hes. *Sh.* 227.

26 For example, τὸν δὲ κατ' ὀφθαλμῶν ἐρεβεννὴ νὺξ ἐκάλυψε ('and down on his eyes came the darkness of night'). (Hom. *Il.* 5.659; trans. Murray).

27 Morrison, 1999: 136.

28 Pease, 1942: 5.

29 Sourvinou-Inwood, 1981: 21, cf. Clarke, 1999: 167n.18.

30 See Hom. *Od.* 4.834, 10.175, 10.491, 10.564, 11.69, 11.164, 11.211, 11.277, 11.425, 11.625, 12.21, 14.208, 15.350, 20.208, 24.204, 24.264.

31 Hom. *Od.* 10.491.

32 Hes. *Th.* 455–456.

33 Hes. *Th.* 851.

34 Pind. *Ol.* 9. 29–35; *LIMC s.v* Hades 22, 24, 121, 137, 140, 146, 147, 148, 149, 151, 156, 161, 162. Pindar comments that Hades uses the staff in a psychopompic fashion. It is also likely that the staff was representative of the journey of the *psyche* into Hades's domain. There are several representations of Hades bearing this sceptre in scenes which are set in the Underworld (for example, *LIMC s.v* Hades 121, 137, 140, 146, 147, 148, 161). In such representations it is clearly not being used to usher the dead into the Underworld, possibly indicating that it had become appropriated into representations of Hades for non-psychopompic purposes, either through the association to the psychopompic staff, or through associ-ation with Plouton.

35 Brumfield, 1981: 108; Clinton, 1992: 105.

36 For example, *LIMC s.v* Hades 39, whom Clinton identifies as Plouton. See, 1992: 109.

37 Persephone will be discussed in detail in Chapter 5.

38 Pl. *Crat.* 403a.

39 For example, and I discuss in Chapter 5, the Lokrian Pinakes depict Persephone in the moments after abduction as well as youth acting out mock abductions in imitation of Persephone and Hades. These often show Persephone or the girl holding flowers.

40 h Hom. *Dem.* 353; cf. 305–311, 332–333.
41 Bremmer, 2002: 6.
42 Hom. *Od.* 11.29; cf. 10.521, 10.536, 11.49. Cf. Sourvinou-Inwood, 1981: 18.
43 Aristoph. *Fr.* 156–157.
44 Sourvinou-Inwood,1981: 17.
45 Sourvinou-Inwood,1981: 18.
46 Clinton, 1992: 114–115.
47 Main inscription *IG* II^2 4701; cf., 1992: 114.
48 Nilsson, 1935: 102, 12–13.
49 schol. AB ad *Il.* 9.158; cf. Burton 2011: 1, 2018: 212.
50 Garland, 1985: 53.
51 Garland,1985: 53.
52 Paus. 1.28.6.
53 Paus. 2.31.2.
54 Paus. 3.19.4.
55 Strab. 9.2.29.
56 Paus. 6.25.3; cf. 5.18.8; Coleman and Abramovitz, 1986: 159, 64–65; Corbett, 1970: 151; Harrison, 1908: 13.There are, of course, some examples of mortals who enter the realm of Hades prior to their deaths – Herakles and Theseus are the most obvious examples. Alkestis also enters Hades and returns to the living again, though unlike the heroes she dies and is resurrected, rather than descending into the Underworld while still living. For Herakles see Hom. *Il.* 8.366–369; *Od.* 11.623–625; Bakchylides *fr.* 5 (Campbell), Aristoph. *Fr.* 468–469. For Theseus see Pl. *Rep.* 391c-d; [Apollod]. *Bibl.* 1.23–24, 2.124. For Alkestis see Eur. *Alk.*
57 Cf. Burton 2018.
58 Paus. 6.25.2; trans. WHS Jones.
59 Paus. 6.25.2–3.
60 Paus. 6.25.3; cf. Hom. *Il.* 5.395–397. Other causes for hostility might include Herakles slaughtering a cow belonging to Hades, the abduction of Kerberos from the Underworld ([Apollod]. *Bibl.* 2.125), or Herakles undertaking to rescue Theseus from Hades ([Apollod]. *Bibl.* 2.124; Diod. 4.26.1; Ael. *VH* 4.5.).
61 Harrison, 1908: 13.
62 Cf. Hom. *Il.* 5.397.
63 Strabo says they 'perhaps' believed, using the word τάχα.
64 Strab. 8.3.15. See also Atherton, 2002: 160, 84 n. 11.
65 Strab. 8.3.15; trans. H.L. Jones.
66 Aisch. *Eum.* 273–275; cf. *Supp.* 228–231.
67 For example, at Aisch. *Cho.* 385–359, *PB* 152–154, *Supp* 156–159.
68 Fate, and characterisations of fate, is a contentious issue even within ancient literature, and this is especially true of issues surrounding the question of who controls men's' destiny. There are examples which show the gods, especially Zeus, as controlling fate, and either examples show that even the gods do not have any control over fate.
69 There is a case to be made for the dead worshipping Persephone, in the context of the 'Orphic' gold tablets, and a fragment of Pindar, as I discuss in Chapter 6.
70 This is most clearly shown by the repeated phrase νεκύων ἀμενηνὰ κάρηνα ('feeble heads of the dead'), which occurs four times in the *Odyssey*: 10.521, 10.536, 11.29, 11.49.
71 For example, in the Homeric *Hymn to Demeter* (481–482) asserts that: ὃς δ᾽ ἀτελὴς ἱερῶν, ὅς τ᾽ ἄμμορος, οὔ ποθ᾽ ὁμοίων, αἶσαν ἔχει φθίμενός περ ὑπὸ ζόφῳ εὐρώεντι ('The uninitiated in the rites, one without part in them, never enjoys a similar portion of benefits, blessings, whatever'). Similarly, Aristophanes's *Frogs* depicts initiates separated from the uninitiated in the Underworld. Eschatological bases for mystery

religion appears to be something of an unwritten understanding between scholars; for example in Albinus, 2000, where the simple inclusion of the Mysteries into this study into Greek eschatology implies a strong connection between them. I suspect that any benefit an initiate hopes to obtain relates to forging a positive (and profitable) relationship with the divinity in question, and they would be hoping that this relationship would serve them primarily in life, with a carryover into death, through their continued relationship with the divinity, rather than any basic 'eschatological' principle (that is 'I will give you x in direct exchange for a better afterlife'). This is discussed in Chapter 4. R. Parker notably ascribes eschatological reasoning to the Mysteries, while J. Bremmer's recent work on Mystery initiation takes the opposition approach. See Bremmer, 2014: 1–20; Parker, 2005a: 354, 73, cf. Bowden, 2010: 47–48.

4 Death and plenty

Agriculture and the underworld in mythology

The way that communities deal with death often reveals something about the values that they collectively hold. For ancient Greeks, particularly, two of the values revealed by death-related rituals (discussed in detail in Chapter 7) are community and continuity, and the intersection of these two things creates an environment in which communities can engage with Underworld gods in interesting and nuanced ways. The most well-known of these engagements is probably the Eleusinian Mysteries in Attica and famously (though not practically) open to any person who spoke Greek. There are several similar interactions people facilitate between themselves and Underworld gods, in which Demeter and her daughter(s) are central. In this chapter I will explore some of the ways that these goddesses are constructed in the mythology that surrounds their relationships to the Underworld.

Persephone, Kore, and the Mysteries

Persephone is, all around, an interesting goddess because she rarely appears alone. Her narrative, as I shall discuss in more detail in this chapter and the next chapter, is intricately tied up in her relationships with her mother, Demeter, and her abductor-husband, Hades. There is one piece of literature that explores both these relationships and yet says very little about Persephone herself – the Homeric *Hymn to Demeter*. But first, on Persephone's name.

In Plato's *Kratylus*, Socrates argues that Persephone's name should actually be something like Pherepapha,[1] because it should describe her wisdom:

> 'Φερρέφαττα' δέ: πολλοὶ μὲν καὶ τοῦτο φοβοῦνται τὸ ὄνομα καὶ τὸν 'Ἀπόλλω,' ὑπὸ ἀπειρίας, ὡς ἔοικεν, ὀνομάτων ὀρθότητος. καὶ γὰρ μεταβάλλοντεςσκο-ποῦνται τὴν 'Φερσεφόνην,' καὶ δεινὸν αὐτοῖς φαίνεται: τὸ δὲ μηνύει σοφὴνεἶναι τὴν θεόν. ἅτε γὰρ φερομένων τῶν πραγμάτων τὸ ἐφαπτόμενον καὶ ἐπαφῶνκαὶ δυνάμενον ἐπακολουθεῖν σοφία ἂν εἴη. 'Φερέπαφα' οὖν διὰ τὴν σοφίαν καὶ τὴνἐπαφὴν τοῦ φερομένου ἡ θεὸς ἂν ὀρθῶς καλοῖτο, ἢ τοιοῦτόν τι – δι' ὅπερ καὶσύνεστιν αὐτῇ ὁ Ἅιδης σοφὸς ὤν, διότι τοιαύτη ἐστίν – νῦν δὲ αὐτῆς ἐκκλίνουσι τὸὄνομα εὐστομίαν περὶ πλείονος ποιούμενοι τῆς ἀληθείας, ὥστε 'Φερρέφατταν' αὐτὴνκαλεῖν.

And Pherrephatta! – How many people fear this name, and also Apollo! I imagine it is because they do not know about correctness of names. You see they change the name to Persephone and its aspect frightens them. But really the name indicates that the goddess is wise; for since things are in motion, that which grasps and touches and is able to follow them is wisdom. Pherepapha, or something of that sort, would therefore be the correct name of the goddess, because she is wise and touches that which is in motion – and this is the reason why Hades, who is wise, consorts with her, because she is wise – but people have altered her name, attaching more importance to euphony than to truth, and they call her Pherrephatta.[2]

Fear, Socrates explains, leads to wilful (and popular) errors in naming, but this can also result in different spellings in order to disguise the meaning of names.[3] The correctness (or more accurately, the incorrectness) of Plato's etymology does not change the point too much: people were afraid of the goddess and accordingly changed her name to make her more palatable.[4] The idea of re-naming or 'un-naming' something to re-channel or mitigate its power is not unusual. Perhaps the most famous paralipsis of modern times is 'He-who-must-not-be-named' in the Harry Potter series.[5] The chorus of Euripides's *Helen* calls Persephone the ἀρρήτου κούρας ('unsayable girl').[6] ἄρρητος applies to something that cannot be spoken or expressed,[7] and so there is a paralipsis occurring here (as in *Harry Potter*), and that this occurs because of an actual fear about her character being manifested as a fear of her name.[8]

Rudolf Wachter has argued that the 'original' name we should be looking for is something like Φερρῶφαττα (that is, with an omega or omicron rather than an epsilon) for which there are nine attestations. Seven of these are found on fifth-century Attic vases, by seven different artists.[9] Most importantly, perhaps, this shows that Pherrophatta/Persophatta, the goddess we know more commonly as Persephone, means 'she who threshes ears of corn' – although as Jan Bremmer points out this does not directly presuppose James Frazer's Corn Maiden, 'but it surely comes rather close!'[10] But Pherrophatta is not an embodiment of corn; she is an assistant in bringing about the full benefit of Demeter's gift to the people. When she retreats beneath the earth, so too the seeds retreat beneath the earth and both the goddess and the seeds mature, together, before sprouting forth to bring life and plenty to the people. In this incarnation, Persephone does not seem like a submissive and deferential goddess, hiding behind her mother or husband. Rather, she is an active participant in the life-cycle of the grain, and therefore of the earth and its population. But this is not always the image of Persephone that this (re)presented.

The date of the Homeric *Hymn to Demeter* is still the subject of debate, although it is likely that it was composed in something like its current form no earlier than the second quarter of the seventh century.[11] The hymn was likely sung, preceding the recitation of other epic poetry,[12] meaning it would have been relatively well known among ordinary individuals. It tells the story of Persephone's abduction and return, and Demeter's intermediary mourning and the establishment of rites for her in Eleusis:

1–3: Opening invocation and establishing subject matter

2–40: Narration of Persephone's abduction by Hades

40–41: Demeter hears Persephone's cry

41–51: Demeter roams the earth looking for Persephone, not eating or drinking

51–80: Demeter is assisted by Hekate and, upon request, by Helios

81–89: Helios tells Demeter to remain calm and that he believes the match is a good one for her daughter

90–304: Demeter goes into the house of Keleos and Metaneira in Eleusis and raises the infant Demophoon

269: (After revealing herself to the household as a goddess) Demeter demands a temple built in her honour

304–314: Demeter, sitting apart from all mortals, inflicts barrenness over the world in mourning for her missing daughter

315–340: Zeus sends the messenger Iris to Demeter in order deliver Zeus's message to return to the world to fertility. After this fails, Zeus sends all the gods, one after another, but she rejects all their advice and relates that she will only relent once her daughter is returned

341–357: Hermes is sent into the Underworld to ask Hades to send back Persephone

358–372: Hades summons Persephone and tells her she is free to leave and puts his case forward for being a good and proper husband. Persephone leaps up at the opportunity to return to the upper world

373–375: Hades gives Persephone a pomegranate seed to eat, in order to ensure her yearly return to the Underworld

376–386: Hermes drives Persephone back to the upper world in Hades's chariot

387–438: Persephone and Demeter are reunited, and Persephone relates the narrative of her abduction to her mother

439–441: Hekate becomes Persephone's servant

442–471: Zeus arranges for Demeter's return to Mount Olympos and decrees that Persephone shall have to spend one-third of each year in the Underworld with Hades

472–473: Demeter returns fertility to the earth

474–483: Demeter teaches her Mysteries to Triptolemos, Diokleis, Eumolpos, Keleos and Polyxenios

484–489: Demeter and Persephone return to Mount Olympos

490–495: The poet's final invocation to the goddesses, Demeter – who shall send Ploutos to distribute wealth to men – and Persephone

The relationship between the myth, the hymn, and the Eleusinian Mysteries is unclear, and certainly not clear enough to elucidate the (unknown) rites that occurred during the Mysteries or whether the hymn can give us any clue to what those are. For instance, we cannot know whether initiates engaged in purification rituals while seated on a ram-fleece covered stool, veiled, simply because Demeter herself sits, veiled, on such a stool, and even though there is what appears to be corroborating iconographical evidence showing famous mythic initiate, Herakles, in the same kind of pose.[13] The other 'elephant in the room' is the association between Persephone and Kore. Are they the same goddess? Certainly, in the classical period they are, by and large, considered to be two names of the one goddess – though this doesn't clear up the identity of Thea at Eleusis.

The Mysteries of Eleusis are dedicated to the 'Two Goddesses' – that is, Demeter and Kore. Κόρη literally means 'girl', and she stands in for Persephone. Are they the same goddess? Yes ...? But things are further complicated at Eleusis by the presence of Thea and Theos – literally 'goddess' and 'god' – who are probably Hades and Persephone. And Plouton. The one thing we can certainly say is that in the evidence that we have available to us, 'Persephone' is not referenced by name at Eleusis. There may have been – and almost certainly were – individuals who underwent initiation at Eleusis that approached 'Kore' or 'Thea' (or even both) *as though they were Persephone*. That is, because 'Kore' and 'Persephone' (and, to a lesser extent and only in the Eleusinian context, Thea), are intricately intertwined in – and between – cultic practices and mythology. Kore and Thea are not the same divinity, but *both* are aspects of Persephone – agrarian and underworld respectively.[14] To start with, then, I will look at Persephone herself and see what detangling (if any) can be accomplished.

Most often, Persephone appears in cult with Demeter, and she is usually – at least superficially – the subservient divinity in the pair. In many such cults, including Eleusis, Persephone has a strong connection to the agricultural seasons due to her association with Demeter.[15] Though neither of the goddesses are solely responsible for dictating the seasonal changes. Of course, seasonal changes occur (aetiologically) because Demeter withdraws her gifts out of grief, chocking the earth's fertility; but it is Persephone's absence from the earth that is the catalyst for Demeter's grief. Going further back, it is Hades and Zeus, who conspired together for the marriage that led to Persephone's abduction. Is it too far to say that there may have been a plan in place from the beginning?[16] Of all these actors, though, it needs to be highlighted that, although it is Persephone who is the intermediary between the earth and the Underworld, she has the least amount of personal agency in the seasonal changes. Her role within the aetiology of the seasons and harvest is of a pawn, perpetually moved from one side of the board to the other by controlling players.

The Eleusinian Mysteries are centred around the two goddesses' agricultural association.[17] Naturally, though, we must imagine that people approaching the Mysteries would also have been thinking of the Underworld association that both Demeter and Persephone command, and therefore that initiation might give them some privilege in their afterlife. But, the main reason for the Mysteries was certainly not eschatological, nor soteriological.[18] The primary purpose was to form (and maintain) a close personal relationship with Demeter and Persephone in order to receive their gifts in life. Primarily, the gift of both goddesses was agrarian fertility, but privilege in the afterlife must be seen as a secondary benefit to be gained. This privilege, however, must be seen as one of a number of possible gifts or benefits, rather than the *raison d'être* of the cult.

It is most likely that people worshipping Persephone anywhere she was presented in an agrarian guise would also understand that she was Hades's bride, and this is especially true at Eleusis given the mythological tradition.[19] But even so, a worshipper would not necessarily think of Persephone as the ἐπαινή ('dread') ruler of the Underworld, even if they had engaged with her in that guises at other times, or in other places.[20] Even Jan Bremmer concedes, in his rigid non-eschatological system for the Eleusinian Mysteries, that 'people will have made their own choices about what to bring home from the festival'.[21] What we would most likely find is that worshipper understood the goddess in both her role as abducted maiden and as Queen of the Underworld. Because she was presented in this guise in so many contemporary sources, either ruling the Underworld in her own right or in conjunction with Hades, people who were so inclined would have viewed the goddess like this. This would have cemented her eschatological aspects, even in agrarian contexts. This would have been the case even though the figure worshipped alongside Demeter in many agrarian-themed cults was named Kore and not Persephone.[22] Further to this, worshippers would have been able to separate out different aspects of a single divinity in their everyday practices, which means that the two identities of Persephone – young victim and Underworld queen – could exist in their minds simultaneously without any specific incongruence.

It is often taken as given that the Persephone of the *Hymn* is the Kore worshipped in Eleusinian cult.[23] The identification of Persephone with Kore is strengthened by the crossover in the (possible) content of the initiation rituals and the *Hymn*, including the potential for a 'sacred drama' enacted during the rite that plays out Persephone's abduction.[24] At the end of the *Hymn* we find out that Eleusis is under the protection of Demeter and her daughter, the κούρη περικαλλὴς Περσεφόνεια ('very beautiful *kore* ["maiden"] Persephone').[25] This may have been the 'definitive identification' that Pausanias claims Homer made,[26] as neither the *Iliad* nor the *Odyssey* make any connection between 'Kore' and 'Persephone'. This lack of association also shows that the Persephone of the epics is not the fertility-focused or agrarian goddess of the Eleusinian Mysteries. And, although the identification between Kore and Persephone is by no means unproblematic or uncomplicated, they are repeatedly presented as one and the same.

Kore does not undertake any Underworld-related or eschatological function at Eleusis primarily because the ritual programme itself has no relationship to the Underworld or eschatological concerns (as noted above).[27] The Underworld is only implied through the association made between the agriculturally concerned Persephone of the Homeric *Hymn to Demeter* and the Queen of the Underworld Persephone (from the Homeric epics, Hesiod, or elsewhere), and this entire, amalgamated Persephone being connected to the Kore of the Mysteries. This has led some, notably Robert Parker, to proclaim that the Eleusinian Mysteries were eschatological.[28] There is no cultic evidence that the Kore of the Mysteries ruled, or co-ruled, the Underworld and she certainly does not become a co-ruler in the Homeric *Hymn*. That the role of 'Demeter's daughter' in the Mysteries is only referred to by the title 'Kore' shows that the primary function, or at least the intended primary function, of the goddess (who might elsewhere be called Persephone) is as a goddess concerned with agrarian fertility.

But if contemporary worshippers did equate the two goddesses then their ideas about one would have influenced their practices dedicated to the other, even unconsciously. It is perfectly plausible that some individuals approached the Kore of the Eleusinian Mysteries as though she were already Queen of the Underworld, or at least that she embodied some of the Underworld characteristics of that particular Persephone. Likewise, it is plausible that other worshippers would have 'compartmentalised' the two distinct personae as belonging to different religious contexts and offering dedication to one would not bring the other to mind automatically.[29] While this may not be a particularly satisfying thought, it does reflect the reality of a non-rigid religious 'system', where there may be as many reasons for participation (and 'take-home' messages) as there are individuals involved. Broadly, though, we might say that in the 'official' guise that Kore is presented in regarding the evidence we have of the Eleusinian Mysteries, she is more closely aligned with the agrarian aspects of Demeter rather than the death-related aspects of Hades. This presentation is echoed throughout the Greek world in agriculturally concerned festivals in which Persephone (or Kore) is partnered with Demeter. Aside from the Eleusinian Mysteries, the most well-known of these is probably the Thesmophoria,[30] and – as Sarah Iles Johnston points out – there is no need to argue for myth-ritual exclusivity, where one myth can only have relevance to one festival, but a single mythic narrative may (appear to) be connected with several different rituals or festivals.[31] Luckily, the myth of Persephone's abduction is perhaps the clearest example of this, and that will be particularly highlighted in the next chapter, regarding the Persephonean cult at Lokroi, and 'chthonic' cults of Demeter (specifically at Hermione).

The Homeric *Hymn to Demeter* does give us one hint of the Persephone who maintains control over the deceased and foreshadows the Persephone that we will find in Pindar and the 'Orphic' gold tablets. This is a Persephone who is not (necessarily) a ruler of the dead, but a goddess who can still manipulate the conditions of death, and the dead. When Hades has agreed to Persephone's return to the earth, he instructs her to go up and meet with her mother, and tells her that:

ἔνθα δ' ἐοῦσα
δεσπόσσεις πάντων ὁπόσα ζώει τε καὶ ἕρπει,
τιμὰς δὲ σχήσησθα μετ' ἀθανάτοισι μεγίστας.

τῶν δ᾽ ἀδικησάντων τίσις ἔσσεται ἤματα πάντα,
οἵ κεν μὴ θυσίῃσι τεὸν μένος ἱλάσκωνται
εὐαγέως ἔρδοντες, ἐναίσιμα δῶρα τελοῦντες.

By being here, you will be mistress of everything that lives and moves, and have the greatest privileges among the immortals, while there will ever be punishment for those who act unrighteously and fail to propitiate your fury with sacrifices, in holy performance, making the due offerings.[32]

As the privileged citizen of the Underworld, Persephone's honours include having the ability to punish mortals who had acted unjustly in life or who had failed to properly propitiate to her fury.[33] This is not the παλαιός πένθος ('ancient grief') that I will discuss shortly in Pindar's representation of this same concept of human propitiation, but Persephone can punish the deceased for acts they have committed in life.

Superficially, this goes against the generally held idea that there is no specific punishment (or reward) in death for things done in life. In this case, punishment is dispensed for failing to propitiation to Persephone, or acting unjustly towards her. This does conform to what we find elsewhere in myth, where there is cause for eternal punishment if you have specifically and severely offended a god in life, but other cases are significantly more extreme transgressions than simply failing to propitiate.[34] This presentation shows Persephone in a particularly harsh light, as a divinity who strictly maintains power over the dead. This is prevalent across various sources, to a greater or lesser degree, even in cases that might cursorily appear to show her in a subservient position. Here, then, she is more like the Persephone shown elsewhere in archaic literature, as Hades promises her a threefold division of privileges: to rule over 'everything that lives and moves', to have honours among the gods, and the ability to enact vengeance upon wrongdoers.[35] Persephone's domain is multifaceted, and she receives honours and has powers in the sky, on the earth, and in the Underworld. She is the child of the king of the gods, Zeus, the supreme Olympian, and has an inheritance over the Olympian-ruled realm of the sky because of this. She is also the child of Demeter, premier agrarian goddess, and she has a claim to the earth and agricultural fertility though this. And she is the wife of Hades, and a ruler of the dead in her own right, and this gives her a claim over the Underworld.

In Pindar, Persephone is the undisputed ruler of the Underworld. The poet never mentions Hades and Persephone together, and the Underworld is very clearly described as her domain, not merely the Ἀιδης δόμος ('house of Hades'), even though Persephone is not always presented in the Underworld, or fulfilling an Underworld-related function.[36] For example, the poet instructs the goddess Echo μελανοτειχέα νῦν δόμον Φερσεφόνας ἔλθ᾽ ('to go now into the black-walled house of Persephone')[37] in order to deliver the news of Orchomenios's Olympic games victory to his deceased father. Persephone's influence over the dead is clearly elucidated in a Pindaric fragment found in Plato's *Meno*,[38] which will be discussed, along with the so-called Orphic Gold tablets, in Chapter 6.

Agriculture and the rape of Demeter

Demeter's capacity for negativity toward mankind in incontestable. She bestows barrenness across the earth, choking fertile lands, and inflicting famine upon her followers.[39] Demetrian worship was a central aspect of society throughout the Greek world, although the connection between Demeter and the individual *poleis* was not always stated explicitly.[40] Nevertheless, agriculture tied Demetrian worship to the prosperity of the city and its citizens.[41] There is no evidence that 'Demeter' has an etymological link to the earth (where, for example, her name might have been an amalgam of μήτρη, 'mother', and δᾱ, supposedly a pre-Greek word for 'earth').[42] Even though there is no explicit etymological legacy, Demeter does have a strong connection to the earth and the wellbeing of cities and people. Primarily, Demeter was an agrarian goddess, and agriculture was deeply connected to the life and death of the city and its populace. Sanctuaries were dedicated to Demeter throughout the Greek world, and although understandably popular in locations that had an affinity for agricultural practices,[43] were still present in less agriculturally-inclined places. As with virtually all Greek divinities, she has both beneficial and harmful characteristics, so while being praised as a giver of life, grain, fruit, and abundance,[44] she was also worshipped in association with the (potential) harm she could inflict on the earth, crops, and the human and animal populations. In Phokis, for example, she was worshipped as Στιρίτιδος ('Barren').[45] In other places she is worshipped with epithets like Χθόνια ('Chthonia' or 'Chthonic'; 'of the Underground'), Μέλαινα ('Black'), and Ερινύς ('Erinys' or 'Fury').[46]

Homer says little about Demeter. The five references in the *Iliad*, and one in the *Odyssey*,[47] detail her connection to agriculture, but say nothing of other aspects of her nature. In the *Iliad* she appears as an agrarian goddess, in charge of both grain and the products produced from it, most specifically bread. Two of the five instances refer to Δημήτερος ἀκτὴν ('Demeter's yield').[48] When Kalypso and Hermes argue, in *Odyssey* book five, about Odysseus's apprehension, they discuss Demeter's sexual relationship with a mortal,[49] linking her to human fertility, although this link is not made explicit. Homer does not mention Demeter and Persephone's relationship.

Demeter's three appearances in Hesiod's *Theogony* predictably centre on her place in the Greek pantheon. They relate the story of her own birth,[50] the conception and birth of Persephone,[51] and the birth of Ploutos, a demigod who is Demeter's child with Iasion.[52] As we might expect from the subject matter of Hesiod's *Works and Days*, which is mostly concerned with agricultural practices, Demeter has a larger role to play in this work. The text is written as a kind of agricultural 'how to' manual for Hesiod's brother Perses, and he utilises Demeter's agrarian associations in his explanations:

ἔργα κομίζεσθαι Δημήτερος, ὥς τοι ἕκαστα
ὥρι' ἀέξηται, μή πως τὰ μέταζε χατίζων
πτώσσῃς ἀλλοτρίους οἴκους καὶ μηδὲν ἀνύσσῃς.

If you want to do the work of Demeter in due season,
So that each crop reaches its seasonal growth, lest hereafter,
Being in want later, you go begging at others' houses and achieve
nothing.[53]

Hesiod also calls her ἐϋστέφανος Δημήτρη ('Demeter beautifully crowned'),[54] an epithet related to plenty that also occurs four times in the Homeric *Hymn to Demeter*.[55] References to Δημήτερος ἀκτήν ('Demeter's grain')[56] and Δημήτερος ἱερὸν ἀκτήν ('Demeter's sacred grain')[57] reinforce her supremacy in agrarian matters. One reference quite explicitly aligns Demeter with the Underworld or underground (linked through the death/agriculture dichotomy), where Perses (and the reader) is urged to:

εὔχεσθαι δὲ Διὶ χθονίῳ Δημήτερί θ᾽ ἀγνῇ
ἐκτελέα βρίθειν Δημήτερος ἱερὸν ἀκτήν,

Pray to Chthonian Zeus and holy Demeter
To make Demeter's sacred grains to ripen heavy.[58]

Although 'Chthonian Zeus' was sometimes used as another name for Hades,[59] that is not the meaning portrayed here. Hesiod does not refer to Hades as 'Zeus Chthonios', and elsewhere the meaning of Zeus-Chthonios-as-Hades is evidence through direct or contextual reference to the Underworld.[60] 'Chthonian Zeus' here should be read as Zeus in an agrarian guise, with the term being used in a more literal sense of 'into the ground' rather than 'underground'. This epithet evokes similar agrarian associations to the image of Demeter hiding seeds beneath the earth in the Homeric *Hymn to Demeter*.[61]

It can be tempting to read an amplified agriculture/death dichotomy into the *Works and Days*. Although Demeter has both agrarian and death-related concerns in various other places, the *Works and Days* is primarily an agricultural text, and the death-related aspects that are encompassed within it do not spread into mythic tropes of death-and-rebirth or other similar established death/life tropes. Fundamentally, however, agriculture *is* death-related because of the necessity of death for the growing of crops (death-related regeneration, for example, or the use of 'dead' organic material as compost) and the obvious concern of famine and the death that results from it through the (potential) failure of agriculture – a failure which is always close at hand. Agriculture is, in many ways, tied up with death because it is an antidote for death. Beyond the burying of seeds there is little in the *Works and Days* to suggest that Demeter has any other Underworld function.

In archaic literature, Demeter is most thoroughly characterised in the *Hymn to Demeter*. This tells the story of Persephone's abduction and Demeter's subsequent search. This story might explain the format of some of the rituals undertaken at Eleusis, although there is no direct or specific aetiological link between the *Hymn* and any Demetrian ritual. Various aspects of the hymn's narrative are embodied in rituals at Eleusis, but this does not indicate a 'forward' aetiological connection between the hymn and the Eleusinian rituals.[62] These aspects include Persephone's abduction,[63] Demeter's frantic search for her daughter,[64] Demeter revealing herself as a goddess to the people of Eleusis,[65] Persephone's return from the Underworld, and the disclosure of her covert marriage.[66] But Persephone is absent in the Mysteries, where Demeter's daughter is Kore – 'the Maiden'.[67] Perhaps Kore is Persephone, and certainly many commenters have aligned the two, from Pausanias to modern scholars.[68] If Persephone is represented at Thea in the Eleusinian cult, this also raises issues, as Kore and Thea are represented together and there is a lack of literary evidence for Thea beyond the First Fruits decree, where she appears alongside Theos, the two Goddesses (Demeter and Kore), Triptolemos, Eubouleus, and Athena.[69] It is not as clear that Thea is an entirely separate divinity from Persephone or Kore. The speculation for separateness rests somewhat on the fact that both Theos and Plouton are represented on the Lakrateides Relief (which, at c. 100 BCE, is late comparatively).[70]

Persephone herself has no impact on the Eleusinian section of the Homeric *Hymn to Demeter*, which tells the story of Demeter's position as the nursemaid of Demophoon, son of Keleos and Metaneira, king and queen of Eleusis. Demeter's stay in Eleusis is an imitation of Persephone's exile to the Underworld, albeit in an inversed form. Demeter exiles herself from Olympos and the world of the immortals.[71] This section of the poem breaks up the narrative cohesion of the opening and closing sections and makes this 'Eleusinian interlude' appear disconnected from the rest of the poem.[72]

This interlude occurs after Helios's speech, and begins with Demeter leaving Olympos in anger, and disguising herself as an old woman. Keleos and Metaneira's four daughters chance upon Demeter sitting next to a well. She introduces herself as Doso and tells the girls that she has been abducted by Kretan pirates and escaped after landing at Thorikos. She enquires after work as a nursemaid, and the girls tell her to visit the homes of several prominent Eleusinian men, including Triptolemos,[73] before suggesting that their mother might be looking for a nursemaid. They depart but return quickly with an invitation for Doso-Demeter to visit their home. As she enters the house, Doso-Demeter 'gleams' with divine radiance. She refuses to sit on Metaneira's couch, choosing instead to sit on a fleece-covered stool. She does not eat or drink, but sits in silence, covered by her veil until Iambe, Metaneira's slave, makes her laugh.[74] She then requests a drink of barley and water mixed with pennyroyal.[75] Metaneira offers Doso-Demeter employment as Demophoon's nurse,[76] and Demeter accepts, her speech foreshadowing her intention for Demophoon's immortality:

παῖδα δέ τοι πρόφρων ὑποδέξομαι ὥς με κελεύεις·
θρέψω, κοῦ μιν ἔολπα κακοφραδίῃσι τιθήνης
οὔτ' ἄρ' ἐπηλυσίη δηλήσεται οὔθ' ὑποτάμνον·
οἶδα γὰρ ἀντίτομον μέγα φέρτερον ὑλοτόμοιο,
οἶδα δ' ἐπηλυσίης πολυπήμονος ἐσθλὸν ἐρυσμόν.

As for your boy, I will gladly take him over, as you request. I will rear him, and I do not anticipate that any supernatural visitation or cutter of roots will harm him through any negligence by his nurse. For I know a powerful counter-cut to beat the herb-cutter, and I know a good inhibitor of baneful visitation.[77]

Doso-Demeter raises Demophoon as though he is the child of a god: she does not feed him, but anoints him with ambrosia, breaths her 'sweet breath' over him, and hides him in the fire each night. And so Demophoon flourishes, but Metaneira apparently grows suspicious and before Demeter can make him ἀγήρων τ' ἀθάνατόν ('ageless and deathless'),[78] she spies on the goddess and her son one evening. Seeing Demophoon in the fireplace, she cries out in alarm, alerting Demeter to her duplicity. Demeter removed the boy from the fire and, putting him on the floor, reveals her true identity and demands that all the people of Eleusis build her a sanctuary, with a large temple and an altar, and perform mystery rites to win her favour, which she will teach them.[79] With Demeter revealed, Metaneira falls to her knees, and her daughters rush to the boy, who is now laying on the floor and crying inconsolably. The women attempt to propitiate the angry goddess throughout the night without success, and in the morning, they report what has happened to Keleos. He summons the Eleusinians and orders them to build Demeter's temple. Once it was finished, the goddess took up a year-long residence, but without performing her divine duties a terrible barrenness took over the land. As the population began to suffer, Zeus sent Iris to appease her, but Demeter was not persuaded.[80] So, one after another, Zeus sent each god down to talk to her. Demeter told them that she would not return to Olympos, nor allow the crops to grow, until her daughter returned from the Underworld.[81] On Zeus's order, Hermes, liminal guide *par excellence*, retrieved the abducted Persephone.[82]

It is worth noting that Demophoon is not directly connected to the historical Eleusinian Mysteries, and herein lies one of the places where we can find a strong divergence between the *Homeric Hymn* and the ritual practices undertaken by real people. What is important to note, and which I hope to have conveyed above, is the spirit of this section is what is important, rather than the character of Demophoon. This is what reignites Demeter's grief, yes, but more urgently this is the episode that gets people involved in the drama of Persephone's abduction. In some versions of the story, Demophoon dies, but in all versions Demeter fails to make him immortal. He can act, both in death and in life, as a conduit between Demeter's grief and people. This is, therefore, the true catalyst for the instigation of the Eleusinian Mysteries in practice.

There are four possible aetiological connections between the *Hymn* and the rituals of the Eleusinian Mysteries (beyond the *Hymn*'s notion that Demeter herself taught the Eleusinian's the ritual programme of the Mysteries). N.J. Richardson identifies these as (1) primary purification, (2) abstention from food and wine, (3) *aischrologia* (obscene mocking or jesting), and (4) the *kykeon*, the 'mix-up' drink modelled on the drink Demeter requested at Metaneira's house.[83] This link has been quite well-established, though I do not think these links are evidence for direct myth-to-ritual aetiology. There is a more useful avenue of enquiry regarding Demeter's Underworld association: the treatment of Demophoon. Demeter's interest in Demophoon's immortality is a direct challenge to Zeus's authority. By sanctioning Persephone's abduction, Zeus played a direct role in Demeter's loss, and by the attempt to make Demophoon immortal (and ultimately adopting him), Demeter can subvert Zeus's rule over the natural condition of mankind.[84] The choice of a male child means that this cannot be viewed as a simple 'replacement Persephone' (quite aside from the other issues such a replacement would raise). What eventually occurs when Demophoon's immortalisation fails is Zeus's domination is reinforced, because Demeter's failure lays in the hands of mortal people.

And yet, Demeter's failure to immortalise Demophoon also forges a strong link between the goddess and Metaneira, the mortal woman whose folly has ultimately reinforced Zeus's (male) supremacy. Metaneira's fear and grief when she sees her son in the fireplace mirrors Demeter's own panic when she discovers that Persephone has vanished.[85] Certainly there is a contrast presented between Demeter's divine knowledge and the ignorance of the mortals affected by her scheme, emphasised by her own reaction to Metaneira's fear for her son:

νήϊδες ἄνθρωποι καὶ ἀφράδμονες οὔτ᾽ ἀγαθοῖο
αἶσαν ἐπερχομένου προγνώμεναι οὔτε κακοῖο.

Ignorant men and senseless, incapable
of foreknowing the lot of coming good or evil.[86]

But Demeter appears to have forgotten that she too had been consumed by fear and grief for her child,[87] and has also forgotten that she needed Hekate and Helios to disclose Persephone's fate to her. So, Jenny Strauss Clay poses the question: 'is it possible that Demeter ... similarly mistakes the plan of Zeus for Persephone and can only conceive of it as signifying a permanent and total separation from her daughter – a kind of death?'[88] But her attempt at immortalising Demophoon has nothing to do with reclaiming Persephone from death. Persephone's residency in the Underworld cannot alter her own inherent immortality. And Demeter does not completely cast Demophoon aside after his immortalisation fails, but she establishes a hero cult at Eleusis for him, showing her care for the infant prince regardless of his mortality. In some ways initiation into the Mysteries creates the same situation for initiates, who cannot achieve immortalisation but, by forging this close relationship with Demeter and Persephone, can ensure that they are treated honourably in the afterlife.[89]

Fundamentally, the *Hymn* asserts Demeter's preeminent control over agriculture in the mortal world. Superficially this is shown by the cycle of barrenness and plenty that occurs in the narrative arc of the *Hymn*, but more thoroughly through the use of motifs that play into the death/agriculture dichotomy, like Demeter hiding seeds in the earth.[90] Demeter also gains a more obvious Underworld pedigree throughout the poem, particularly as the mother-in-law of the Lord of the Underworld. Her care of Demophoon shows an image of the goddess attempting control over the fate of death, and her failure to complete Demophoon's immortalisation reflects only on the aspects of the mortal realm which she cannot control. In fact, it might be more pertinent to view the barrenness she spreads across the world while camped out in the Eleusinian temple as a declaration of her ability to influence aspects of the mortal world in retaliation to mortals causing her personal failure. There is no reason to assume that Demeter would not have succeeded in immortalising Demophoon had she not been found by Metaneira. So, although she is ultimately foiled in her attempted control over death, she does have charge over aspects of death: postponing it in the case of Demophoon, or quickening it through inflicting agrarian infertility.

Concluding note

Although Demeter does not have significant Underworld characteristics in the Homeric *Hymn*, it does establish her connection to the Underworld. The most obvious of these is the actual cause of her search: Persephone's forced residence in the Underworld. Demeter's haste to drive infertility across the mortal world, even though her quarrel is with Zeus, is a subtler incarnation of this connection. In the largely Underworld-themed Hymn, Demeter is the only divine character (except the very brief appearance of Helios) who has no strict, pre-established Underworld connection.

Persephone's relationships to both the Underworld and to her mother are fraught with tension that does not easily play out in either the Homeric *Hymn to Demeter*, nor in cult practices that are associated with that myth – namely the Eleusinian Mysteries, where she only appears under the pseudonyms Kore and Thea, and the Thesmophoria where she is relegated to a subservient divinity. There are a few instances in which Persephone appears alone, or on equal footing with Hades (discussed in the next chapter), though the majority of her mythological story is as a secondary character.

Notes

1 Plat. *Crat.* 404c-e.
2 Plat. *Crat.* 404c-d; trans. Fowler.
3 Cf. Riley, 2005: 65.
4 This is also true of Hades's amalgamation with Plouton, in order to make him less frightening (cf. Plat. *Crat.* 403a), and more relevant to worshippers needs. See the discussion in Chapter 3.
5 Harry is presented as 'equal' to Lord Voldemort, which is shown in two main ways: (1) by Harry also having his name publicly redacted (he is, after all, 'The Boy Who Lived') and (2) because he, almost alone of all the characters dares to utter the name 'Voldemort'. See Nilsen and Nilsen, 2009: 64.
6 Eur. *Hel.* 1306–1307, cf. *fr.* 63 (Kovacs), and to Hades as an 'unseeable' god, see discussion in Chapter 3.

7   In the notes to *The Unspeakable Girl: The Myth and Mystery of Kore*, the translator
    (from the Italian original), L. de la Durantaye, comments on the translation of this as
    'unspeakable' that 'It should be noted that neither the Greek term not the Italian one
    with which the author [Agamben] translates it possesses the English word's sugges-
    tion of impish or malicious misbehaviour. Given the alternative between the idiom-
    atic *unspeakable* and the calque *unsayable*, I deemed the former truer to the
    original'. The Italian word used to translate ἄρρητος was *indicibile*. See Agamben
    and Ferrando, 2014: 48, n. 41.
8   As Professor Albus Dumbledore says in *Harry Potter and the Philosopher's Stone*:
    'Fear of a name only increases fear of a thing itself' (the saying is given to Her-
    mione Granger in the film version).
9   Wachter, 2006: 139–144.
10 Bremmer, 2013: 44. For Persephone as the embodiment of corn see Frazer, 1912:
    39–40, cf. Preller, 1837: 128–129.
11 Richardson, 1974: 6.
12 Foley, 1994: 28; Parker, 1991: 1.
13 h.Hom. *Dem.* 197–198. For visual representations of Herakles assuming this pose
    see *LIMC* s.v. Cares 145, 146. Herakles is also shown in other representations
    indicative of Eleusis, for example carrying a purificatory piglet; see Clinton,
    1992: 78. I should note that these scenes of Herakles's initiation are from the
    Roman period.
14 Cf. 1992: 106.
15 Cole, 1994: 201. A large number of Demeter's epithets reflect her connection with
    agriculture: Chole ('Green Shoot'), Sito ('Grain'), Himalis ('Abundance'), Ompnia
    ('Nourisher with Grain'), Achaia ('Reaper'), Ioulos ('Goddess of Grain Sheaves'),
    Haloïs ('Goddess of the Threshing Floor'), Megalartos ('Goddess of Wheat Bread'),
    Megalomazos ('Goddess of Barley Bread'), Hamalophoros ('Bearing Sheaves of
    Grain'), Plousoros ('Rich in Piles of Grain'), Sotitis ('Giver of Heaps of Grain'),
    Karphphoros ('She who brings forth fruit'), Anesidora ('She who Sends up Gifts'),
    Kalligeneia ('She who brings forth beautiful offspring'); see also Farnell, 1907:
    311–320; Nilsson, 1906: 311–312.
16 I recently read Madeline Miller's novel *Circe*, which presents an image of the gods
    I feel is probably consistent with how the gods would have behaved had they been
    real – which is to say, there must be enough given to humans to keep them alive
    and hopeful, but not so much that they have no need to propitiate the gods and god-
    desses (particularly of Olympus, but more generally, in whole).
17 Bremmer, 2014: 1–20 has recently stressed this point in his new reconstruction of
    the Eleusinian festival.
18 This has been very convincingly argued by Bremmer 2014, and by and large
    I follow his reasoning set out there.
19 That is, Hades's bride without the connotation of ruling the Underworld, as she is
    presented in the Homeric *Hymn to Demeter*.
20 This is clearly not the case in cult that purposefully evoke both agrarian or fertility
    and Underworld queen aspects, as is the case at Lokroi, discussed in Chapter 5 and
    cf. Mackin Roberts, 2018.
21 Bremmer, 2014: 20.
22 For example, the Haloa, a mid-winter festival that was held in Eleusis in the month
    of Poseideon (around December/January) was a festival of Demeter and Kore
    (Brumfield, 1981: 104), as was the Thesmophoria (Brumfield, 1981: 70), so too the
    Stenia (Dillon, 2002: 109) and the Greater and Lesser Mysteries.
23 For example, Walter Burkert comments that 'Kore's own enigmatic name is Perseph-
    one' (Burkert, 1985: 159) and 'the mysteries of Eleusis were devoted to the 'Two
    Goddesses,' Demeter the grain goddess and her daughter Persephone, locally called

Pherephatta or just 'the Maiden,' Kore. (Burkert, 1987: 4). Erica Simon, in an arch-aeological study of Attic cult, uses the term 'Kore-Persephone to describe the Eleu-sinian goddess, and the index states 'Persephone, *see* Kore', indicating that the two are one and the same. (Simon, 1983: 25). The same hyphenated name is used, again with no explanation, in Ugo Bianchi, 1976: e.g. 2. Fritz Graf does not go so far as to create a direct amalgam of Kore and Persephone but does register 'Kore (s. auch Persephone)' and 'Persephone (s. auch Kore)' in his index (Graf, 1974). Claude Calame, in the discussion of the myth of Persephone's rape in *Greek Mythology: Poetics, Pragmatics and Fiction*, seems arbitrarily to switch between referring to Persephone and Kore (for example, on page sixty he refers to 'the story of the abduction of Persephone' while two pages later says 'the hymn that tells the story of Core's abduction', both in reference to the content of the Homeric *hymn*) (Calame, 2009: 60–62). Helene Foley's *The Homeric* Hymn to Demeter: *Translation, Com-mentary and Interpretive Essays* comments that 'the *hymn* honours the Greek god-dess of grain Demeter, and her daughter Kore ("maiden") or Persephone' (Foley, 1994: 79). Ava Avagianou directly addresses the problematic situation in identifying Kore: 'the name Kore for Persephone: The question that arises is not whether Kore and Persephone were one or two goddesses. I think undoubtedly they must be identi-cal' (Avagianou, 1991: 131). Lars Albinus repeatedly refers to the goddess of the Homeric *Hymn* as Kore (Albinus, 2000: e.g. 168, 70). Some scholars, particularly those outside Greek religious studies proper, do not even attempt to acknowledge that there are multiple 'names' that could refer to one (or several) divinities, for instance, 'The Eleusinian Mysteries of Demeter and Persephone: Fertility, Sexuality, and Rebirth' (Keller, 1988: 27–54). Lewis Farnell deduces that the name Kore was simply an abbreviation of the fuller title 'Persephone-Kore', and that the two god-desses were one and the same, citing parallels including the cultic title of Hera at Stymphalos being Ἥρα Παῖς ('Hera the girl'). He goes on to comment that 'the ritual-testimony compels us to say that the young corn-maiden was always indistin-guishable from the chthonian goddess, that at no period is Kore shown to be the former only and not also the latter' (Farnell, 1907: 120–121).

24 See Clinton, 1992: 84–90.
25 h.Hom. *Dem*. 494.
26 Paus. 8.37.9.
27 Cf. Bremmer, 2014: 84. Hugh Bowden (2010: 47–48) hints that he agrees with the notion that there was no eschatological basis for the Eleusinian Mysteries, by separ-ating out the personas of Persephone as Queen of the Underworld and Kore as maiden, although he does not explicitly state that the Mysteries are not eschatological.
28 Parker, 2005a: 354.
29 For further discussion on this see Chapter 1.
30 For more on the Thesmophoria see Versnel, 2011: 110–120 inc. references.
31 Johnston, 2013: 371.
32 h.Hom. *Dem*. 364–369; trans. West.
33 See also Richardson, 1974: 269–270.
34 The two most well-known of these, Sisyphos and Tantalos, demonstrate this clearly. Sisyphos repeatedly violated the guest-host relationship that was enshrined in Zeus's domain, and Tantalos – among other things – served his own son, Pelops, to the gods.
35 Richardson, 1974: 270.
36 Pindar usually presents Hades as blending into the scenery of the Underworld, as, for example, at Pind. *Pyth*. 5.96.
37 Pind. *Ol*. 14.20–21.
38 Pind. *fr*. 133 (Race) = Pl. *Men*. 81b.

39 There are numerous examples of Demeter causing barrenness across the earth. The most well-known is arguably found in the Homeric *Hymn to Demeter*, and I will be discussing another prominent example in this chapter.

40 Bremmer, 2012: 26; Parker, 2005a: 280.

41 Cole, 1994: 201.

42 Beekes, 2010: 324–325. Although it is common for divine names to have no traceable etymology, cf. Burkert, 1985: 159. Having said that, the names of gods still communicate something about the nature of those gods, even if that is not though a kind of 'spoken' etymologisation (where the name directly translates into something about the god). This is because of the foundation that is built underneath the characterisation of a god in the mind of the person when they are called out in a story, art piece, or conversation, and storytellers can use this to make their audiences think about their characters in specific ways by, for example, using a patronymic to evoke the story of their ancestry.

43 Cole, 1994: 201.

44 Such epithets include Χλόν ('First Shoots', for example *IG* II² 4748, 4750, 4777, 5400; Erythrai 60), Πλουτοδοτείρα ('Giver of Wealth', for example IScM III 259), and Καρπόφορος ('Bearer of Fruit', for example DAW 46.6 (1896) 16).

45 Paus. 10.35.10, cf. Cole, 1994: 202.

46 The epithets will be discussed in detail below. The Erinyes were Underworld-dwelling, death-related goddesses of vengeance, and Demeter's association with them hints at a strong connection between her and the Underworld.

47 Hom. *Il.* 2.969, 5.500, 13.322, 14.326, 21.76; *Od.* 5.125.

48 Hom. *Il.* 12.322, 21.76.

49 Hom. *Od.* 5.97–144.

50 Hes. *Th.* 454.

51 Hes. *Th.* 912–913.

52 Hes. Th. 969, cf. Diod. 5.48.2, Hyginus *Astronomica* 2.4. (where Ploutos is the twin brother of Philomelos), see M.L. West 1966: 422.

53 Hes. *WD.* 393–395.

54 Hes. *WD.* 300.

55 h.Hom. *Dem.* 224, 308, 385, 471.

56 Hes. *WD.* 300, cf. Hom. *Il.* 13.322, 21.76; Hes. *Sh.* 290.

57 Hes. *WD.* 597, 805.

58 Hes. *WD.* 465–466. Most translates Zeus Chthonios as 'Zeus of the land', emphasising the agrarian aspect of this sentiment.

59 For example, Hom. *Il.* 9.457, Aisch. *Sup.* 231, *Ag.* 1386–1387. See Calame, 2008: 242, 45; Schleiser, 1997: 1187. Also see Chapter 3 above.

60 See Chapter 3, n. 7 above.

61 h.Hom. *Dem.* 354.

62 For example, Demeter pointedly asks for a temple to be constructed in her honour and teaches high-standing Eleusinian citizens her mysteries (h.Hom. *Dem.* 474–483). One of these citizens is Triptolemos, who is honoured in Eleusinian cult. See Clinton, 1992: 13; Penglase, 1994: 126. There is an undoubtable narrative link between the two, although it is unprovable to say that the similarities between the ritual and hymn are not the result of what I would call a 'reverse aetiology' rather than a 'forward aetiology'. I do not think that there is a forward aetiological relationship between the hymn and the rituals of the Eleusinian Mysteries – that is, that the hymn was written before the rituals at Eleusis took a form which mirrors aspects of the hymn. It is clear that there is some relationship between the two, but this must be, I think, that certain aspects of the ritual were included within the hymn to create this link.

63 h.Hom. *Dem.* 15–30.

64 h.Hom. *Dem.* 47–50.
65 h.Hom. *Dem.* 256–275.
66 h.Hom. *Dem.* 371–372, 412.
67 Clinton, 1979: 5.
68 Paus. 8.37.9, Bianchi, 1976: at e.g. 2; Burkert, 1985: 159, 1987: 4; Keller, 1988: 27–54; Simon, 1983: 25.
69 *I Eleus.* 28a: 37–40.
70 Cf. Clinton, 1992: 114.
71 Clay, 1989: 222 and n. 68. This is not Demeter's only instance of self-exile. See, particularly, sections below on Phigalia and Thelpousa.
72 As commented on by several scholars, but notably Parker, 1991: 7–9; Richardson, 1974; Von Wilamowitz-Moellendorff, 1932: 50; Zuntz, 1971: 79.
73 Although he is not given a privileged position in the poem and appears among the other prominent Eleusinian men. There is no indication here of his role within the cult.
74 h.Hom. *Dem.* 202–204. Iambe's name is certainly related to etymologically to ἴαμβος, and so is connected to the idea of mocking or insulting. Although the hymn does not tell us what Iambe actually says to make Demeter laugh, we can surmise that it is probably sexually charged mocking, perhaps about the abilities of men.
75 h.Hom. *Dem.* 208–210. The hymn calls this drink the kykeon, the 'mix up'. This is the same as the name for the drink used in Eleusinian ritual practices.
76 Although he is not named until line 234.
77 h.Hom. *Dem.* 225–230; trans. West.
78 h.Hom. *Dem.* 242.
79 h.Hom. *Dem.* 269–274.
80 h.Hom. *Dem.* 315–331.
81 h.Hom. *Dem.* 333–334.
82 h.Hom. *Dem.* 341–357. For discussion on Hermes's role as a guide across liminal boundaries, see Chapter 7.
83 Richardson, 1974: 211, cf. Shelmerdine, 1995: 43–44.
84 Cf. Clay, 1989: 226, 39.
85 Clay, 1989: 240.
86 h.Hom. *Dem.* 256–257; trans. Clay.
87 It is easy to read this 'Eleusinian Interlude' as a time when Demeter has forgotten about Persephone's abduction. J.S. Clay has very convincingly argued that she neither forgets about her daughter, nor releases her anger and grief during her stay in Eleusis. See Clay, 1989: 225–226.
88 Clay, 1989: 240.
89 Though, as I have said, I do not think that the Eleusinian Mysteries are primarily eschatological, rather that people undergo initiation to form and strengthen their relationship with the two goddesses. More immediate benefits can be gained though this relationship, and a 'better afterlife' is perhaps only an extension of the strength of the relationship formed.
90 h.Hom. *Dem.* 307–308.

5 Rites-of-passage and metaphorical death

Speaking about rites-of-passage in ancient Greece is problematic. This is true both in historical rituals that signify the transition from one status to another and in discussing mythic narratives of those transitions. There are two reasons for this: first, there is no real scholarly consensus of what transitory or 'initiatory' rites are, and second, the rituals and narratives themselves are different – sometimes vastly so – and use different vocabulary and imagery. There is no universal vocabulary that covers these various rites of passage, each of these rites conforms to various regional vocabularies, such as the Spartan *Krypteia* and the Athenian *Ephebia* and *Arkteia*. Just as it is unproblematic that there is no Greek word for 'religion', it is similarly unproblematic that there is no umbrella term for 'coming-of-age rites-of-passage'. This, then, raises the issue of which rites can be classed as 'rites-of-passage'. For instance, there is little difference between the function of the *Ephebia* and *Krypteia* – both are aimed at transforming boys into men.[1] In some ways there are overlaps in form, also – both include some military service and forced liminality (which will be discussed later in this chapter). However, they cannot be linked together in any phenomenological way, because they are highly localised practices. The important connection is that they represent the same transitory period for young men and women within the context of their own society and socio-political roles. I am not here interested in creating a definition of rites of passage[2] but at looking how gods related to the Underworld assist young men and women in the ancient Greek world to shed one identity and to gain another. The inclusion of Underworld gods in such rites is understandable, because these rites can be cast (in both modern interoperative frameworks and in ancient narratives) as stories of 'death and rebirth'.

All rites-of-passage represent crossing of one stage of life to another. This was first articulated by Arnold van Gennep in *Les rites de passage* (1909), who argued that all these rites of passage share three common and distinctive stages.[3] His schema is widely applicable to other transitory passages. The schema's first stage are the rites of separation 'or pre-liminal rites that remove people from their prior status'. The second stage represents transitional or liminal rites 'that subject them to transformative operations inside a symbolic border zone'. Finally, the third stage represents rites of reintegration or 'reaggregation or post-liminal rites that reintroduce them to society and insert them in new stations'.[4] Although van Gennep's schema is perhaps oversimplified, it can be applied to all cases of 'initiatory rites' and underwent vigorous testing in *Les rites de passage*. The employment of a simple yet specific base schema is advantageous in this situation, wherein the myths and rituals that represent transition or initiation are, themselves, so complex and different from one another, that these disparate rites can then be more easily compared. So even when there is no overarching vocabulary describing 'coming of age' rites, we can clearly identify rites that are concerned with the crossing of status boundaries, and which include a necessarily liminal stage. One example of this is the transitionary process undertaken from maiden, to fiancée, to wife.

In the process of getting married, a girl leaves her family with whom she has belonged as a girl (separation). She then enters an in-between period of ritual liminality (transition) during the marriage rites themselves, during which she is formally transferred from her father's *oikos* to that of her new husband. Finally, she then re-enters society in a different role and a different status (re-incorporation) as a wife and a member of a new household. Classical Athenian wedding customs reflect this schema, as they were undertaken in three parts, each of which directly correlates to one of van Gennep's stages. The first stage is the ἐγγύη, or betrothal of a girl by her father. This stage represents the metaphorical separation of the girl and her former life, and although she does not formally leave her family home during this stage of the initiatory process, it signals that she is becoming a disparate entity. The second stage is the ἔκδοσις, wherein the girl is transferred from her father's house to the house of her new husband. This transformation between houses represents the liminal period of transition; she leaves her father's home as a girl and enters her new husband's home as a woman and wife and this intermediary period is a physical representation of the metaphysical change occurring in her status. Finally, the γάμος, the actual wedding ceremony, which includes the consummation of the marriage on the night of the wedding, is representative of her acceptance of her new role and her re-incorporation into society.[5] In this final stage, change is characterised by a private physical change in condition, the girl transforms from maiden to woman. This – along with several other transitory rituals, including the *Arkteia* in Athens[6]– were the girls' equivalents to the boys' *Ephebia* (in Athens). The connection between war and age transition is well established. For example, the Athenian army was divided into forty-two sub-groups based solely on age differentiation. The youngest class were the *epheboi*, and they moved up through the groups as they aged and, alongside this, gained military and political experience: the transition from boy to soldier.

In initiation myths, death is often used as an image for the intermediary liminal period – the pause between realised statuses. Sometimes this is represented as a physical death, as in the case of Iphigeneia (discussed below), but often it is only a metaphorical death. Sometimes the death is final, and the new status is achieved once the protagonist has finally settled into death and reached the Underworld. But usually there is a rebirth of sorts. This is what happens in Orestes's unusual death narrative that I will discuss below.

By briefly examining the girls' marriage transition and its connection to the tale of Iphigeneia, we can see that initiatory paradigms are visible in the mythic narratives surrounding the House of Atreus, and Aischylos himself used them extensively. From these examples we can see that, although both rituals of 'initiation' and initiatory mythic narratives do fit van Gennep's tripartite schema of initiation, myths of initiation are usually more complex to tease meaning from. Furthermore, '[o]ne may argue that these mythical examples have little to do with the real life of the ancient Greeks, but then one forgets how these stories represent the very foundation upon which the various rites of passage were based'.[7]

Fritz Graf identifies three categories of such initiation myths. The first group includes myths that are aetiologies for rites contemporary to the myth that we would still label as initiatory in nature. This subgroup provides a quite straightforward analysis wherein each myth has a clear initiatory function for the peoples that use that myth.[8] The second group includes myths that correspond to rituals that are initiatory in character, but which have been transformed into something else. In this group the methodological problems arise when attempting a reading of a non-initiatory myth as an aetiology of an initiatory ritual.[9] The third category includes myths which do not directly correspond to initiatory rituals in antiquity, but which scholars read as having initiatory characteristics, and whose initiatory background belongs to the prehistory of each specific myth. 'The real challenge is the third subgroup, myths that are assumed to be initiatory but without existing initiation rituals.'[10] Graf identifies two examples of such myths of this third category, Theseus' trip to Krete, which will be discussed below, and the myth of Iphigeneia in Aulis.

In this narrative, Iphigeneia, a young Argive princess and daughter of Agamemnon and Klytaimestra, travels from Argos to Aulis on the promise of marriage. In reality, her father has been commanded by Artemis to sacrifice the young virgin in exchange for agreeable winds for the combined Greek armies, under the command of Agamemnon, to sail to Troy for war. Eventually, Iphigeneia is sacrificed to the goddess and the Greeks sail to war. Euripides's version of this myth, told in *Iphigeneia Taurica*, sees Artemis exchange Iphigeneia with a deer at the moment of her death;[11] however, Aischylos mentions no such exchange in the text of the *Oresteia*.[12] Agamemnon's false promise of marriage to his daughter corresponds to the first stage of the schema, during which the young girl's betrothal signals the beginning of separation from her family. Although Iphigeneia is unaware that her betrothal is to D/death and not to a suitor, she readies herself for marriage and for the process of becoming a wife. The transitionary stage occurs during her journey from her home in Argos to the Greek army camp in Aulis. This occurs in the same fashion as the young girl travelling from her father's house to her husband's house. In both the historical and the mythic examples, the physical journey signifies not only a metaphysical alteration, but the physical journey is the origin of the metaphysical journey.[13] During this time – whether it is a short trip from her father's oikos to a husband's within the same *polis* or the longer trip from a home *polis* to a foreign one as undertaken by Iphigeneia – the young girl uses this time to begin her mental preparation for the deeply personal change she is about to undergo. This includes not only a change in duties or status within the community, but a personal physical experience of this process of transition. For the young girl this is signalled by the loss of her virginity, but for Iphigeneia it means the loss of her life. Rather than experiencing re-integration, Iphigeneia becomes a 'bride of death'[14] and transforms ritualistically, rather than re-entering society like the young girl following her wedding rites and the consummation of her marriage. This also represents the motif of death and rebirth found within narratives of initiation, which will be discussed in greater detail below.

Though Iphigeneia's sacrifice is a well-known component of this myth, especially from Euripides's later treatment of it, Aischylos says little of it directly.[15] However, it is indirectly referred to throughout the *Oresteia*, and the *Agamemnon* alludes directly to this myth. The chorus of Argive elders remember the prescription that Kalchas delivered to the king and Agamemnon's deliberation over whether to sacrifice his daughter to the goddess. Finally, they comment that ἔτλα δ᾽ οὖν θυτὴρ γενέσθαι θυγατρός ('he brought himself to become the sacrificer of his daughter').[16] After slaying her husband, Klytaimestra refers to the sacrifice of Iphigeneia a number of times, calling herself δικαίας τέκτονος ('a crafter of justice').[17] During interrogation from the Argive elders for her murder of Agamemnon she says: μὰ τὴν τέλειον τῆς ἐμῆς παιδὸς Δίκην, Ἄτην Ἐρινύν θ᾽, αἷσι τόνδ᾽ ἔσφαξ᾽ ἐγώ ('by the fulfilled Justice that was due for my child, by Ate and by the Erinys, through whose aid I slew this man').[18] Later, Orestes and Elektra both comment directly on and indirectly allude to the sacrifice of their sister, but either neither of them understands or neither acknowledge that it has provided the catalyst for Agamemnon's death.

Euripides's *Iphigeneia at Aulis*, possibly the fullest contemporary account of this narrative, reports that unfavourable winds have stranded Agamemnon and the Greek forces in Aulis. Agamemnon consults the seer Kalchas who replies that the king must sacrifice his daughter, Iphigeneia, to the goddess Artemis in order to gain favourable winds to sail to Troy. After much anguish the king, Agamemnon, sends for his daughter under the pretence of offering her in marriage to Achilleus. However, he later changes his mind and sends a second message instructing Klytaimestra to ignore the first letter. Menelaus intercepts the second letter and Klytaimestra and Iphigeneia arrive at Aulis. Klytaimestra and Achilleus eventually discover the plot and together they attempt to stop the sacrifice, but to no avail. In the end, Iphigeneia willingly offers herself up for sacrifice and is killed by Agamemnon.[19]

The narrative of Iphigeneia provides an example of an initiatory myth that presents an initiation-style transition that subverted the sequence of these status-altering rituals, although they generally still present van Gennep's three-stage schema. Though her narrative is normally read as a myth of initiation it is not explicitly so, nor does it present an overt display of an initiatory ritual. This is the category of initiation myths into which all narratives of initiation and transition within the *Oresteia* belong, and this is especially evident in an examination of Orestes's initiatory process.

One of the key points to highlight in this third subcategory of myth is the experience of marginalisation. However, we must be careful to recognise that, as Lincoln points out:

> there is nothing necessarily liberatory anti-structural, or communitarian about this stage of a ritual process. Asymmetries of power and status do not evaporate in the liminal period. Rather ... a condition of the communitas experienced among novices is the absolute authority elders exercise over them.[20]

It is also important to remember that 'initiatory experience is not derived from ritual; rather the ritual is derived from the experience, which it aims to clarify, motivate, normalise, support, and explain'.[21] This period of marginality is implied in the process of transition from the status of recognised future-citizen (or, more accurately citizen with future political rights) to politically active citizen in Athens. Becoming a full-citizen is, for boys, the same process as the step from maiden to wife for girls. Although there is no single formal rite of initiation that transforms the boy from one status to another, there is a process of 'becoming a citizen' that includes 'induction into a *phratry*, induction into a deme, and swearing the oath of citizenship [which] took place on three separate occasions over a period of two years'.[22]

The formalised occurrence of male coming of age initiation rituals in classical Athenian society is, however, a highly contentious issue. Certainly, there were aspects of the process of 'coming of age' that may be described as ritualistic in nature and later developed into formalised rituals. In the *Athenaion Politeia*, written around 350 BCE, Aristotle describes a series of presentations and oaths that occur in order for the eighteen-year-old ephebe to be admitted into the deme as a political member. Though he describes these as 'ancient' practices, there is insufficient evidence to confirm a classical era ephebeia as a stand-alone ritual passage. Admittance to the military marked the beginning of two years of military training, after which the young cadet was admitted into the citizen body of the *polis* and attained rites to represent themselves as political adults.[23] The epheboi – young men between sixteen and eighteen – were also involved in a number of Athenian religious festivals, including the festival which celebrated Athenian victory at Marathon,[24] demonstrating the strong ties the young ephebes had with the military past of Athens, and the Mounychia, a festival dedicated to Artemis during which the ephebes participated in a mock sea-battle or regatta on ships that are described as being 'sacred'.[25] Athenian ephebes also acted as processional escorts during a number of other religious festivals, including processions between Athens and Eleusis, the accompaniment of the cult statue of Athena Polias and of the peplos offered to the goddess during the Great Panathenaic festivals that occurred every four years.[26] The 'ephebeia' as a stand-alone ritual, which was undertaken by young men in fourth-century Athens,[27] is certainly not an aspect of the classical Athenian model of 'coming of age' or any requirement of citizenship. It is more likely that these later rites represent a blending of customs, which includes a form of private military training undertaken by a select group of classical Athenian boys. In the classical period this aspect was probably an institution that the rich upper classes afforded to their sons to complete their 'coming of age' rites, which was later transformed into a general requirement for all ephebes to undertake.[28]

Hermes the transgressor: on passing through the Underworld

Being taken to the Underworld seems, on the surface, like a relatively easy business – and that is probably true when you die. If you happen to die on the Homeric battlefield your *psyche* might wing its way out of your body and down to the Underworld as Hektor's does: ἄρα μιν εἰπόντα τέλος θανάτοιο κάλυψε, ψυχὴ δ' ἐκ ῥεθέων πταμένη Ἄϊδόσδε βεβήκει ('He spoke, and as he spoke the end of death closed in upon him, and the soul fluttering free of the limbs went down into Death's house').[29] A person in the classical period might have their *psyche* taken into the Underworld by Charon's boat, or by Hermes himself. But if you wanted to get into *and* out of the Underworld then Hermes was probably the safest bet. It was Hermes who was able to retrieve Persephone from the Underworld, after all.

The Homeric *Hymn to Demeter* does not elaborate on why Persephone needs a guide, whether she can navigate back on her own and chooses not to, or even if she does not try. The hymn does say that she is 'reluctant' (ἀεκαζόμενος)[30] because she longs for her mother. On the other hand, she also takes Hades's chariot,[31] putting Hermes in the role of black-suited chauffeur[32]– fitting for the new wife of the Lord of the Underworld. There is the odd mediation between Persephone as the rebellious teenager who is playing both sides – telling her mother she was *definitely forced*, yet also indulging her new husband.[33]

Hermes's guidance comes with the explicit permission to travel out of the Underworld, but the one figure whose opinion really matters here is Zeus. Hermes is sent on Zeus's authority and relays this command to Hades,[34] who then allows Persephone to leave.[35] Similarly – though without the same explicit permission – Hermes leads Herakles up from the Underworld after he captures Hades's three-headed dog Kerberos. When Herakles recounts this to Odysseus, he credits Hermes for bringing him back to earth.[36]

Hermes is not a character in Aischylos's *Eumenides*, which may seem irrelevant to both this discussion and any discussion of that play. Hermes has, I think, one of the most important roles in the *Eumenides*, and that role perfectly illustrates the ephemeral nature of Hermes as an Underworld-and-Back-Travelling god. This is because he is the single most important figure in getting Orestes purified, and so also in undergoing the coming-of-age rite that underlies his purification from bloodguilt. And, therefore, Hermes is instrumental in the conclusion of the trilogy. This is interesting because it demonstrates how death can be used in narratives to show a status change (other than from alive to dead). It also clearly shows how a god's Underworld function is often just an extension of their wider persona.

This all comes about because Apollo asks Hermes to guide (πομπαῖος) Orestes from Delphi to Athens, a usually straightforward trip that is anything but for the young killer. Hermes's role in the play has not been the subject of much scholarship, probably because he is almost entirely absent from it. Many editions of the tragedy mention his entrance, at line sixty-three, with Orestes and Apollo, and mention that he departs at line ninety-three with Orestes.[37] We obviously cannot know if Aischylos meant Hermes to physically appear but, regardless, the god has not warranted a speaking role. Editors probably suppose that Hermes is on stage because Apollo directly addresses him at line ninety: Ἑρμῆ, φύλασσε ('Hermes, watch him').[38] I do not think that direct address should automatically mean he is present. As people pray to absent gods and expect that they will be heard, it does not seem unreasonable to assume that a god could call upon another god who is not present.[39] There is a good reason why Hermes might not come on stage at the beginning of the play: if he were present at this point then why would he be absent when Orestes reaches Athens? While this perhaps makes it seem like he is just a guard escorting a prisoner to court, his involvement says something more meaningful about Orestes's liminalised journey to Athens. This is simply down to Hermes's profile as a ritualised boundary crosser. When we account for this it is both appropriate and unsurprising that Hermes should lead Orestes. Not only does Hermes excel at crossing liminal physical boundaries, but also those that govern other kinds of liminalities, including the barrier between youth and old age.[40]

When Orestes and Hermes leave Delphi for Athens, they go on a seemingly unnecessary sea voyage.[41] This is mentioned twice in the play: first when Apollo commands Orestes to flee ὑπέρ τε πόντον ('over the water'),[42] and again when Orestes tells Athena that he arrived in Athens by ὅμοια χέρσον καὶ θάλασσαν ἐκπερῶ ('crossing over sea and land alike').[43] Orestes then uses the term πόρος to describe his purification by 'flowing streams', a term that also connotes crossing water or travelling across water.[44] So, although the trip from Delphi to Athens would not typically require a sea crossing, Orestes has spent at least part of his journey at sea. This geographically unnecessary voyage can only be explained by the vastness of transition that Orestes is attempting. The sea crossing motif only appears occasionally in narratives of purification, and even when it does appear it often refers to very specific circumstances, like purificatory colonisation. The theme often appears in coming-of-age narratives, like those of the young male dolphin riders, or an analogous motif in girls' coming-of-age stories in which they are exposed to the sea locked in a chest.[45] But here Orestes must undergo several simultaneous transitions: from polluted to 'ritual normalcy',[46] from outsider to citizen, from adolescent to adult, and from (brand new) citizen to king, to gain legitimacy and reclaim his father's throne. And, crucially, he must undergo all these changes at once. Orestes's travels are designed to bring about this mass status transition in the shortest time possible.

Crossing the sea is like crossing between the worlds of the living and the dead and is a particularly apt motif for transition narratives that play out a death and rebirth. By crossing the sea, Orestes is travelling *through* the Underworld; the 'old' Orestes dies, and the 'new' Orestes (re)enters the living world in his place. Hermes's affinity for boundary crossing makes him well suited to leading the young Orestes over this boundary, so it does not matter that the god has no particular expertise in water-crossing. He is, however, well known not just as a transgressor of taboos, or a crosser of nominal age-boundaries, but also – and quite prominently – as a crosser into (and out of) the Underworld. This is the truly exceptional thing about Hermes, and what makes him particularly able to guide Orestes through his unnecessary sea journey: boundary crossing for Hermes is a two-way path.

By the time he is appointed as Orestes's guide, Hermes's connection to the Underworld has already been made explicit in the *Oresteia*. The first words of *Choephoroi* invoke the god as Ἑρμῆ χθόνιε – Hermes of the Underworld, as Orestes prays to him while standing at the stone pile of his father's grave.[47] Hermes represents the physical and metaphysical marks of death: the stone *herm* that marks Agamemnon's grave, his physical remains, and the perpetual reminder of his journey into the Underworld.

Apollo's command to Hermes reinforces his ability to guide Orestes through the dark, liminal (physical and metaphysical) space of transition and back to the living world, and he says this very explicitly:

Ἑρμῆ, φύλασσε, κάρτα δ' ὢν ἐρώνυμος
πομπαῖος ἴσθι, τόνδε ποιμαίνων ἐμὸν
ἱκέτην – σέβει τοι Ζεὺς τόδ' ἐκονόμων σέβας -
ὁρμώμενον βροτοῖσιν εὐρόμπῳ τύχῃ.

Hermes, guard him, and, true to your title, be his escort, shepherding this my suppliant – for Zeus respects the sanctity of wayfarers like this one – who will have the blessing of a good escort as he starts his journey back to human society.[48]

By using the word βροτός ('mortal'), Apollo is making a very clear and deliberate claim for Orestes's travel to Athens. That Orestes must go back to βροτός society shows that he has entered a world of otherness, undefined but decidedly not mortal. If he had not left the human world there would be no need for a guide to return him to it. It reminds us – (ancient) audience and (modern) reader – that Orestes is himself mortal and the act of traversing the Underworld will put him into a category of people who are super-human.

And so, Hermes guides Orestes 'back to mortal men', just as he had returned Persephone from the Underworld in the Homeric *Hymn to Demeter*.[49] Hermes's role in Persephone's return is quite small (not unlike his presence in the *Eumenides*). The

Hymn reports that Zeus asked Hermes to ἀγαυὴν Περσεφόνειαν ἐξαγαγεῖν Ἐρέβεσφι ('lead noble Persephone back from Erebos').[50] Persephone's return demonstrates the link between Underworld visitation and status transition, and this connection is perfectly mediated by Hermes – leading into and out of the Underworld being representative of his ability to return his charges to a status of normality, even though that is a new kind of normalcy. For Persephone, that change is to wife; for Orestes, it is to ritually normal, adult, citizen. Persephone's inability to return to the earth (whether because she could not find her way out of the Underworld on her own, or for another reason), necessitated the assistance of a suitable guide: Hermes.[51]

Hermes's inclusion in the *Eumenides* is particularly noteworthy because Apollo has a well-reported and strong connection with ephebes and their transition to full adulthood.[52] The Homeric *Hymn to Hermes* even has the arch-ephebic god guide Hermes through the transition from adolescence to adulthood![53] If Apollo already has both the capacity and the reputation as a god who leads ephebes through transition then why include Hermes in the plot at all? I think it must be because of his singular ability for two-way travel across tricky, metaphysical boundaries that others – even other gods – cannot cross.

Hermes's profile as a leader over boundaries is not confined to leading the dead or coming back from the Underworld. He is also known to guide over age-related boundaries, mediating between adolescent and adult.[54] This is shown clearly in the iconographic record at the temple of Hermes at Kato Syme, on Krete (although this is admittedly a fairly unique context).[55] A large hoard of figurines shows two distinct guises of Hermes: the beardless adolescent, and the bearded adult. This double-guise shows his transgressive nature, not only mediating between the two phases but easily crossing back and forth between them, and able to guide other across this threshold.[56] He does not simply lead the youths *up to the point of transition*, but rather he takes them *across the border* between the old and new states. The 'double guise' motif, in which images of the adult god and the adolescent god appear in the same place, during the same time-frame, and using the same iconographical formulae in their construction is also found elsewhere, notably in Corinth.[57] What we have is a god who can shift both ways between adolescence and adulthood, just as he can cross through the Underworld and return to the earth. Hermes is not only a figurehead but a true guide, someone who can pass through the barrier with the initiand rather than remaining at the precipice watching his followers step through.

Hermes is a transgressor of both physical and symbolic markers. He is the god who can safely traverse into the Underworld, who can shift from adolescent to adult and back and is in the exceptional position to guide Orestes through his enormous liminal transition. While this does relate to Hermes's profile as an Underworld god, it demonstrates how this Underworld-related position is a portion of the god's wider aspect to go beyond borders, lines, and limits.

Marriage and death: Persephone at Lokroi and Hades in Athens

In mythic rites-of-passage, death can be used as a stand-in for the intermediary 'liminal period' of rites-of-passage in the real world. Dying is the process that changes a person from 'before' to 'after'. This is sometimes represented as a physical death, as in the case of Iphigeneia, which I will discuss briefly below. More usually, however, it is only metaphorical. Death sometimes occurs alone, as an ending, but more usually is narrated with some form of rebirth. One of the most prominent uses of death-and-rebirth in marriage mythology is the story of Persephone, a goddess who is literally snatched away and driven down into the Underworld to become a wife. Mock abduction forms a part of some marriage rituals and abduction-as-marriage (so-called 'bridal theft') was common in myth.[58] This role of 'mock abduction', and its link to Persephone's abduction, in marriage rituals practice is particularly evident in the southern Italian settlement of Lokroi Epizephyrioi.[59] Somewhat unusually, Persephone here is characterised as both the victim of bridal theft and the Queen of the Underworld. That is, Lokrian Persephone is both the archetypical abducted maiden and the ruler of the Underworld.[60] Both aspects are strongly related to fertility through the link between agriculture and the Underworld. This is intimated in the Homeric *Hymn to Demeter* in, for instance, the connection between Persephone going into the Underworld and the burial of seeds.[61] It is also brought out at Lokroi using fertility-related iconography (like grain stalks) alongside Underworld-related iconography (like pomegranates), particularly in the homage and 'still life' pinakes (discussed below). Persephone's cult was a major religious focus for the *polis*.

The pinakes were most likely votive tablets dedicated by young girls in the lead-up to their weddings. In this sense, it is understandable that the chosen god does not completely undergo the transition process. The dedications served the function of seeking Persephone's blessing and protection for their marriages,[62] and they were dedicated before the marriage had taken place. So, the image of the goddess that was being invoked and imitated in the abduction scenes was the goddess in the same state as the dedicating girls: the state immediately before marriage.[63] Persephone as a protector of marriage appears to be local to Lokroi, and there is no evidence that people came from outside the city to make marriage-related dedications to Lokrian Persephone.

The most common pinax types are the 'divine' and 'imitation' scenes. In both cases, these range from unambiguous abductions where the maiden clearly struggles against her captor to images in which it appears the girl is complicit in her own kidnapping – sometimes even taking charge of the chariot herself. The range can be accounted for because, as James Redfield points out, 'no doubt some brides felt more abducted than others'.[64] This position, of course, supposes that the girls themselves were responsible for picking out the image for their pinax. This may well have been the case, and I tend to think (partly following Redfield's intimation) that the image chosen reflected the feelings of each girl, and probably also her mother, about the upcoming marriage. There are many examples of women dedicating objects in the Greek world,[65] so it is certainly not implausible to suggest that a female (either the girl, or her mother in consultation with her daughter) would have chosen the image. If the girl's *kyrios* is selecting the image there may be fewer that show the bride's dissatisfaction, worry, or fear at the impending marriage, given the role they would play in selecting the groom to begin with, though this does not discount a father or brother being sensitive to his daughter or sister's feelings. In the context of Lokroi, this does relate to the apparently matrilineal transference of religious practice.[66]

Feelings towards marriage-abduction are echoed on some southern Italian vases, showing Persephone leaning back, stretching out for Demeter and a final attempt for help.[67] But, unlike these dramatic scenes, the majority of the pinakes show a middle ground, where the girl is neither totally cooperative nor being forcibly torn away from her family: she is a captive, but her abductor is soft and adoring. Persephone was torn between acceptance and horror in her own abduction, and although Zeus had permitted the marriage Persephone screamed when Hades snatched her, and the hymn describes her as being ἀέκων, 'constrained' or 'unwilling'.[68] But, her victimisation is not necessarily that clear. In any case, consent in the ancient world was highly problematic,[69] but a girl who had been genuinely sexually assaulted (without her or her father's permission) would have had legal recourse against her attacker.[70] The *Hymn* challenges Persephone's victimhood by having her *self*-identification change from aggrieved victim to accepting wife. Hades had a genuine desire to marry her and was not just attempting to rob her of her chastity: just like the grooms, who are all depicted as abductors on the pinakes, who imitate him in Lokroi. Persephone's agreement to her marriage is represented in the homage pinakes, where she calmly sits by her husband, receiving dedications.

The content of the imitation scenes has been greatly contested in the past, with identification ranging from prematurely dead girls[71] being taken into the Underworld by Thanatos,[72] a youthful Hades,[73] or Hermes,[74] or one of the Dioskouroi snatching Persephone on Hades's behalf,[75] or a local indigenous hero who was amalgamated into the Persephone-and-Hades abduction story due to similarities with the pair.[76] It has also been suggested that the divine abduction scenes could show Persephone being kidnapped by Eubouleus,[77] rather than Hades. This is unlikely: the abductor(s) are iconographically different from Eleusinian Eubouleus,[78] and there is no reason for him to appear in southern Italy, especially in a cult not connected to Eleusis or to mystery rites. The case for the young abductor and his bride imitating Persephone and Hades was made convincingly by Christiane Sourvinou-Inwood.[79] She argued that these must represent an idealised form of actual bridal couples because of the quantity and variety of depictions, and because they primarily relied on marriage-related iconography (rather than non-marriage-related abduction iconography[80]), and due to the relationship between mock abduction and marriage rituals.

There is no evidence that mock abductions occurred in marriage rituals at Lokroi, although whether they did or not is irrelevant.[81] That rites-of-passage were often mythically conceived of as death-and-rebirth, and in religious practice this was symbolised as a kind of death of the person's former status. In the context of marriage rites, which are essentially coming-of-age rites for girls,[82] Persephone's narrative is a perfect model. When Persephone is married she is literally snatched up and taken into the Underworld, and when she returns she is no longer a girl, but a woman with all the connotations that go with that change in status. This change happens while she is in the Underworld – at the moment she swallows the pomegranate seeds – not during her return or when she is back on the earth. So, when young Lokrian girls on the precipice of wifehood dedicated images of themselves looking and acting like Persephone, they were being written into Persephone's narrative, and her divine experience was appropriated into their mortal experience. These images do not need to be illustrations of an actual ritual to give them meaning. They are images of girls (metaphorically) dressing up as Persephone and acting out her story, being taken into the Underworld by their own groom-to-be, in order to undergo the change from girl to woman. So, it is important that Persephone is always shown before the conclusion of the marriage rite. The girls dedicating these images are preparing to enter the Underworld – that is, for their 'old' status to die – but they cannot yet envision the 'other side' of this change. In this way, Persephone is the perfect figure for emulation. There is the promise of a safe return to the 'known-ness' of their present lives. After marriage, these girls would still, in some ways, be under the control of their familial homes, just as Persephone is still under the control of her mother. A woman can always be retrieved, a marriage nullified. She does not completely integrate into her husband's home.[83]

The prominent role played by Hades in this cult, or at least in its iconography, is significant. In other cults that might be aetiologically linked to Persephone's abduction narrative (like the Eleusinian Mysteries or the Thesmophoria), the main narrative elements relate to Demeter's loss and Persephone's recovery. There is little (if any) reference to Persephone's abduction or marriage. These cults are predominantly agrarian-themed and represent Demeter's grief at the loss of her daughter, and the joy she exhibits upon her recovery, which plays out the cycle of barrenness and plenty that covers the earth. To achieve this, Persephone could have gone *anywhere*; for the narrative, however, the Underworld is the best place, because it cannot be easily entered, even by the gods. There is no indication that fertility aspects of these cults might be represented by the marriage of Persephone and Hades, perhaps because the couple is extraordinarily barren. But at Lokroi the abduction and marriage are the central aspects of the cult. This marriage cannot occur without Hades – perhaps an obvious observation, but nonetheless an important one in the context of a marriage-related dedication.

It is not just this point, though. Persephone is also presented here as Queen of the Underworld, not just a girl on the precipice of marriage. This symbolises what happens after the abduction, when the young girl leaves her familial home for that of her new husband, and in doing so takes over the duties of running her own household. The homage pinakes, in particular, feature death-related iconography, and Persephone is given the prominent position – at the front of the scene, with Hades seated behind her. But, the girls do not depict themselves in this guise – they are still on the other side of the transition.

The idea of girls playing Persephone is not unique to Lokroi. There are several examples of young girls imitating the goddess in her guise as Hades's wife.[84] This is, therefore, a flexible identification: where the girls at Lokroi present themselves as Persephone being taken into the Underworld, these girls are instead dressing up as brides to forego the direct experience of premature death. Following premature, and often horrible or violent, deaths, many girls become 'Brides of Hades', and their deaths are described as marriages. All these girls are being written into Persephone's abduction and marriage narrative to tell us something about their present context. There is a significant contextual difference between the cultic dedications at Lokroi and the tragedy of fifth-century Athens.[85] Yet this is an idea that appears in both contexts and, as I will discuss below, is also translated into Athenian funerary rituals. While the 'Persephone' that is being invoked in each case is slightly different, it is her more widely 'global' attribution that colours each interpretation.

Death and marriage rites were similar in many ways,[86] and they are connected by the typological motif of separation and reunion. Funerary epitaphs of young unmarried girls often comment that they had not experienced married life, and sometimes they include references to abduction by Hades.[87] Their tombs are likened to bridal chambers, and images often depict the dead girl as a bride being unveiled.[88] Iphigeneia is probably considered to be the archetypical 'Bride of Hades', although there are many other examples in classical literature. Iphigeneia, according to Euripides, is called to meet the combined Greek army waiting at Aulis under the pretence of marriage to the hero Achilleus,[89] but – we later learn – instead finds her husband in Hades.[90] The marriage ruse ensures that Iphigeneia undergoes the normal ritual preparations carried out by any young girl readying herself for marriage. However, this activity only serves to highlight her impending death to the all-too-knowing audience. Her mock marriage, and death, is a mythic exemplar for the rite-of-passage that each young Greek girl undergoes. Like Persephone, Iphigeneia dies and is transformed into a bride in the Underworld. She therefore embodies each possible outcome for young girls: marriage, or premature death. Young brides must prepare themselves for the end of childhood and to take up the responsibility of adulthood – that is, the metaphorical death of their former selves in order that they may be 'reborn' as wives. Iphigeneia's story draws out the mental preparation required of young girls about to undergo this status shift and the physical preparation for death that informs the mythic death-and-rebirth of this moment, reinforcing Persephone's double-edged marriage narrative.[91]

This is the role of the rite-of-passage, and the reason this idea embodies the motif of separation and reunion required in coming-of-age rites.

Antigone also prepares for her marriage only to find herself wed in Hades. She is betrothed to Haimon, son of her uncle Kreon. But instead she is entombed alive by her would-be father-in-law as punishment for attempting to bury her brother, Polyneikes.[92] That her crime relates to her own direct participation in Polyneikes's burial foreshadows her own imminent live burial, and her obsession with her brother's burial keeps her from the normal preparations for a young girl about to be wed. This is particularly pronounced given that her first burial attempt would have been ritually successful in the eyes of the gods.[93] But Kreon does think of Antigone's marriage to his son when he uncovers her plan. Or rather he considers that Antigone will no longer become his son's wife – commenting that Ἄιδης ὁ παύσων τούσδε τοὺς γάμους ἔφυ ('Hades will bring an end to this wedding for me').[94] And it does, but not in the way that Kreon initially intends. Because, protesting his fiancée's condemnation, Haimon kills himself. Antigone – now a bride without a mortal bridegroom – declares that the 'Ἀχέροντι νυμφεύσω ('I will marry Acheron'),[95] and she calls her own tomb a νυμφεῖον ('bridal chamber').[96] Through this explicit series of references, Sophokles writes Antigone into Persephone's narrative, exploiting the deep-rooted connection between marriage and death. Although, unlike Persephone, we know that Antigone will not return to the upper world and so she has no choice but to make her marriage in the Underworld. This is possible even though Antigone has not yet even mentioned Persephone. Repeated references to marriage in, and to, Hades is enough to place her in this narrative context.

Several characters clearly struggle with the idea that Antigone will be unwed, but Antigone is the one who drives this connection home. When she is led into her living tomb, she cries out – finally invoking Persephone:

> ὦ τύμβος, ὦ νυμφεῖον, ὦ κατασκαφὴς
> οἴκησις ἀείφρουρος, οἷ πορεύομαι
> πρὸς τοὺς ἐμαυτῆς, ὧν ἀριθμὸν ἐν νεκροῖς
> πλεῖστον δέδεκται Φερσέφασσ' ὀλωλότων·

> O Tomb, bridal-chamber, ever-lasting deep-dug home, where I go to join my own, who have been destroyed in the greatest numbers, and Persephone has received among the dead![97]

Judith Butler suggests the first lines of this speech indicate that Antigone marries one of her close family members, either Polyneikes or her father-brother Oidipous.[98] This follows her family's (mythic) heritage but does not necessarily fit into the concept that is being invoked by Antigone; namely, marriage in death. Haimon's mother, Eurydike, believes her son still marries Antigone in the Underworld, saying:

κεῖται δὲ νεκρὸς περὶ νεκρῷ, τὰ νυμφικὰ
τέλη λαχὼν δείλαιος εἰν Ἅιδου δόμοις

He [Haimon] lay, corpse enfolding corpse, having won his marriage rites,
poor boy, not here, but in the house of Hades.[99]

Kreon also refers to Antigone finding her husband in Hades but does not say
directly that she will marry the god (or, indeed, anyone else).[100] Even taking
these references alongside Antigone's own explicit reference to her marriage *to
Hades* we must acknowledge that her marriage is still made in the Underworld.
This demonstrates that the idea of a young woman of marriageable age dying,
without undergoing the experience of marriage, still needs to undergo this status
change. That is: every character with a stake in Antigone's outcome determines
that she will marry in the Underworld. Young women who die without marrying
in the mortal world get married in the Underworld. This is the effect of Persephone's narrative being used to discuss girls like Antigone. None of the girls –
Antigone included, despite her direct reference – attempt to subvert Persephone's position in the Underworld. They are not claiming rulership, or divine
status, or consortship. They are attempting to undergo the normal status change
that their adolescence has been building towards.

Because of this, the honour of taking up the mantle of 'Hades's Bride' can
be extended to Polyxena. She is sacrificed over the grave of Achilleus, to be his
wife in the Underworld.[101] Unlike Iphigeneia and Antigone, Polyxena is never
represented as *Hades's* bride, but her sacrifice takes the form of the 'reversed
wedding' apparent in other Brides of Hades.[102] The sole reason for her death is
marriage. For Polyxena, marriage is not a pretence that 'softens the blow' of
a more horrific reality. Antigone finds marriage in the Underworld only because
she disobeys a public edict and is punished with entombment. Otherwise, she
would have married Haimon and, presumably, helped provide the next
generation of Thebans. Likewise, Iphigeneia would have grown and married
(perhaps even married Achilleus) and lived a normal life if Agamemnon had
not been required to sacrifice her to wage war against the Trojans. Although
marriage is used to entice Iphigeneia to the camp, by the time she is killed
there is no marriage charade. In comparison, Polyxena's death is blunt and
brutal. Marriage in the Underworld is not the consolation she wins for her
untimely death: it is suddenly the prize. Polyxena's intended husband is already
dead and she cannot claim her position as his wife without following him.[103]

Euripides's *Hekabe* tells us that Polyxena entered the underworld a virgin,[104]
and was not united with Achilleus in death,[105] but she was, nevertheless, no
longer a virgin. And even Polyxena herself recognises the inevitability of her
union in Hades when she says she was being sacrificed *for* the god.[106] The
firmer ground in Polyxena's case is the distinct wedding-like motifs found in
her sacrifice. She is, for instance, led to her grave by the wrist,[107] a gesture
used in marriage rituals as a symbol of possession. This is a distinct feature of
wedding iconography in vase paintings from the archaic and classical periods,
and usually shows the groom leading the bride. John Oakley and Rebecca Sinos

comment that 'early classical vases tend to portray a fairly realistic scene from one moment in the wedding ... The groom seizes either the hand or the wrist of his bride to lead her away'.[108] But Polyxena's groom is already dead. So, she is pulled along by his son, Neoptolemos, like a bride to her bridal chamber, which is – like Antigone's – actually a tomb. Polyxena bravely offers her own neck, willing no man to touch her,[109] although the custom is for sacrificial victims to be held aloft by ephebes.[110] This is how Polyxena is more normally shown in visual representations,[111] and how Iphigeneia's sacrifice is described in Aischylos's *Agamemnon*.[112] The clear parallel between Polyxena and Persephone is their figurative loss of virginity. Polyxena can, therefore, be seen as a bridge between the mythic 'Brides of Hades' and the ritual custom of treating girls who have died prematurely as though they were brides. Although we cannot lay out a claim that these prematurely dead girls lost their virginity when entering the Underworld, they are afforded the opportunity to undergo the process of becoming a wife. The mythic examples can achieve this in full, particularly as virginity-loss was an important physical marker of the transition: on one side she was a girl and afterwards, a woman. But mythic heroines can achieve something that real girls cannot – in death, they 'live' the experience of being wed, but not fully. This takes us back to the choice of Persephone for imitation at Lokroi. There, as her final scenes were prior to the point the bride was taken into her new husband's home, she also is a bride who has not (yet) undergone this physical process.

In Athens, prematurely dead girls were buried wearing wedding clothing and given grave goods that resembled wedding gifts.[113] A brief examination of some examples of grave markers also shows that they play on the idea of girls being wed in (or to) Hades. One of the most famous examples is Phrasikleia, whose grave marker was a kore statue bearing an epigram, from around 540 BCE. The epigram makes it clear that Phrasikleia died unmarried, and that she had a special status in the Underworld because of this:

σῆμα Φρασικλείας·
κόρε κεκλέσομαι
αἰεί, ἀντὶ γάμο
παρὰ θεὸν τοῦτο
λαχōσ' ὄνομα

The tomb of Phrasikleia, I shall be called maiden forever,
Because I won this name from the gods instead of marriage.[114]

The kore stands tall on her inscribed base and would have been brightly painted.[115] She holds a closed lotus flower in her hand, a symbol of her unmarried state. But the lotus crown on her head portrays both closed and half-open lotus flowers, giving the impression that she is in the liminal state between maiden and wife – she is, as it were, mid-wedding ceremony, and she will stay in that state forever. Her desire is plain to see in the open rosettes printed on her peplos.[116] Phrasikleia, and other girls like her, are not portrayed as 'Brides of Hades' – there is no notion that she will marry Hades in the Underworld. They are, in a way, being presented as a metaphorical image of the maiden Persephone.[117] But they are 'incomplete Persephones' because they can only undergo half of her journey. Phrasikleia's tomb makes it explicitly clear that she is a κόρη and that she will remain so forever. She does not lose her virginity, like Polyxena. She does not find a husband in Hades, like Iphigeneia or Antigone. And this is the special status that she attains. In playing at being Persephone the young maiden in some ways falls short, but her specialness is retained because she is perpetually in the state of being wed. She lives in the Underworld in her wedding attire, always on the precipice of marriage. Like Persephone, she does not actually undergo consummation: she never has sex and never becomes a fully-fledged wife. Like Persephone herself, she is infertile. She cannot bear children, so her 'marriage' in death is a failure in practically every sense.

These prematurely dead girl brides, like those presented on the Lokrian pinakes, are imitating a specific part of Persephone's mythic heritage. The Lokrian girls imitate the moment of her abduction; they briefly become the powerful Queen of the Underworld who is shown on the homage pinakes at Lokroi. And the dead Athenian girls imitate Persephone in another way, as the helpless Kore, snatched away by death, present in the Underworld. They are not granted Persephone's honours. That is to say that these girls – all of these girls, even the mythic girls who do marry Hades or lose their virginity – imitate Persephone but they cannot take her place.[118] The girls who were buried with bridal objects and iconography were not being offered to Hades as brides by their parents – that is, their death rituals were not a 'substitute' for marriage rituals – rather the form of burial can be read as a way of giving these girls the opportunity to undergo an experience that defines the life of a woman.[119] Mythic variants of ritual practices often present protagonists in ways that do not reflect actual practice, particularly related to their social status.[120] The difference here is not the girls' position in life, but their perceived position in the Underworld, after death. They are not Hades's bride in the same way as mythic or literary figures, because they cannot (much like the girls of myth) replace Persephone's position in the Underworld, whether as a ruler or simply as a wife.

Persephone's marriage is, in one sense, a failure. She spends a significant portion of her time away from her husband, and she does not have a child. This is partly because the Underworld is a place where no life can grow, but this cannot be the only factor. Persephone spends two-thirds of the year on the fertile earth,[121] and her return from the Underworld induces the earth's fertility – when she is in the Underworld the seeds are buried in the ground, seemingly lifeless, and when she returns to the earth they bloom in growth. Her never-ending journey brings the earth's alternate fertility and infertility, but she remains infertile. Persephone had, inadvertently or not, caused her own infertility by swallowing Hades's pomegranate seeds. The moment Persephone takes the pomegranate seeds from Hades,[122] she assents to her marriage.[123] This is the moment that she has sex and is no longer a chaste girl; when she emerges from the transgressive period in between 'girl' and 'woman'. Her liminal status ends, and she begins to be reintegrated into society as 'wife'. This takes place in the Underworld, so her new status is predicated on this position. Her marriage, an archetype held up for girls to mimic is flawed and subverted by her environment, rather than her own behaviour or – perhaps crucially – that of her husband. It is not until well after the classical period that Hades takes another lover. Her marriage conveys status, power, and influence upon her, as Queen of the Underworld, and this also represents a successful match. It is a match that she did not choose and, at least in the beginning, actively resisted. It demonstrates that her father, in particular, made a wise choice for his daughter and that this turned out well for her after the initial shock of the marriage (and the inherent violence of the beginning of a marriage, at least for girls). This might be part of the reason she is a prime candidate for imitation by precariously positioned young girls, who are in a place where the success of their own marriages is unknown – perhaps it is better to prepare for the worst and be gracious when success comes.

So, these girls – both at Lokroi and in death – get to play at being Persephone temporarily, in order to form a relationship with her, and to win her blessings in their marriages or their afterlife. Building a relationship with the gods is important in all cult settings (and all religious practice feeds into the common goal of relationship-building). Creating an association between yourself (or your deceased child) and the goddess is a way of strengthening that relationship. Worshippers playing at being Persephone for a while give themselves access to all aspects of the goddess. By undergoing her experiences, these girls put themselves in a position to receive the goddess's favour.

Concluding note

Rites of passage are problematic to define. But we can define them, *if* we trust that 'knowing' and 'seeing' give us insight into these rituals. So, because the individual who is undergoing a rite of passage is the only one to experience, directly, their own transition it might be easier to define rites of passage by looking for instances when people, truthfully, describe a status change. But individual experience has another problem. Because experiences differ, sometimes very widely, between individual participants in the same ritual then perhaps we cannot even trust that someone else's experience will match our own.[124]

It is not too far to say that a similar thing occurred in the ancient world. If you are then one of the girls who felt more, rather than less, 'abducted' in your impending marriage you might wish to turn somewhere to gain solace and understanding. And, if you were a girl in Lokroi in the fifth century BCE, that place would have been to Persephone, and you might have articulated your longing for connection in your own pre-marriage pinax. The fact that there is not a standard mould for the pinakes shows that some kind of personalisation was desired. But this still does not answer the question of why an Underworld god, specifically, might be right for this sort of moment. In the context of Lokroi that might mean: why not Hera?

Hermes is an appropriate guide for Underworld crossings, and so also for rites of passage, and this might hint at the reason why Persephone was a good choice for girls on the precipice of marriage. When one part of you symbolically changes, and you are regenerated, then death is a useful psychological tool for characterising that change in your own mind. Thinking of rites of passage as a 'death and rebirth' allows a person to mourn their 'old' self and to celebrate their 'new' self. This is not an intrinsic part of either Persephone or Hermes, but a part of the motif of death and rebirth and explains why gods who are related to the Underworld in some way are in prime positions to deal with these liminal periods.

Girls in Lokroi form their attachment to Persephone during preparation for their marriages because she underwent a traumatic wedding that turned out well. Hermes guides people into and through the Underworld because he is unrivalled in the ability to traverse boundaries. These things alone would, I think, not be enough to give these gods the privileged position they have in these contexts. Without the link to the Underworld, the metaphorical death and symbolic mourning, there would not be a satisfactory psychological conclusion. It is not about the death or the rebirth, but the concession to mourning and celebration that this motif provides.

Notes

1 This comparison was made by Vidal-Naquet's (not unproblematic) work on the 'Black Hunter' narrative (1986: 106–128); cf. Ma, 2008.
2 For a general introduction to the background of 'initiation' rites – which 'rites of passage' come under – see Calame, 1999: 278–307; Graf, 2003a; Lincoln, 2003: 241–254; Padilla, 1999: 15–21.
3 van Gennep, 1960: 11.
4 Lincoln, 2003: 246.
5 Beaulieu, 2008: 42.
6 Though this was most likely a representative ritual, wherein some girls participated on behalf of all the girls in their age cohort.
7 Øistein Endsjø, 2002: 245.
8 Graf, 2003a: 16.
9 Graf, 2003a: 16.
10 Graf, 2003a: 16–17.
11 Eur. *IT.* 28–31. Near-sacrifice is an important component of the narrative of initiation in Eur. *IT.*; on this see Tzanetou, 1999.
12 For other treatments of the Iphigenia narrative see Dowden, 1989: 17. For an analysis of where Euripides's narrative on Iphigeneia originates see Hulton, 1962: 364–368.
13 Øistein Endsjø, 2002: 236; van Gennep, 1960: 22.
14 Loraux, 1987: 38–39, 42–47.
15 Aischylos wrote an earlier play called the *Iphigeneia* that likely dealt with this portion of the myth, but it is totally lost except for one small fragment.
16 Aisch. *Ag.* 225–226, trans. Sommerstein.
17 Aisch. *Ag.* 1406.
18 Aisch. *Ag.* 1432–1433.

19 Euripides, in *Iphigeneia Taurica*, explains that Artemis substituted the young girl for a deer in the final moments. No such substitution is mentioned or alluded to in the *Oresteia*.

20 Lincoln, 2003: 250. The term *communitas*, coined by Victor Turner, denotes the liminal period of initiation. This is a period in which the initiate is not only able to learn and grow, but it also serves as a safe haven from considerations of status: it is a place and time during which the initiate can experience intimacy, egalitarianism, spontaneity and humane authenticity, without the trappings of a fixed status

21 Redfield, 2003a: 257.

22 Leitao, 2003: 109.

23 Arist. *Ath. Pol.* 42.1–3.

24 Parker, 1987: 54–55.

25 *IG* II² 1101.16. Cf. Simon, 1983: 82. The significance of the ephebe's involvement in sea-crossing rituals will become clear during a discussion of Orestes's sea cross-ing, below.

26 *IG* II/III² 1006; 1008; 1011. Cf. Burkert, 2001: 86; Simon, 1983: 59–60.

27 For a full and current discussion of the ephebeia as a formal ritualised event see Friend, 2009: specifically 99–146.

28 Xen. *Mem.* 3.12.4. Cf. von Reden and Goldhill, 1999: 269.

29 Hom. *Il.* 22.361–362.

30 h.Hom. *Dem.* 345.

31 h.Hom. Dem. 376–377.

32 Innes and Sunstrum, 2016: 49:30.

33 This will be discussed further below.

34 h.Hom. *Dem.* 334–338, 347–356.

35 h.Hom. *Dem.* 360–369. For this purpose, his permission to *leave* is the important aspect, not the trick he plays to affect her return, as discussed above.

36 Hom. *Od.* 11.625–626; cf. [Apollod.] *Bibl.* 2.71, 2.123.

37 By way of very brief example: Headlam and Headlam (1909: 277) includes 'Hermes is in the background' in the stage directions, the same idea is found in Slavitt, 1998: 117 and Weir Smyth (1930: 277), similarly we also find Hermes 'standing next to' Apollo in, for example, Thompson (1966: 193), and this is reflected in the 'translation of translations' of Lowell (1978: 96).

38 Aisch. *Eum.* 90.

39 Cf. Taplin, 1977: 364–365.

40 Cf. Marinatos, 2003: 141–142.

41 Many male coming-of-age myths involve dangerous journeys, often though the wil-derness. Journeys over, though, or under the sea show heavily marginalised youths. As per the usual structure of male coming-of-age narratives, these journeys always involve parental separation. In Orestes's narrative, this is symbolised by matricide, and he undertakes his dangerous coming-of-age journey under the guise of purification.

42 Aisch *Eum.* 77.

43 Aisch. *Eum.* 240.

44 Aisch. *Eum.* 452.

45 The myth of legendary Athenian hero and king Theseus, illustrates the motif of transitionary myths. In regard to specifically Athenian mythology, Theseus is the arch-ephebe – the paradigm that all Athenian youths follow. 'The myth of Theseus is a case in point. In a fragmentary second-century BC inscription, Theseus' exploits during the Cretan expedition as well as those during his return from Troe-zen were compared to the ephebic education: as an ephebe, Theseus is a paradigm of the ephebes who imitate him' (Graf, 2003b: 18; cf. IG II² 2291a). As a dolphin-

rider, Theseus' descent into the sea was a symbolic death and rebirth and it is well attested by the fifth century. Bakchylides relates the story of the young Theseus, sailing to Krete and defending the maiden Eriboia against the unwelcome advances of Kretan King Minos. In a show a force, Minos called out to his father, Zeus, who responded by illuminating the sky with lightening. Minos then issued the challenge to the young hero:

> Θησεῦ, σὺ τάδε
> μὲν βλέπεις σαφῆ Διὸς
> δῶρα· σὺ δ' ὄρνυ' ἐς βα-
> ρύβρομον πέλαγος· Κρονίδας
> δέ τοι πατὴρ ἄναξ τελεῖ
> Ποσειδὰν ὑπέρτατον
> κλέος χθόνα κατ' ἠΰδενδρον.

Theseus: you see my clear gift from Zeus. Now you must leap into the loud-roaring sea. And lord Poseidon, Kronos' son and your father, will give you supreme glory over the forested earth.

(Bakchyl. 17.75–80)

Once so challenged, Theseus dove into the sea with unwavering conviction, distressing his Athenian companions who began to cry out for their hero. Almost as soon as the young hero is in the water, dolphins arrive to carry him safely to his father Poseidon's underwater palace, where he is adorned with gifts. Finally, Theseus emerges from the sea and appears at the ship's side, completely dry and adorned in the finery he had been given under water, much to the astonishment of Minos and his fellow sailors. Thus, Poseidon is proved to be Theseus's father.

For the link between dolphins, male coming of age rituals, and Apollo, for which see Calame, 1996: 229–2230. For women and girls being locked in chests, see, for example, the story of Danae and her son Perseus; Eur. *Arch. fr.* 228b.7 (Kannicht); Paus. 2.23.7, 10.5.11, and for an excellent discussion of this see Beaulieu, 2016: 90–118.

46 I use the rather awkward term 'ritual normalcy' deliberately, to emphasise that Orestes is not attempting to become 'pure' through purification, but to shed pollution and return to a state of normality in a ritual and religious sense. This is the same state that a person would be in prior to purification at the entry to a sanctuary, for instance.

47 Aisch. *Cho.* 1–9, cf. Johnston, 1999: 45.

48 Aisch. *Eum.* 90–93 (trans. Sommerstein)

49 h.Hom. *Dem.* 335–383.

50 h.Hom. *Dem.* 348–349; cf. Sourvinou-Inwood 2003: 31.

51 h.Hom. *Dem.* 340–388; cf. Sourvinou-Inwood 2003: 61.

52 See, for example, Hom. *Od.* 19.86; Hes. *Th.* 347, and discussion in Bierl, 1994; Harrison, 1912: 441; Parker, 2005a: 393, 436; Versnel, 1993: 290–334.

53 This is emphasised in the changes between Hermes's first and second songs (24–64, 423–433). Hermes's maturation is relayed through the extended story of the cattle raid (which occupies most of the *Hymn*), and the relationship between Apollo and Hermes plays out the story of the older male and younger male found in coming-of-age narratives, for extended discussion see Johnston, 2003: particularly 157–161, 65.

54 Although I will only be discussing one example, this is much attested in literature as well, though his *kourorophic* and *pedophoric* roles in several mythic narratives. For example, Hermes snatches the infant Asklepios from death (Paus. 2.26.6) and delivers the infant Dionysos to Olympos (Paus. 3.18.11). These roles are also

evident in Attic vases, dating from at least the sixth century BCE, see Siebert, 1990; cf. Johnston, 2003. Boys also dedicated their childhood toys to Hermes, see Beaumont, 2012: 129.

55 Larson, 2007: 148; on the cult more generally see Marinatos, 2003. The sanctuary was also the location of coming-of-age rituals for girls, see Lebessi, 2010: 198.

56 Marinatos, 2003: 138.

57 Marinatos, 2003: 138–140. Examples of images of Hermes in multiple age guises on Corinthian vases see *LIMC* s.v. Hermes 237 (unbearded) and 230 (bearded).

58 In Sparta, for example, where Plutarch relates: ἐγάμουν δὲ δι' ἁρπαγῆς, οὐ μικρὰς οὐδὲ ἀώρους πρὸς γάμον, ἀλλὰ καὶ ἀκμαζούσας καὶ πεπείρους ('for their marriages the women were carried off by force, not when they were small and unfit for wedlock, but when they were in full bloom and wholly ripe' (*Lyk.* 15.3.). Cf. Avagianou, 1991: 116.

59 For further background see Mackin Roberts, 2018.

60 Cf. Redfield, 2003b: 349; Sourvinou-Inwood, 1978: 101.

61 h.Hom. *Dem.* 353, cf. 305–311, 332–333.

62 Sourvinou-Inwood 1973: 18. For the pinakes being predominantly dedicated by girls, also see Redfield, 2003b: 252–253.

63 We might draw a parallel with Apollo, the 'arch-ephebe' who never himself becomes truly 'adult', for instance see Bierl, 1994.

64 Redfield, 2003b: 357.

65 See Dillon, 2002: 9–36 for detailed discussion on women dedicating.

66 Cf. Greco, 2006: 173; Larson, 2007: 83.

67 Jenkins, 1983: 142, pl. 18b, *LIMC* s.v. Persephone add.5b, add.5c; cf. Beazley, 1942: 647.

68 h.Hom. *Dem.* 19. Zeus's permission – representing the ἐγγύη ('betrothal') – is vital for the legitimisation not of the marriage but any resulting children (of which we know there are none) (see Ferrari, 2003: 27). The ἐγγύη is a pledge made by a father, brother, or grandfather and is attested in several places, including Athens (Dem. 46.18) and Sparta (Hdt. 6.57.5). This point is important regarding the use of Persephone as a figure for emulation, which I will discuss below.

69 As is our 'scholarly' reading of it. For discussion on concept in the ancient world see see Cohen, 1993; Omitowoju, 2002: 26–28.

70 Carey, 1995: 414; Harris, 2013: 286–289, 90–91, 98–300; 2015: 300.

71 That is, girls who have died before marriage, and were therefore considered 'special' in death; for further discussion of 'special dead' see Garland, 1985: 77–103.

72 Quagliati, 1908: 158–159, cf. Bianchi, 1976: 12.

73 Scheurleer, 1932: 334.

74 Richter, 1949: 184–185.

75 Zancani Montuoro, 1955: 9–10.

76 Prückner, 1968: 73–74.

77 Bonnechere, 2003: 181.

78 Clinton, 1992: 73.

79 Sourvinou-Inwood, 1973.

80 There is a loose connection with other types of abduction scenes found throughout the Greek world, the so-called 'erotic pursuit' scenes (identified primarily by Sourvinou-Inwood, 1991: 59). The main difference between the Lokrian abduction scenes and 'erotic pursuit' scenes are the protagonists. In many other examples the main abductor is Theseus (Sourvinou-Inwood, 1991: 60, cf. 29–51), although they are also unidentified youths similar to those found in the Lokrian examples. These youths often carry spears, which are never present in the Lokrian examples. The prominent 'grabbing motif', which carry a strong connotation of violence or forceful marriage, is also not found in the Lokrian scenes.

81   Contra Sourvinou-Inwood, 1973: 17.
82   Ferrari, 2003: 36.
83   Cf. Ferrari, 2003: 29.
84   The examples of Iphigeneia, Antigone, and Polyxena will be discussed in this sec-
     tion, but see also Cassandra (Eur. *Tro.* 444), and Medea relating this notion to
     Glauke (Eur. *Med* 985). For greater detail and links with other Indo-European
     mythologies see Janakieva, 2005; cf. Ferrari, 2003: 35; Jenkins, 1983: 142.
85   Debate about the extent to which tragedy itself was a religious phenomenon is
     ongoing. Certainly, tragedy was presented during a religious festival but we cannot
     automatically assume that it was a 'religious act', for further discussion see Scul-
     lion, 2008.
86   For a full discussion of marriage and funeral rites see Rehm, 1994: 11–29.
87   This will be discussed below.
88   Ferrari, 2003: 35.
89   Eur. *IA*. 100.
90   Eur. *IA*. 460–462; cf. *IT*. 369.
91   I would also like to flag the possibility that an ongoing mental preparation for mar-
     riage has the potential to fill-in for the physical preparation for death – presuming
     that at least some deaths of a young teenagers would be sudden and therefore give
     no time for physical or mental preparation. However, this idea is purely speculative
     on my part.
92   Soph. *Ant.* 883–890. It is important that Kreon does not directly kill Antigone, but
     by burying her alive he sentences her to a 'living death'. See Butler, 2000: 27.
93   Soph. *Ant.* 245–247. See discussions in Held, 1983: 193; Rose, 1952: 219. For
     a more general overview of the issues here see Margon, 1972. This is important
     because Antigone's insistence on burying her brother rests in the fact that she
     believes it is her familial duty and not undertaking it would contravene the laws of
     the gods, see *Ant.* 450–470.
94   Soph. *Ant.* 575.
95   Soph. *Ant.* 815.
96   Soph. *Ant.* 891.
97   Soph. *Ant.* 891–894.
98   Butler, 2000: 23–24.
99   Soph. *Ant.* 1240–1241.
100 Soph. *Ant.* 654; cf. Ferrari, 2003: 37.
101 Eur. *Hek.* 40–44, 189–190.
102 Loraux, 1987: 37.
103 There is an obvious parallel between Iphigeneia's false groom and Polyxena's
     intended husband, Achilleus. As Ken Dowden (1989: 68) eruditely points out: 'mar-
     riage to Achilles is a dangerously genuine motif for Iphigeneia and for Polyxena'.
104 Eur. *Hek.* 416.
105 Eur. *Hek.* 612; cf. Loraux, 1987: 39, 40–41.
106 Eur. *Hek.* 207–210.
107 Eur. *Hek.* 523.
108 Oakley and Sinos, 1993: 45, and figs. 86, 87. An excellent example is Oakley and
     Sinos's figure 86 (= Boston, Museum of Fine Art 13.186), an Attic red-figure *sky-
     phos* by Makron that shows Paris leading Helen by the wrist. Cf. Bremmer,
     2007a: 62.
109 Eur. *Hek.* 548–549.
110 Bremmer, 2007b: 63–64.
111 For example, the c. 570–560 BCE black-figure amphora showing Polyxena held in
     the air by a group of warriors while Neoptolemos pushes a sword into her out-
     stretched neck, her blood spurting out over the altar below (British Museum GR

1897.7–27.2), or the sarcophagus of Polyxena at Gümüşçay from c. 520–500 BCE, again showing Polyxena being held up by ephebes, this time upside down, while her throat is slit, see Sevinç, 1996: 255–258, figs. 56, 59, 510b.

112 Aisch. *Ag.* 231–237.

113 Garland, 1985: 87.

114 *IG* I³ 1261, trans. Dillon.

115 A reconstruction, based on surviving paint fragments on the statue, was undertaken in 2010 by O Primavesi of the German Research Foundation, and can be viewed here under 'Painter as Sculptor: A Cult Image Comes to Life', https://buntegoetter.liebieghaus.de/en (accessed 10/10/2019).

116 Cf. Stewart, 1997: 115.

117 Cf. Sourvinou-Inwood, 1995: 249–252.

118 This is partly because Hades is, in this period, perpetually faithful to Persephone. The figurative connection between marriage and death might be more understandable if this was not the case. This is an attribute of Hades that remains constant throughout many different representations, or more accurately perhaps, there is no strong evidence that he was thought to have taken lovers – at least in the archaic and classical periods. That (many) other gods do so provides enough evidence that divine infidelity is not unusual and that the Greeks (whichever Greeks that might be) had no fundamental problem with the philandering ways of their gods.

119 Cf. Vermeule, 1979: 55–56. A parallel might be drawn between this practice and the advent of the 'Solo Wedding' in modern Japan, which allows single women to have a 'wedding package' without the marriage that normally accompanies it; see Japan Today 2014.

120 Mythic *pharmakoi*, for example, are often kings or beautiful women – they are always individuals of high standing in society, which obviously gives their death significantly more meaning and weight in relation to the dispelling of pollution. In real life, however, those chosen to be *pharmakoi* are often criminals, or other people with particularly low standing in society. Their deaths have very little impact on the day-to-day life of the city. For further discussion, see Bremmer, 1983: 31–37; 2007b: 88–89; Versnel, 1990: 53.

121 h.Hom. *Dem.* 446.

122 h.Hom. *Dem.* 372.

123 There is much to say about whether or not Hades had forced or tricked Persephone into eating the pomegranate seeds, but before she leaves the Underworld she does agree to the marriage, this is evident though the use of words like ἀκοίτης ('husband' h.Hom. *Dem.* 363). The ingestion of the pomegranate seeds marks the moment of consummation in Persephone and Hades's marriage, if this were forced the union would be regarded as rape. Rape victims, at least in classical Athens, were not shamed or punished for wrongdoing like women who had been seduced (and were therefore consenting partners), so if she felt truly violated she would have recourse to deny the union with Hades, rather than consenting to the marriage. For further discussion on consent and rape see Carey, 1995; Harris, 2013: 90, 98–300; 2015.

124 An oft-cited example in academia is the doctoral viva voce. It is, technically, the same experience for everyone but you can almost guarantee that each person's experience will be different and have possibly very different outcomes. Because the people who publicly comment on their experience are a self-selecting group, you cannot even trust that savvy internet skills will pop up a result that might match your own. A quick search for 'my viva experience' produces more negative than neutral or positive experiences, with the second most common type being the extremely positive results. This means that although most candidates receive some minor corrections, this category of experience is almost entirely missing from viva discourse on the internet. It

is understandable that wading through the mass of contradictory personal experience and advice might make a religiously inclined person toward a divine being to offer some comfort. Although I could not find a Saint of the Viva Voce, I did find five different saints that are given over to various types of college students, summarised by Sam Grace: Saints Jude Thaddeus (lost causes and desperate situations), Catherine of Alexandria (scholars, librarians, and the like), Jerome (scholars, archaeologists, translators), Ursula (students and teachers, especially women), and Joseph Calasanz (universities and schools for the poor), see Grace, 2013.

6 Personal interactions with Underworld gods

The most common way that people sustained their relationships with the gods was though one-to-one interaction. This mainly involved prayer and the offering of votives, even where this occurred during large-scale civic festivals.[1] Votive offerings collectively make up the largest body of religious artefact from the Greek world, so we know that this is something that people are doing consistently. And, to a certain extent it is true that people maintained their relationships with Underworld gods through one-to-one interaction as well. But the most striking difference between Underworld gods and other gods is that there were no large-scale civic festivals held in their honour, and no temple precincts in which to leave votive offerings – the Eleusinian Mysteries, perhaps, and the sanctuary dedicated to Hades at Elis, notwithstanding. Of course, this is a generalisation, but it holds that *most* Underworld gods never received the kind of large-scale community worship that we have come to expect in Greek religion and *many* Underworld gods had a significant amount of one-to-one religious activity performed in their honour. In this chapter I will look at three kinds of religious practice that rely on the relationships that individuals build with the Underworld gods: curses, the so-called 'Orphic' gold tablets, and necromancy.

Curses! Underworld gods and the *katadesmoi*

Katadesmoi are related to the Underworld for two main reasons. First, they are usually buried in the ground, often in graves (sometimes even placed in the hand of the deceased), or in sanctuaries of gods associated with the Underworld, particularly Demeter.[2] Second, they often directly name gods who are associated with the Underworld, like Hermes, Persephone, Demeter, and Ge ('Earth').[3] A god's presence on a *katadesmos* represents a kind of religious practice where there is little or nothing of what we might call 'orthopraxic performativity' – the 'being seen to do the right thing'-ness that is inherent in many other types of more public religious practice. The ritual processes involved with the burying of a curse tablet is a deeply private experience, between a person and the god or gods they are addressing (as well as any non-divine intermediaries, like ghosts). There is no 'showing off', no sense that the outward performance is more important than the inward performance.

That is, the performance itself comes from a position of personal devotion and belief primarily because the only audience members are the practitioner themselves, the divinities being called, and any supernatural subsidiaries (like ghosts) who are also involved in the process. The act is one of immersive personal theatre.

It could be said that there are many such objects of private dedication or communication between the practitioner and the divine: devotional inscriptions and votive offerings, for example. But these are still public declarations. A small offering might be intended primarily for the pleasure of a god, but there is a rather obvious secondary audience in the friends and strangers who witness the dedication ritual (perhaps including a sacrifice) or the physical offering after it has been left in a sanctuary. For those burying a *katadesmos* in the night, the hidden and immortal audience evokes a different facet of the individual's religious practice than the publicly-concerned facet of the individual who is worried with 'right acting',[4] rather than 'right believing'. This points to individuals who *do* genuinely believe in the gods they are invoking. This evidence of belief can and does extend to the more publicly visible offerings that those same practitioners dedicate. And even though we have a relatively small number of extant *katadesmoi* there were most likely far more curse-performances (with or without a physical object) than we have found, and therefore this may be used as evidence for belief within Greek religion more widely.

Many of the examples of *katadesmoi* that go into detail about the gods are later in date than the period I am primarily concerned with in this book, and the later date of many examples of *katadesmoi* also accounts for the presence of some gods – most notably Hekate – who do not have a strong connection to the Underworld any earlier than around the third century BCE,[5] with a few small exceptions, including her relationship with Persephone (for which, see the Afterword). They do show us that some gods, notably Hermes, have a continuing importance in Underworld-related activity. Hermes features prominently on *katadesmoi* during the time that he (mythically) begins to deal more directly with the dead.[6] He is called Hermes, Hermes of the Underworld, Hermes the Trickster, Hermes the Binder, Lord Hermes, and Erionios; several tablets give him multiple epithets, sometimes in rapid succession. For example, side A of *DTA*93, from Patissa in Athens, dated to the classical or Hellenistic periods says:[7]

Ἑρμῆ [χθόνιε· λά] βοι ψυχὴν
Ἑρμ{ῆ} δόλιε· τῆς Πύρρου γυναι{κὸσ}
Ἑρμ{ῆ} κάτοχε· μαμμίας Ἱεροῦς
τὰ]ς χεῖρας καρδίας πόδας
. . μαμμί{α} Ἱερ{ώ} . . . .
. . . Τ Ι κάτοχ[ε . . . . . .
. . . . . Τ Ι Ο . . . .

Hermes of the underworld; may you take the spirit, Hermes the Trickster, of the wife of Pyrros, O Hermes the Binder. The titties of Hieres, the hands, hearts, feet, titties of Hieres ... O Binder ...[8]

While the functions Hermes's epithets hint at are specific to the requirements a person might have of a god who will enact their curse: binding, tricking, and being χθόνιος, but his presence on the *katadesmoi* are because he is a messenger to the Underworld,[9] and therefore stem directly from his more general function as a messenger.

There are some gods we might expect to find on *katadesmoi* who are largely absent, notably the Erinyes.[10] But not all the gods named on the tablets have a link to the Underworld. Perhaps there was an idea that gods who did not have direct 'cursing' functions (like the binding or trickery of Hermes, or Artemis as a doorkeeper),[11] had some authority to engage vengeance deities like the Erinyes or Praxidikai to actually enact the curse. We can see something akin to this in Aischylos's *Eumenides*, in which Klytaimestra enlists the Erinyes to assist in her quest for vengeance against Orestes.[12]

The other main group that appear on *katadesmoi* are the dead themselves.[13] They are not intended to act out the curses, but perhaps they are included because they are the audience meant to lend these requests power. The small, inscribed, mainly lead or lead alloy tablets[14] are not buried in graves because the dead have any power, but rather because they are useful messengers to the Underworld gods who are able to act on the requests they contain. Delivery of the request is the first function of the shade in the curse transaction. The second function is to pass on some of their *miasma* through the close contact between the physical body of the deceased and the name of the curse's victim.[15]

The dead have another function in the tablet, one that I have already alluded to, and that this can also say something about the people who decided not to include the dead as intermediaries upon their tablets. Werner Riess comments that:

> Rituals typically require an audience in order to be effective; thus, at first glance, the lack of observers seems to be a defining feature of magic. Indeed, the audience of a magical ritual is often thought to be identical to its performer, making the performer and the recipient of a magic ritual one and the same person. On this view, the message of a collective ritual is directed at an entire group, but the message of a magician is relevant only to himself. Given the information we have today, however, this can hardly be true.[16]

The dead, then, can be seen not only as messengers or enactors of curses but also the audience that gives the ritual power. This is reflected in the way the dead are introduced in the tablets, for example in *DT68*, an Attic curse from the fourth century,[17] that says that the victim, Theodora, is bound 'in the presence of the unhappy dead'. But the text also puts Hermes in the same position; the god is present as both enactor and bystander, giving the god a more emotive role in the transaction of the curse. Most curses do not invoke the dead, leaving the writer as both architect and viewer on – at some level – equal footing with the gods who are included as co-ritual actors. Does this change the way that people interact with these gods?

Sarah Iles Johnston hypothesises that the *katadesmoi* demonstrate the changing attitudes towards the dead in the fifth century BCE.[18] They certainly do show that people (or, at the very least, the people who are engaging with this religious activity) are allowing ever-increasing contact between themselves and the dead. In turn, this shows that people are investing the dead with autonomy, rather than being the unthinking hoard portrayed, for instance, during Odysseus's necromancy in the *Odyssey*.[19] But there are limits to the power that the dead have – they are messengers to the Underworld gods, not actors who control direct influence over the living. This is reflected in the prevalence of legal vocabulary found on *katadesmoi*,[20] which both hints at the subject of some curses (that is, that they were deployed in response to litigious concerns), but also gives a litigious role to the ghosts who are cast as intermediaries between people and the Underworld god, in much the same way that legal appeals were directed through the prosecutor, for the *dikastai* ('judges') to rule on. The expectation was that the god or gods addressed would take note of the request and set the curse in motion, if they felt it was warranted. The only duty of the shade in the curse transaction was to ensure that it was delivered. Here, although the shade does not take part in enacting the curse, they are clearly not the 'witless' dead that we hear about in Homer and other early literature. A person would not entrust their curse or binding spell to a ghost who is not able to hear, read, see, or understand their role in the transaction. I think we must assume that the people placing these tablets into graves would have thought about the dead as having – at a bare minimum – a semblance of understanding.

How to get to the Underworld: the gods on the 'Orphic' tablets

From around the late fifth century we begin to find small gold tablets throughout the Greek-speaking world, inscribed with a variety of invocations. These are the so-called 'Orphic' gold tablets. There are around forty longer tablets, plus a 'undisclosed number' of tablets from fifteen fourth-century BCE cist-graves that only contain personal names, presumably that of the deceased, and placed in the deceased's mouth.[21]

There are some methodological problems that are necessarily encountered in studying these tablets, most notably a lack of contemporary literary evidence.[22] There might be a connection between these tablets and the *katadesmoi*, which start appearing around the same time.[23] The longer tablets can be designated either as mnemonic tablets, seemingly designed to instruct the recently dead on their first steps in the Underworld, or introductory tablets, acting on behalf of the dead to introduce the Underworld rulers.[24] Most of these longer tablets contain what appear to be instructions, advising the deceased how they can enter the Underworld. They follow the pattern a relatively straightforward Underworld journey – Radcliff Edmonds calls this the 'obstacle-solution-result' framework.[25] Several of the tablets refer to Dionysos or Bacchus, and there is some indication that these may be references to Persephone's son, Dionysos

Zagreus and related to the Orphic mysteries.[26] This cult may have been a sub-category of a more widely practised Bakchic cult, though just as likely they could have been particularly Orphic, rather than being a subsidiary cult of a wider or more inclusive set of practices. This could be due to their heavy eschatological nature, which is not necessarily a feature of other Mystery cults.[27] Perhaps Orphism in general, and this cult in particular, was, as Edmonds thinks, a 'countercultural' religion, particularly in the context of how 'mainstream' religion (if such a thing existed) as organised around the structure of the *polis*.[28] As various societies had different 'protests' against mainstream religion, the beliefs expressed in the gold tablets make a number of different, but comparable, comments about this 'countercultural' religious movement. As such, we should not view the Orphic gold tablets as commenting on congruent systems which exist alongside 'mainstream' religion, but rather as a tool for understanding several potentially disparate responses to religious ideologies.

Most of the mnemonic tablets that include geographical features of the Underworld are concerned, at least in part, with helping the deceased to obtain water, describing the locations of various good and bad springs from which to drink.[29] These springs are directly related to remembering (by drinking from 'good' springs) and forgetting (by drinking from 'bad' ones).[30] Although there are various ways of interpreting this – including the soul requiring memory of their previous life to 'do better' in the next one, Sarah Iles Johnston's final justification for the connection is that, by remembering their previous lives, good souls 'will be able to enjoy their rewards fully'.[31] Mnemosyne, the personification of memory, is mentioned in several of the tablets, strengthening the connection between the focus on memory and the notion of the tablets as part of an Orphic mystery rite, as she was mythically Orpheus's maternal grandmother. This also demonstrates the full circle of life: through memory, the soul comes to know their own identity and begins to remember more and more about their life. This idea has roots in earlier eschatological practices, whereby grave markers were used as 'memory inducers', connected to the soul having access to their wider memory through the remembering of their own name.[32] It is obvious that the 'memory' of the tablets is supposed to be the deceased's memory rather than the memory of the deceased in the world of the living, because the tablets are buried rather than being displayed. In this context, memory is utilised as a way for the soul to ensure that they are paying dues, are receiving rewards as appropriate to his conduct in life, and therefore, memory becomes their salvation.[33]

The deceased's ability to retain memory of life while in the Underworld presents a marked shift from the initial ideas expressed by 'older' beliefs presented in Homer, namely that the shades of the dead were witless and without knowledge.[34] Edmonds makes a connection between quenching thirst and memory to the story of Er in Plato's *Republic*, in which those souls who refrained from over-drinking did not suffer their memories being erased.[35] He views the tablets as being predominantly about identity, which relies heavily on memory to be established. The various components of the tablets correspond to various statements of identity which culminate in the deceased being allowed entry into the Underworld. Any difference within the identity statements found within the corpus of the tablets corresponds to differences in the eschatological hopes of the participants.[36]

Several tablets include what appear to be passwords, which Johnston hypothesises would have been spoken to Persephone herself.[37] Thus, the password functioned as a way of being recognised and admitted into the inner sanctuary of the Underworld.[38] The proxy tablets normally only include the name of the deceased, and sometimes also a dedication to a god (usually Persephone) or a declaration of initiation – for example, Φίλων μύστας, 'Philon, the initiate'.[39] The presence of these tablets indicate that, for the groups who utilised them, initiation would be sufficient to guarantee a good afterlife.[40]

Many of the tablets specifically mention Persephone in her role as ruler of the Underworld, but the first extant instance of this is in Pindar's Odes. Here, Persephone and Hades are never mentioned together, and although she is not always referred to in relation to the Underworld and her role within it, she is presented with attributes commonly associated with Hades in contemporary or near-contemporary literature. For example, in the *Hymn to Persephone*, the goddess is addressed: Πότνια θεσμοφόρε χρυσάνιον ('O Law-bringing mistress of the golden reins').[41] The epithet χρυσάνιον ('with reigns of gold') is, according to Pausanias, more ordinarily applied to Hades and so the reference here is to Persephone's rape:

> ἐν τούτῳ τῷ ᾄσματι ἄλλαι τε ἐς τὸν Ἅιδην εἰσὶν ἐπικλήσεις καὶ ὁ χρυσήνιος, δῆλα ὡς ἐπὶ τῆς Κόρης τῇ ἁρπαγῇ.

> Among the epithets he applied to Hades in this song is 'golden-reined', which clearly references Kore's rape.[42]

Pindar very plainly describes the Underworld as being Persephone's domain, rather than simply as Ἀΐδης δόμος. For example, Orchomenios's Olympic victory is instructed, by Pindar, μελανοτειχέα νῦν δόμον Φερσεφόνας ἔλθ' ('to go now into the black-walled house of Persephone')[43] so that Orchomenios's deceased father could learn of it.

Persephone's influence over the dead is further elucidated in a fragment of Pindar found within Plato's *Meno*[44] which speaks of the goddess accepting recompense for her παλαιός πένθος ('ancient grief')[45] from certain individuals, whom she will then send back to the mortal world:

> οἷσι δὲ Φερσεφόνα ποινὰν παλαιοῦ πένθεος
> δέξεται, ἐς τόν ὕπερθεν ἅλιον κείνων ἐνάτῳ ἔτεϊ
> ἀνδιδοῖ ψυχὰς πάλιν, ἐκ τᾶν βασιλῆες ἀγαυοί
> καὶ σθένει κραιπνοὶ σοφίᾳ τε μέγιστοι
> ἄνδρες αὔξοντ'· ἐς δὲ τὸν λοιπὸν χρόνον ἥροες ἁ-
> γνοὶ πρὸς ἀνθρώπων καλέονται.

> But for those from whom Persephone accepts requital for the ancient grief, in the ninth year she returns their soul to the upper sunlight; from them

arise proud kings and men who are swift in strength and greatest in wisdom, and for the rest of time they are called sacred by men.[46]

The more theological/eschatological issues[47] aside, what this passage clearly shows is an extension of the power that Persephone held over the dead, which we see originally in Homer where the goddess was able to change the natural condition of death for one of her charges and manipulate the movements of others. In this fragment from Pindar, too, she has the power to control and change the natural condition of death, but here she is changing the state of death itself.

The passage challenges the idea that the dead did not need a god to whom they could devote worship, which we have seen very clearly in the discussion relating to the worship dedicated to Hades. Here the souls of the deceased are offering some form of devotion to the goddess and she is, in turn, offering them not only the chance to live again but also the promise of a rewarding and blessed afterlife following their subsequent, second death. It is fairly certain that they are not attempting to gain forgiveness for wrongs they have committed during their own lifetimes, and that Persephone's παλαιός πένθος ('ancient grief') is her own private grief and has not been caused by any transgression of these individuals in life.[48] A number of scholars agree that Persephone's grief should be explained as the grief she herself experiences following the murder of her son Dionysos, the result of his murder and consumption by the Titans, and as narrated in Orphic mythology:[49]

> *Dionysus was the child of Zeus and Zeus' daughter Persephone.* Dionysus succeeded Zeus; *Zeus himself placed the child on his throne and declared him the new king of the cosmos.* The Titans, jealous of Dionysus' new power and perhaps encouraged by Hera, *used various toys, and a mirror, to lure Dionysus away from his guardians, the Curetes,* and dismembered him. *They cooked his flesh* and ate it. Zeus, being angry at this, killed the Titans, and from their remains, humanity arose. *Because humanity arose from material that was predominantly Titanic in nature, each human is born with the stain of the Titan's crime,* but a remnant of Dionysus leavens the mixture. *Each human must expiate the Titan's crime by performing rituals in honour of Dionysus and Persephone, who still suffers from the "ancient grief" of losing her child; by doing so, humans can win better afterlives.* Meanwhile Dionysus was in some matter revived or reborn.[50]

Persephone's rape and abduction by Hades may provide another possible interpretation for her grief. Although both readings would provide equally eschatological responses, this alternative interpretation may account for earlier conceptualisations of Persephone as the sole, powerful ruler of the Underworld, rather than as a bereft mother, and this may also explain the description of her grief as being 'ancient'. Rose argues against this possibility as no mortals were involved in Persephone's rape narrative, and although a number of mortals were in fact involved in the overall story, their contact was all with Demeter. Thus, he says, 'no human soul could be expected to make requital to the goddess for what she underwent then'.[51] There has, however, been a move away from the 'traditional' Orphic interpretation of the Dionysos Zagreus myth argued notably by Edmonds,[52] Zuntz,[53] Linforth,[54] and Brisson.[55] It seems, as Edmonds points out, obvious that the Zagreus myth fits the model presented both in the 'Orphic' tablets and in this Pindaric fragment. However, as he also points out:

> This myth of Zagreus provides a seductively simple and neat explanation of the cryptic gold tablet; it is unfortunately a modern creation that could not have been known to the 'Orphics' of Timpone Piccolo. Indeed, I shall demonstrate that this Zagreus myth is, in fact, a modern fabrication dependent upon Christian models that reconstruct the fragmentary evidence in terms of a unified 'Orphic' church, an almost Christian religion with dogma based on a central myth – specifically salvation from original sin through the death and resurrection of the suffering god.[56]

It is noteworthy that the term of servitude for the deceased is nine years. This is the term of banishment ascribed to both mortals and gods who have committed 'a serious offence, homicide or, at least in the case of a god, perjury'.[57] One prominent example of this term being applied to the punishment of a god is the mythic case of Apollo's exile from Delphi to Thessaly following the murder of Python.[58] Either abduction and rape or murder would fit this type of punishment, so whether Persephone's own rape or the slaughter of her son were the cause of her grief, the term of punishment would be the same. In this case the exile is from the mortal world, rather than from the *polis*: the deceased serve out their period of banishment in death and, after some or all have completed the requisite time, they are returned to the mortal world and restored with life, just as the banished murderer would again be allowed to enter the *polis* and reclaim their possessions. The Persephone that is presented here is the goddess purely in her role as Queen of the Underworld, and she can not only change the condition of death but change the inevitable and eternal fate of death as well. Hades needs no mention as, even when he is a well-defined character and not merely blending into the scenery of the Underworld,[59] he is not a divinity who can bring about such a change.

There are similarities in the way Persephone is presented in this fragment and her characterisation in the so-called 'Orphic' gold lamellae, and there may be some connection between the fragment and the ritual activity associated with the gold lamellae. The Orphic gold lamellae are small, inscribed amulets that have been found in grave-burials throughout the Greek world,[60] and the earliest examples might be reasonably dated to the late fifth century, although the majority of depositions appear to occur in the fourth and third centuries.[61] Early scholars of the tablets described them as belonging to some form of eschatological based, Orphic cult.[62] The link to an 'Orphic' cult is through the mythological narratives that form the background of the tablets; that is, narratives involving the murder and eating of Zeus and Persephone's son, Dionysos Zagreus, and the expiation that man must pay to Persephone for this crime.

We should be wary of using this mythic correlation to ascribe a uniform belief system to the owners and users of the gold lamellae as being 'Orphic' or members of an 'Orphic' cult or a particular, undeviating, 'mystery' cult. The term Orphic, according to Herrero de Jáuregui, 'tends to be said and understood, no matter how much one nuances it, as reflecting a sect or a least a uniform type of people holding similar ideas and practices'.[63] There are elements in the lamellae that appear to reflect earlier linguistic and stylistic nuances, perhaps even dating back to the Homeric poems,[64] and this hints at a long heritage for the content of the lamellae. The inscription style is also consistent with the evolution in other tablet types. For example, many of the earliest curse tablets are found usually containing only names, and tablets become more and more complex in content the later they appear (though this is not a universal rule). It has been suggested that this 'extra' content represents material that was still being used in the case of the earlier tablets, but represents something that would have been spoken, rather than inscribed, as the tablet was being prepared or buried.[65] Persephone appears on a curse tablet with Hermes Chthonios in Tangara, Boiotia.[66] For this reason, we can use the tablets as evidence for earlier practices as long as one does so tentatively and with the knowledge that the tablets represent what is likely an evolution of earlier ideology.

How to get the Underworld to come to you: necromancy

Getting to the Underworld seems incredibly simple, if we take Kirke's very exact instructions to Odysseus:

> μή τί τοι ἡγεμόνος γε ποθὴ παρὰ νηὶ μελέσθω,
> ἱστὸν δὲ στήσας, ἀνά θ᾽ ἱστία λευκὰ πετάσσας
> ἧσθαι· τὴν δέ κέ τοι πνοιὴ Βορέαο φέρῃσιν.
> ἀλλ᾽ ὁπότ᾽ ἂν δὴ νηὶ δι᾽ Ὠκεανοῖο περήσῃς,
> ἔνθ᾽ ἀκτή τε λάχεια καὶ ἄλσεα Περσεφονείης,
> μακραί τ᾽ αἴγειροι καὶ ἰτέαι ὠλεσίκαρποι,
> νῆα μὲν αὐτοῦ κέλσαι ἐπ᾽ Ὠκεανῷ βαθυδίνῃ,
> αὐτὸς δ᾽ εἰς Ἀΐδεω ἰέναι δόμον εὐρώεντα.
> ἔνθα μὲν εἰς Ἀχέροντα Πυριφλεγέθων τε ῥέουσι
> Κώκυτός θ᾽, ὃς δὴ Στυγὸς ὕδατός46] ἐστιν ἀπορρώξ,
> πέτρη τε ξύνεσίς τε δύω ποταμῶν ἐριδούπων.

> Zeus-nurtured Laertiades, resourceful Odysseus,
> don't let the absence of a guide bother you beside your ship,
> but set up the mast, spread the white sails,
> and sit. North Wind's breath will bear her for you.
> But when you drive through Ocean with your ship,
> there will be a rough headland and groves of Persephone,
> tall poplars and willows losing their fruit.

Land your ship at that spot, by deep-eddying Ocean,
but go yourself to the dank house of Hades.
There Pyriplegethus and Cocytus, which is a branch
of the water of the Styx, flow into Acheron,
and there is a rock and the junction of two roaring rivers.[67]

He goes, and there it is. He is face to face with the dead. The journey was treacherous, of course – but all sea travel was. Perhaps it might be that easy for us, as well, to locate the Underworld. After all the place that Krike sends Odysseus is a real place – a Nekyomanteion, or an oracle of the dead, in Elis on the western coast of the Peloponnese. But if we travel to this place and follow in Odysseus's actions, will we enter the Underworld ourselves? Obviously not. Either because a living person cannot enter the Underworld or because we are not actually at an opening or because the opening is not meant for us (and therefore cannot be meant for Odysseus).

'The Underworld' is never really where the Underworld is located. The ancient Greeks had a curious relationship with the Underworld, and (as we have seen in part of this book already) with its principle divinity Hades. The dead go there, but they are also at their burial place. Funerary ritual does not invoke Underworld gods, so while the Underworld and its divine citizenry have a place in people's afterlives, they do not play a role in the transporting them between the two. But this is complicated by ideas of *psychopompoi* – mainly Hermes and Charon – who *are* involved in stories and myths about dead people travelling to the Underworld.

I began this book – in the Preface – with a short piece of pseudo-historical fiction that I wrote as an experimental 'guided meditation' for a seminar paper I gave at the University of Leicester in the summer of 2017. It is a necromancy – a type of ritual that is usually called 'chthonic' and certainly fits into the category of death-and-Underworld ritual practice. But what we think of as necromantic ritual is not always about communing with the dead, but sometimes also related to divining from Underworld gods. But who, and why?

It is probably best to start with the easiest question: where did necromancy take place? Nekyomanteion – sanctuaries that were designed to be oracles of the dead – were considered to be entrances to the Underworld, where people could go and communicate with the dead. There are four major Nekyomanteia in the Greek world: at the Acheron in Thesprotia, Avernus in Campania, Herakleia Pontike on the southern Black Sea coast, and Tainaron on the tip of the Mani peninsula.[68] The most probable consultation method was oneiromancy, where the consultant spent the night in the nekyomanteion in order to encounter ghosts in their dreams.[69] There is some evidence that during necromantic rites a pit was dug out around the hearth-fire as a form of reversed altar to the Underworld gods.[70] If we consider that this practice might also occur in all, or at least some, other types of Underworld-related religious practices, it accounts for the absence of permanent, established altars dedicated to these gods.

As offerings to Olympic gods were (usually) focused upwards, with the main offerings being burnt and the smoke rising up to the gods, it makes sense that offerings given to Underworld gods should be directed downwards, with the main offerings poured into the earth.[71] One prominent (literary) example of this occurs in *Odyssey* book eleven, where Odysseus digs a pit with his sword and pours his libations to the dead into it. This libation consists of milk, honey, sweet-wine, water, barley meal, and finally blood.[72] So here, the inverted altar, dug into the ground, aids in the delivery of the offerings, which were now flowing in the right directions. A better-established parallel can be seen in the practice of supplication of Hittite Underworld gods. The Hittite Underworld gods, like those in Greece, generally had no established cults and were only supplicated to in direct response to specific problems or situation, and so the lack of permanent altars is not troublesome. Temporary, downward facing altars were made by digging a pit in the earth, sometimes along the riverbank (which is what occurs in the *Odyssey*).[73] There is evidence that these pits could sometimes be dug out with a dagger (as, again, occurs in the *Odyssey*).[74] There is an obvious link between Odysseus's ritual and the evidence for Hittite rituals to Underworld gods, but there is also a strong link to Greek necromantic rites.[75] Odysseus's ritual is potentially based on a real-world ritual, and it does not represent a mythic *katabasis*. These *katabasis* episodes do not generally include a realistic religious ritual, let alone a necromantic ritual. They involve direct descent into the Underworld, without the shades of the dead being used as intermediaries. Odysseus begins in the living world, and the shades rush up, out of Erebos (ὑπὲξ ʽΕρέβυς),[76] to greet him, rather than the other way around. This alone shows that Odysseus is performing a necromantic rite, and not a descent into the Underworld. Odysseus's 'descent' is easily explained by the same performed 'false' *katabasis* that happen in necromantic rites, including entering the Nekyomanteion as a proxy for entering the Underworld.[77]

When Kirke advises Odysseus to travel εἰς ʽΑΐδαο δόμους καὶ ἐπαινῆς Περσεφονείς ('into the house of Hades and dread Persephone'),[78] the place that she sends him to matches the description of the Nekyomanteion near the Acheron in Thesprotia. Pausanias tells us that Homer had seen the Thesprontian Nekyomanteia and described it in the Nekyia of the *Odyssey*:

Ὅμηρός τέ μοι δοκεῖ ταῦταἑωρακὼς ἔς τε τὴν ἄλλην ποίησιν ἀποτολμῆσαι τῶν ἐνʽΑΐδου καὶ δὴ καὶ τὰ ὀνόματα τοῖς ποταμοῖς ἀπὸ τῶν ἐνΘεσπρωτίδι θέσθαι.

I think Homer had seen these places and boldly ventured to describe Hades's realm in his poem and further named the rivers after those in Thesprotia.[79]

Homer, of course, does not say that Odysseus visits an established site that he himself had visited, but in addition to Pausanias's claim, the archaeological evidence indicates that this Nekyomanteion survives in the location that Homer

described.[80] Homer might have included specific details about the Nekyomanteion because of the local emphasis on the worship of Hades as ruler of the
Underworld, and a feeling that the site was especially connected to the Underworld because of both the Nekyomanteion and the cult of Hades.

We must also remember that the Greeks themselves had no single set of
vocabulary for so-called 'chthonic' practices.[81] Like all religious vocabulary in
Greece, the kinds of sacrifices that might be made to the gods and other divine
denizens in an Underworld- or death-related context are described using
specialist terms. ἐναγίζειν refer to sacrifices made to the dead or to heroes, but
it is never used of a sacrifice made to a god.[82] Sacrifices to Underworld gods
can be described using terms like ὁλοκαυτεῖν (bring a burnt offering or offer
whole), καθαγίζειν (devote or dedicate, especially of burnt offerings, or
dedications for the dead), καρποῦν (offer by way of sacrifice), and ἁγίζειν
(make sacred, especially by burning a sacrifice). The fifth-century BCE Greek
could conceive of different types of sacrifice, and different categories of
sacrifice – those to heroes as opposed to gods, for instance.[83] That there is no
explicit vocabulary for a distinct type of sacrifice that might be viewed as
'chthonic' only indicate that this was not seen differently from sacrifice to other
gods. Small details might change, but these changes are not necessarily greater
in number or significance than the changes in rituals between two other cults,
or even differences in cult of the 'same' god. There is no reason that we should
find a strict distinction being made in the sacrificial calendars because they are,
by nature, lists rather than complex how-to guides for sacrifices.

Concluding note

What do cursing, participation in an eschatological-based mystery cult, and
talking with the dead have in common? They are all intricately tied to the way
that people – real people – interact with the gods, and specifically with the
Underworld gods. In a space where most of what we know about religious
practice in archaic and classical Greece deals with public and civic rituals,
finding the personal – even the private – is a rare and wonderful glimpse into
the lives of these ordinary people. What does it say that these glimpses
involved the Underworld gods?

I do not want to imply that there are not similar personal expressions that
involve non-Underworld gods. There are. But that some of these private
experiences involve Underworld gods is important. People do not go to the
trouble of building relationships with divinities that will not benefit them in
some direct way. That is to say, people expect that the relationships they build
with gods will be two-way. The individual is getting something back from their
religious performance: damage being inflicted upon a rival business, an
opportunity to not lose their memories in the Underworld, information.
Underworld gods can give people something that non-Underworld gods cannot,
and for that reason alone they should be included in mainstream religious
practices, rather than sidelined.

Notes

1 Mackin Roberts, 2019.
2 For instance, DT1, DT4-5, DT10, and cf. Ogden, 2008: 139.
3 For references see Appendix 1.
4 Right acting is so pervasive that Werner Riess goes so far to say that 'rituals typically require an audience in order to be effective' (2012: 187). This is used as a way of distinguishing between 'religion' and 'magic', but whether such a distinction should be drawn is another argument. There are significant enough overlap between 'religious' and 'magical' practices to consider that they stem from the same foundation.
5 For example, Hekate appears on *DTA* 104–108; *DT* 72; *SDG* 170.
6 Johnston, 1999: 74.
7 Faraone, 1991: 28 n. 59.
8 *DTA*93, side A (trans. Eidinow)
9 h.Hom. *Herm.* 572–573.
10 However, Johnston (1999: 140) does claim that the Erinyes are the invoked subject of *katadesmoi*. Although there are few, an example can be found at *DTA* 108 – which invokes the Erinyes on Side B: καὶ Ἐρινύσιν ἠλιθιώναις.
11 Jordan, 1985
12 Aisch. *Eum.* 115–136, and see discussion in Chapter 6.
13 For example, see Jordan, 1997.
14 Lead was probably used because it was cheap and readily available, and there is also evidence that other materials might have been used to make *katadesmoi*, including bronze, wax, and papyrus, see Eidinow, 2007b: 45.
15 Cf. Jameson, Jordan and Kotansky, 1993: 129.
16 Riess, 2012: 187.
17 Jameson, Jordan and Kotansky, 1993: 130.
18 Johnston, 1999: 75, 85–86.
19 This will be discussed more thoroughly in the next section.
20 The connection between *katadesmoi* and legal practice is particularly strong – a large portion of the texts seek to bind the tongue, words, actions, or similar of a person who is in legal battle with the dedicants of the curse. For further discussion, see Eidinow, 2007a: 165–190; Faraone, 1999: 111; Gager, 1992: 116–150; Graf, 1997: 123–124.
21 Johnston, 2013: 46.
22 Edmonds, 2004: 31.
23 Edmonds, 2004: 31–32.
24 Johnston, 2013: 94–95.
25 Edmonds, 2004: 35.
26 Johnston, 2013: 4–5.
27 Cf. Bernabé and Jiménez San Cristóbal 2008: 185.
28 Edmonds, 2004: 41, cf. 45–46.
29 Bernabé and Jiménez San Cristóbal 2008: 30.
30 Graf and Johnston, 2007: 98–100.
31 Johnston, 2013: 120.
32 Discussed in Chapter 7; and cf. Edmonds, 2004: 34.
33 Bernabé and Jiménez San Cristóbal 2008: 17; Edmonds, 2004: 53.
34 Bernabé and Jiménez San Cristóbal 2008: 33.
35 Edmonds, 2004: 51.
36 Edmonds, 2004: 80–82.
37 Johnston, 2013: 130.
38 Bernabé and Jiménez San Cristóbal, 2008: 152–155.

39   Edmonds F5 496c. Edmonds' *F* group is made up of such tablets; and see Edmonds, 2011: table 2.7.
40   Johnston, 2013: 135.
41   Pind. *fr.* 37 (Race), trans. Race.
42   Paus. 9.23.4.
43   Pind. *Ol.* 14.20–21.
44   Pind. *fr.* 133 (Race), cf. Pl. *Men.* 81b.
45   Pind. *fr.* 133 (Race), cf. Pl. *Men.* 81b.
46   Pind. *fr.* 133 (Race), cf. Pl. *Men.* 81b. trans. Race.
47   These issues include the nine years exile. reincarnation, incarnation into a better position in the new life, and reincarnation depending on the payment of recompense.
48   Rose, 1936: 84–85; cf. Bernabé and Jiménez San Cristóbal, 2011: 80.
49   Bernabé and Jiménez San Cristóbal, 2008: 72; Bluck, 1961: 278–279; Edmonds, 2013: 304, 306; Graf and Johnston, 2007: 68–69, 157; Ionescu, 2007: 51–52.
50   Graf and Johnston, 2007: 67. Italicisation is from Johnston's chapter, and indicates portions of the narrative that are embellished from the version found in Olympiodorus, which constitutes the fullest version of the story available and dates from the sixth century CE, additions are from various fragmentary sources. Cf. Bernabé, 2002: 403; Gantz, 1993: 118–119; Morford, Lenardon and Sham, 2011: 318.
51   Rose, 1936: 85.
52   Edmonds, 1999; 2013: 305–306.
53   Zuntz, 1971.
54   Linforth, 1941 Although Linforth himself did not consider the gold lamellae as belonging to strict Orphic cult, choosing only to deal with material that directly named Orpheus.
55   Brisson, 1985; 1992; 1995.
56   Edmonds, 1999: 36. However, see also Bernabé (2002: 402), who strongly disagrees with Edmond's assertion.
57   Rose, 1936: 86; cf. Parke and Wormell, 1956: 8.
58   Plut. *Mor.* 421c; Ael. *VH.* 3.1; Kall. *fr.* 81 (Trypanis). This is not the only instance of Apollo being exiled from Delphi for purification from bloodguilt. He was forced to serve a year in exile by Zeus for the killing of the Cyclops, [Apollod]. *Bibl.* 3.10.4.
59   As, for example, at Pind. *Pyth.* 5.96.
60   Though it should be noted that there have been no tablets found in Attica, Boeotia, the eastern Peloponnese, the Cycladic islands, or Rhodes, and there is probably only one example of a table that may have been deposited in Asia Minor. See Parker and Stamatopoulou, 2004: 23.
61   Parker and Stamatopoulou, 2004: 23.
62   For example, Dietrich, 1893: 84; Harrison, 1903: 572–574. For a full study on the history of the scholarship of the gold lamellae see above; Johnston, 2013: 50–65.
63   Herrero de Jáuregui, 2011: 273.
64   Eidinow, 2007a: 141.
65   Eidinow, 2007a: 144.
66   Audollent, 1904: 81; Schachter, 1986: 200.
67   Hom. *Od.* 504–515.
68   For an introduction to the Nekyomantia see Caskey and Dakaris, 1962: 85; Ogden, 2001: 17; Ustinova, 2009: 69–81.
69   Paus. 9.39.6–13; and see Ogden, 2001: 18–19.
70   Heli. 6.14; Stat. *Theb.* 4.451–452; Ap. Rho. 3.1034; cf., 2001: 168.
71   For types of altars connected with 'chthonian' and 'Olympian' sacrifices, and Olympian sacrifices being partially burnt and 'chthonian' sacrifices being wholly burnt see

van Straten, 1995: 166. However, we must remember that there is no uniform 'style' of sacrifice to any 'type' of god, so these cannot be taken to relate to all sacrifices.

72 Hom. *Od.* 11.25–29, 11.31; cf. 10.517–520.
73 Collins, 2002: 225.
74 Collins, 2002: 228.
75 Steiner, 1971: 265.
76 Hom. *Od.* 11.37.
77 Tsagarakis, 2000: 275.
78 Hom. *Od.* 10.491.
79 Paus. 1.17.5. See also, 2000: 35 n. 104.
80 Dakaris, 1973: 148. Tsagarakis (2000: 43) disagrees with the claim that the site of the Odyssean Nekyomanteion is historical, saying: 'despite its fictional setting, our *Nekyia* has links with the historical world. But the necromantic link is further fictionalized in the sense that the necromantic ritual does not take place in one of the historical oracles but across the ocean, at the edge of the world, where the dead gather to enter Hades *proper*, i.e. in the land of the dead'. Regardless of the historical claim of the Odyssean Nekyomanteion, what appears as a common theme in both arguments is that the scene is based in historical *ritual* practice.
81 Cf. Parker, 2005b: 39.
82 See Parker, 2000: 38 n. 33; Pfister, 1912: 466, 80. The only exception to this is a vague reference to ἐναγίζειν and 'chthonians' in scholia. See, for example, schol. Ap. Rh. *Argo.* 1.587.
83 Parker, 2005b: 37–38, 39. For example, Herodotos, when discussing the dual nature of Herakles comments:

> καὶ δοκέουσι δέ μοι οὗτοι ὀρθότατα Ἑλλήνων ποιέειν, οἳ διξὰ Ἡράκλεια ἱδρυσά-
> μενοι ἔκτηνται, καὶ τῷ μὲν ὡς ἀθανάτῳ Ὀλυμπίῳ δὲ ἐπωνυμίην θύουσι, τῷ δὲ
> ἑτέρῳ ὡς ἥρωι ἐναγίζουσι.

> I think the best practice is that of those Greeks who have established two shrines of Herakles, and in the one case sacrifice as to an immortal under the title of Olympian, and in the other make offerings as to a hero (Hdt. 2.44.5, trans. Parker).

However, it has been suggested that double-cults of Herakles were actually very rare. This does not necessarily change the picture of differentiation which is expounded in Herodotos Histories. See Verbanck, 1989: 43–65. The *Lex Sacra* from Selinous contains three explicit references that indicate that a sacrifice is to be made following a set pattern; one 'as to the heroes' at line A10, one 'as to the gods' at A17, and one 'as to the immortals' at B 12–13. See Jameson, Jordan and Kotansky, 1993: 14–17, 29, 45.

7   The dead – belief and reality

By and large, religious or ritual practices about death are actually about life. That is, ideas about death are informed directly by concepts of life, and most of what occurs in death-related ritual is focused on the living, rather than the deceased. Beliefs about death are about living people trying to process what will occur after death – both their own death and that of their loved ones. Along with any theological considerations, there are very real emotional difficulties that people face when thinking about death. Through this emotional, religious, and philosophical turmoil, suppositions about the 'life' of the dead come about. These might result in ideas about the dead being 'differently alive' and perhaps still capable of interacting with the living world. In part this is reflected as a denial of mortality, through which, as Diana Burton comments, 'we are able to deny death and maintain the fiction of our own immortality or of the continued existence, in some form, of significant others who have died'.[1]

There are three main considerations of death-related belief, which interact but are not interdependent, and which often demonstrate incongruity. These are: the way the living regards the dead; ideas about what happens after death; and the actual funerary or burial practices. While these considerations do inform and change one another, they also act independently, and a single society may concurrently hold contradictory views relating to different aspects of death. One place where these considerations seem to have crossed into one another was in ideas about the length of death – that is, how long it actually took for a person to die. Death was a journey, of varying length, during which the living person crossed through some kind of liminal space and arrived, dead, into the Underworld. Aspects of this journey changed over time, of course, but the general idea remained an integral component of death-belief. The *psyche* of the man killed on the Homeric battlefield fled his body for the Underworld,[2] just as the deceased classical Athenian travelled from this world into the netherworld by way of boat. The two worlds were separate and only the dead could enter the lower world, except in particularly exceptional circumstances. For instance, both Herakles and Theseus enter the Underworld alive, and in the cult of Hades in Elis the priest enters the temple – thereby symbolically entering the Underworld – once per year.

In Chapter 5 I discussed van Gennep's tripartite theory of rites-of-passage, and this is a good place to reflect on that theory and how it may be applied meaningfully outside rites-of-passage. There are, in Greek death practices, a number of tripartite systems. The main one I will discuss further in this chapter is that of the funerary ritual itself – the three phases of ritual practice that allow the living to bid farewell to the deceased and allow the deceased to travel into the Underworld. Another fruitful way of examining this is less corporeal – the tripartite of the body, the soul, and memory. Bodies are, through cremation or inhumation, disposed of and cease to be the link between a person and the physical world. This link is severed during the liminal phase – between the exact moment of death (or, as I discuss further below, the beginning of the elongated process of death) and the end of that process, and the burial and ceremonial activities that accompany burial (this is itself a process that may last up to a year). This is the point when the body is made into a soul – the *psyche* – and this *psyche* might move between the Underworld and the living world at various points of ceremony. Finally, the immediacy of the *psyche* fades as direct relatives also die or move on, and the person becomes memory. Again, each of these phases is not really about the deceased themselves, but about the people who are left behind. They are the ones who care for the body, who nourish the *psyche*, and who tend to their memory.

What happens to the dead?

This section aims to set out a blueprint for general death-related beliefs found across the Greek world roughly during the archaic and classical periods. However, even with the creation of a very general map we must be wary of ascribing a system of beliefs that is too invasive to the privately held, shifting, and changing ideas about death and the Underworld that occur across the Greek world in these periods.

To the Greeks, death was a journey during which the deceased left the world of the living and arrived into the world of the dead. Although certain aspects of this journey changed over time, the general idea remained as an integral component of death-belief. The two worlds were separate and the 'other' world was only accessible to the deceased, except in particularly exceptional circumstances.[3] Preoccupation with creating a clear distinction between life and death is a feature of many cultures,[4] and efforts to create an increasingly stronger delineation between the living and the dead, in archaic and classical Greece, include the propagation of the idea that the deceased had a polluting influence to those who encountered them and, following this, legislative changes to funerary rites.

The Homeric dead were presented as weak and ineffectual, although this is an over-simplified explanation of their representation within the epic poems, and it does not indicate that archaic Greeks felt this way about the deceased. The idea of 'weak dead' is found in other literary and visual sources from the archaic and early classical periods, although not usually to the extent of the

Homeric 'witless' dead. The weak-dead trope is shown in mythic examples where the dead must enlist divine assistance to avenge themselves against living people who have caused them injury in life. This concept was appropriated into society and this was demonstrable in the procedures of Athenian law courts, where citizens placed trust in the courts to act on their behalf. By doing so, rather than attempting to enact justice themselves, they enshrined the court to provide just punishment and retribution. Examples of this include individuals and families prosecuting people accused of murdering one of their relatives or slandering their deceased relative's name.[5] In these cases, the living family members took on the role of the slighted party, although they were officially acting on behalf of their deceased relative. This shows that the concern was for the reputations and livelihoods of surviving family members and that the deceased had little or no power to avenge wrongs against him in life.[6] The 'weak dead' motif is reflected in other aspects of interaction between the living and the dead. For instance, as I discussed in Chapter 6, the process of burying *katadesmoi* in cemeteries[7] does not indicate that the dead have any particular power over the living, but that they can act as messengers between the living and the Underworld-dwelling gods who *were* in a position to be able to punish the living.

But the dead must *also* seek assistance from powerful Underworld divinities to enact revenge upon the living. For example, Klytaimestra must appeal to the Erinyes to assist her quest for vengeance against Orestes. Aischylos's *Eumenides* certainly depicts the shade of Klytaimestra relying on these goddesses of vengeance to assist her, but – perhaps paradoxically[8]– she is not subservient to them. On the contrary, she stands as their ruler, issuing demands that they carry out obediently. And, when they do not meet her high expectations she chides them. Her position over them is obvious in her language. For instance, when attempting to rouse them from sleep she uses her own name to call them, indicating that this holds power over them: φρονήσατ', ὦ κατὰ χθονὸς θεαί. ὄναρ γὰρ ὑμᾶς νῦν Κλυταιμήστρα καλῶ ('be mindful, you goddesses from beneath the earth: I call you now in your dream, I am Klytaimestra').[9] Elsewhere, she threatens them with violence for failing to submit to her will: ἄλγησον ἧπαρ ἐνδίκοις ὀνείδεσιν: τοῖς σώφροσιν γὰρ ἀντίκεντρα γίγνεται ('feel a stab of pain in your liver at these reproaches: to the wise they act as goads').[10] Her reproach is not empty; her words inflict physical pain on them in punishment. The liver is the seat of emotions – the heart of the ancient world – and Klytaimestra's words here more likely represent her ability to inflict psychological pain on the Erinyes. This fits with her lack of corporeality here but is no less violent or physical than if she were literally stabbing the Erinyes here. Aguish and anxiety cause real physical pain and discomfort, and psychological violence can be just as physical, and even more damaging, than purely physical violence. Far from demonstrating the ineffectual character of the shades, what this actually shows is the power and influence that Klytaimestra wields over the Erinyes. While we cannot take this to mean that there was a belief that all shades had the power to instruct divinities like the

Erinyes, what it does show is that there was a clear consideration that some shades, in some circumstances, were very powerful. If a shade has a level of power over divinities then theoretically that shade must also have power to change the living world, but this is where the geographical limitations of the Underworld are perhaps best shown.

What the *katadesmoi* show, when taken as a genre of religious text, is one aspect of the overarching shift in contemporary ideas about the dead and death throughout the archaic and classical periods. At the beginning of this period, the shades of the dead may have been considered by some to be weak, with no power to harm or influence the living, and this is what is represented in literary representations at the time. The gradual increase in *katadesmoi* throughout the period demonstrates an increased level of respect for the power and position of the dead. By the middle of the fifth century there was an increased amount of interaction with the dead. Sarah Iles Johnston argues that this shows the living had started to believe that the dead had certain inherent powers that they had not previously had.[11] The way the dead are characterised in the Homeric epics certainly shows that they are, generally, witless, weak, and powerless to assist the living in all but the most exceptional of circumstances. Representations of the dead contemporary to Homer still exhibited the weak-dead motif, although this often manifests as powerlessness rather than witlessness. The major changes that are being presented include both the increasing awareness of the deceased themselves and that the living are soliciting their assistance, even in some cases in which the living person was not related to, and had no other association with, the deceased person.[12]

This shift is demonstrative of a wider social restructuring and widespread changes in religious beliefs and practices. Christiane Sourvinou-Inwood argued that this began to take place because of pervasive social restratification. This included the move from small, isolated villages into larger settlements that were increasingly well-connected with one another, taking place throughout the early eighth century.[13] Such social reorganisation was necessary because of a boom in population in the closing decades of the dark ages and into the early archaic period, which forced the creation of the '*polis*'. Alongside this, advances in technology, including the reintroduction of writing, helped to create a more 'panhellenic mentality', particularly in religious practice.[14] This was further facilitated by inclusive, inter-state 'Greek' sanctuaries, like Delphi and Olympia, where cultural and religious interchange was fostered, and the mentality was heavily influenced by the spread of the works of Homer and Hesiod. But counter to Sourvinou-Inwood, I do not feel with any conviction that there was such a 'panhellenic mentality' created, even by the spread of Homer and Hesiod's works. That the Greek *poleis* considered themselves to be a unified whole was minor and although they did share some large-scale religious events, this hardly qualifies as a reason to imagine that there was a conscious attempt at wholesale cohesion. Any congruence is probably by-product of the network of macro- and micro-communities that served to influence one another's semiotic language and ritual.

Literary works, like Homer and Hesiod, spread ideas about the gods and religion and so also spread ideas about death, particularly as different societies would have placed their own inflection over the belief system represented in the poems. As such, the final 'versions' of the Homeric epics, which are now extant, probably represent an amalgamation of disparate beliefs from various settlements in the Greek-speaking world. The views expressed about death and dying within them are not the ideology of a single person or group, but represent a conflation of beliefs that loosely, as Sourvinou-Inwood says, 'corresponds to the actual nexus of attitudes of the eighth century'.[15] As the belief system evolves over time, society passes through a transitory phases in which both 'older' and 'newer' beliefs may be simultaneously considered to be influencing cultic activity depending on the appeal of each separate belief.[16]

One of the most prominent contradictions about death-related beliefs centre on how the dead themselves are imagined – as I mentioned above, this is demonstrated within the Homeric epics themselves. If we adopt a system of inter-community belief 'conflation' this contradiction becomes easy to explain; the dead are imagined as being mute and witless in some communities and, elsewhere, are believed to appear as they did in life. However, if we examine representations of the deceased in the poems through the lens of memory construction we find that they can be simultaneously remembered in multiple ways – in much the same way that the gods can be conceptualised simultaneously in different guises. It is not contradictory that the dead are represented as being both mute and lifeless, as they would have been after death during funerary rituals, and animated and appears to be alive, as they would have been throughout their lives. For instance, in the *Iliad*, the recently deceased Patroklos appears to Achilleus exactly as he was in life;[17] here, Achilleus' memory of his deceased friend is so strong that there is no trouble in Patroklos appearing to him *exactly* as he would have in life. Nevertheless, over time memory fades and, as Jan Bremmer comments, 'it is understandable that the more personal traits gradually withdraw behind a more general idea of the dead as opposed to the living'.[18] A person might find it easier to construct a 'living' memory for a person they had known in life, rather than for a deceased stranger unless the imagination is allowed to construct the dead. Odysseus has no trouble recalling the likeness of Achilleus and Agamemnon when he talks to them in the Underworld, who – at this stage – he had not seen for many years. He recalls his mother, Antiklea, though he has not seen her for some fifteen years. Tireseus, the seer he is there to consult, is someone he has never met. So, it is not necessarily about time, but also memorial strength – Achilleus and Agamemnon were influential players in his life, his mother similarly. Tireseus's image is important to Odysseus, but it is *not* important that the figure Odysseus conjures represents what Tireseus was meant to have looked like in life. Thus, an individual may find it easier to construct a 'living' memory for a person they had known well, than for a deceased stranger, but that the imagination may fill in the gaps if it is important to see a well-constructed shade. The change in representation between the mute and witless shade and those who are or become during the course of exchange with the living person, more lifelike (either through drinking blood, as occurs in *Odyssey* eleven or through other means) is not a conflation or amalgamation of older and newer death-related beliefs. It is rather that socially constructed memory is likely to fade over time but also be reignited through the consciousness of the living participant. This functions alongside ideas constructed and shared by overlapping religious communities and are (sometimes liberally) altered to suit the context of each community's need.

Memory has another important function in death-related beliefs: the way people envision the dead remembering their life. Essentially that when you die you need to self-construct your own being and your past through memory recall. We see things like people writing the name of their dead relative on the grave marker in the hopes that this might jog the dead person's memory and lead to the retention of other mental faculties.[19] Similarly, the so-called 'Orphic' gold tablets[20] present memory, and its deified personification Mnemosyne, as paramount to the deceased gaining entrance into the netherworld. Tablets often include instruction on how to properly select the correct spring to drink from in order to regain memories from life.[21] One tablet begins Μνημοσύνας τόδε ἔργον ('This is the work of Mnemosyne [Memory]'),[22] another echoes this further in the text,[23] a number of other tablets refer to τῆς Μνημοσύνης ἀπο λίμνης ('the lakes of Memory'),[24] and one refers to the bearer of the tablet being asked to δέχε<σ>θε Μνημοσύνης τόδε δῶρον ('accept this gift of Memory').[25] Mnemosyne is invoked to enable Orphic initiands to 'remember the ritual' that allows them entrance to the afterlife.[26] Given that we have a notion that simply remembering one's own name can trigger a memory-instigated retention of faculties exhibited in life, a similar 'chain of memory' is at work here. As we saw in the case of Achilleus' memory of recently deceased Patroklos in the *Iliad*, recent or special memories create a sharper picture of the dead; and keeping the memory of a loved one alive enhances their reputation. Mnemosyne, in the 'Orphic' tablets, fulfils the function of the remembering relative or friend left behind[27] and enables the deceased to begin to regain their own memory.

Dying into death: how to die

Dying was a multi-stage process, during which your relatives were required to perform the appropriate rituals at the appropriate times to make sure that you actually *finished* dying. The process was an on-going separation from the living world, and only after the completion of the ritual process could your shade enter the Underworld.[28] All this is to say, death is not instantaneous.[29] Although complex in structure, funerary rites were often performed without the assistance of a religious professional, and legal reforms regarding activities associated with the funerary rites demonstrate that Athenians, at least, liked to show their grief loudly and publicly. These reforms along with the wholesale demolition of earlier grave monuments in the classical period provided an avenue for publicly speaking out against the privileged position of past aristocracy.[30] In this way, death could be seen as an equaliser, and it certainly becomes more socio-economically equal following the reforms, which included legislated cost prohibitions, noise reduction, and the banning of professional mourners.[31] These reforms, though, also point to places where death is not about equalisation but is used, in socio-political terms, as a way for living families to use their wealth to advance the social perception of their lost loved one. And, of course, themselves as the living relatives who have sacrificed a portion of their wealth to the memorialisation of their relative (and therefore have enough to sacrifice).

Funerary ritual and burial rites can be roughly broken into three main acts; *prothesis* (laying out the body; see Figure 7.1) and including washing or cleaning both the body and the deceased's house, *ekphora*, or conveyance to the place of interment, and finally deposition of the cremated or inhumed remains.[32] Washing the house and body formed an important aspect of the funerary ritual and acted as a way to start cleansing away the pollution created both by the act of death and the corpse itself. But death-related pollution was not necessarily a negative force, it was one aspect of mourning.[33] How much pollution a person incurs from death and a corpse almost directly corresponds to the relationship between the two in life, and in some cases, this was regulated by legal codification. In Figure 7.1, a black-figure Attic pinax, we can see family members surrounding a corpse during

Figure 7.1 Attic black-figure terracotta pinax (decorated plaque) showing the prosthesis ('laying out') phase of funerary rites, with family members surrounding the corpse. Attributed to the Gela Painter. Second half of the sixth century BCE. The Walters Art Museum, 48.225.

the *prosthesis*. At the head of the corpse, three women – or two women and a female child – tear at their hair in grief. Three men and a child stand at the foot of the bed in discussion. They are not only physically further from the corpse but depicted as emotionally further from it as well. It was not their place to undertake conspicuous acts of grief, even in the private space of the home. Though male family members may well have been, and acted, physically grieved it would not have been displayed in public, or even on publicly displayed images of private household scenes such as this one. Women lament the dead and men greet them.

Death itself pollutes the living who interact with the corpse. That is to say, it is not the body itself that was considered to be polluting, but the death that lingered in it. The body itself was considered to be a pure, or even sacred, object.[34] Death pollution was not just sentimental, but founded in practical, physical, and hygienic considerations that need to be accounted for when moving – and living! – around a decomposing corpse.[35] And this is not just the decomposing adult corpse that we might consider when imagining a scene of mourning. Sacred laws from Kyrene, in Libya, describe the pollution caused by a miscarriage, even delineating different strengths of pollution by how far the pregnancy had progressed:

αἴ κα γυνὰ ἐβάληι, αἰ μέγ κα διάδηλον ἦι, μ[ι]-
αίνονται ὥσπερ ἀπο θανόντος: αἰ δέ κα μὴ
διάδηλον ἦι, μιαίνεται αἰτὰ ἀ οἰκία καθάπε[ρ]
ἀπὸ λεχός.

If a woman miscarries, if it is recognisable, they are polluted as if by a corpse. If it is not recognisable, the house itself is polluted as if by childbirth.[36]

And different kinds of death created different levels of pollution, even beyond the 'normal' pollution that any corpse would impose upon a household – a suicide can pollute implements and objects so forcefully that they need to be expelled or destroyed. Death by lightning creates almost no pollution at all. Similarly, the way the body is treated can have an effect on pollution levels. Failure to undertake proper burial, even for strangers, had a strong pollution effect on those who neglected the task.

The sentimental nature of pollution concepts attached to the body of the deceased were mirrored in the ways in which personal grief was performed. Although there was an acceptance of personal grief over the loss of a family member this was tempered by an understanding in the inevitability of death. Grief, then, was not a long-lasting personal trauma that overtook a person indefinitely, but rather was, at least in public, highly controlled and channelled into a ritualistic outpouring. Violent outbursts involving ripping at hair and clothing are a good demonstration of this. On the surface, they appear to be spontaneous acts of overwhelming grief, but they are actually a highly ritualised performative aspect of formal grieving and lamentation.[37] This is why the women in the *pinake* in Figure 7.1 are shown tearing at their hair – not because they necessarily would have done this, but because this would have been read by others as an over grief performance.

Often, these grief performances focused on personal disadvantage and loss to the surviving relatives, rather than the deceased.[38] 'Real' personal grief may be separated from these highly ritualised acts of grief and lamentation, which were considered to be owed to the dead as part of the γέρας θανόντων – the honour for the dead – and as Christiane Sourvinou-Inwood comments: 'lament was one of the ways through which the deceased's social personal was articulated and given value, and his importance stressed'.[39] As well as being highly disrespectful against the deceased's surviving relatives, to leave the deceased without such praise and honour was also a grievous insult against the gods, who may then turn the deceased upon the living. When Odysseus speaks with the dead in the *Nekyia* of the *Odyssey*, Elpenor pleas with the hero that he should not be left ἄκλαυτον ἄθαπτον. μή τοί τι θεῶν μήνιμα γένωμαι ('unwept and unburied … I might become a source of the gods' wrath for you').[40] Lamentation, and therefore both public and personal grief, were traditionally connected to the *ekphora* phase of funerary rites, and this is where they were most publically expressed. However, lamentation began during the *prothesis* phase, after appropriate sacrifices and offerings had been made to the deceased.[41]

Grief could also be expressed through intentional physical defilement. This was not the same type of pollution that naturally surrounded the body of the dead, but an outward representation that could help align the mourner with their dead loved one. In a literary example of this, upon learning of Patroklos' death, Achilleus covers his face and hair with dirt, performing a physical act of his internal grief:

> ἀμφοτέρῃσι δὲ χερσὶν ἑλὼν κόνιν αἰθαλόεσσαν
> χεύατο κὰκ κεφαλῆς, χαρίεν δ' ᾔσχυνε πρόσωπον:
> νεκταρέῳ δὲ χιτῶνι μέλαιν' ἀμφίζανε τέφρη.
> αὐτὸς δ' ἐν κονίῃσι μέγας μεγαλωστὶ τανυσθεὶς
> κεῖτο, φίλῃσι δὲ χερσὶ κόμην ᾔσχυνε δαΐζων.

> and with both hands he took the dark dust and poured it over his head and defiled his fair face, and on his fragrant tunic the black ashes fell. And he himself in the dust lay outstretched, mighty in his mightiness, and with his own hands he tore and marred his hair.[42]

And, he refuses to wash the marks and stains of fighting from his body until Patroklos' death is avenged, and his funerary rituals are complete.[43] Achilleus' initial self-defilement is not met with shock: self-pollution was an excepted way of physically expressing emotional pain. Following Hektor's death, Priam similarly aligns himself with the state of his son's body when he κυλινδόμενος κατὰ κόπρον ('wallowed in the muck')[44] and when Iris delivers the gods' message to him, she finds him similarly defiled:

ἀμφὶ δὲ πολλὴ
κόπρος ἔην κεφαλῇ τε καὶ αὐχένι τοῖο γέροντος
τήν ῥα κυλινδόμενος καταμήσατο χερσὶν ἐῇσι.

and on the old man's head and neck was filth in abundance which he had gathered in his hands as he grovelled on the earth.[45]

Physical pollution was aimed at assimilating with the state of the deceased, particularly when that person had not yet undergone proper funerary rites and was, therefore, still in a transitory position between the worlds of the living and the dead. Eleanor Guralnick asserts that 'dirtiness, which compromises a person's physical integrity, is a visible sign of the existential disorder affecting those who have lost someone close'.[46] In other words, it is nothing more than physical lamentation.

Achilleus's assimilation to Patroklos' state goes further than a simple physical representation of his grief. Bathing in dirt is symbolic of death on the battlefield, as the body is ground into the dirt, mud, and blood, and mutilated by the enemy forces. So, his self-defilement begins the process of total integration between Achilleus himself and his lost friend's body, and this assimilation is completed when Achilleus's re-enters the battlefield and, refusing to wash, his body is further stained with mud and – perhaps crucially – blood. Integration between Achilleus and Patroklos is reinforced by Thetis and the Nerieds's lamentation, wherein they act as though they are grieving for Achilleus himself, appearing to confuse Patroklos's death with Achilleus's own upcoming demise which, of course, they know is coming up.[47]

While this situation is certainly atypical of normal death-rites, his actions can tell us much about the funerary process. The first ritualised act of Patroklos's funeral occurs some time after Achilleus's initial outpouring of grief and is manifested in a distinct way. If we look at the episode from the first act of actual funerary activity proper, then the expected elements of funerary ritual are all there, albeit not in the order we would expect. This is completely unproblematic for two main reasons. First, the *Iliad*, as a piece of oral poetry, was shaped by voices from many different communities who may have done things differently than classical Attica, from where we have the most evidence. Second, the *Iliad* is a piece of literature, and it serves us well to remember sometimes that literature does not have to conform to ritualistic conventions that we may think of as 'unbreakable' in the real world. There is feasting alongside Patroklos's lifeless body, and then the γέρας θάνατον, or ritual lament,[48] with an *ekphora* beginning Patroklos's separation from the world of the living as his body is removed from Achilleus's hut and toward the ritual space of the funeral. Holding the feasting out of place (we would normally expect it at the end, not the beginning, of a funerary ritual), is done to facilitate Achilleus's alignment to the dead Patroklos. Prior to this point, Achilleus has refused to eat, but does so here because it is appropriate for the dead to partake in food: he has taken on the characteristics of being dead through metaphysical amalgamation with Patroklos and can, therefore, participate in the 'normal life' of the dead. More practically, however, eating here gives Achilleus the nourishment needed to facilitate his killing spree. The Myrmidons are told not to lament Patroklos's death, to allow him to move swiftly into the Underworld, but by perverting and prolonging the necessarily funerary rites Achilleus is himself keeping Patroklos in the mortal world longer than necessary – and Patroklos appears in Achilleus's dream to rebukes him for the delay. Only after this dream-apparition does Achilleus agree to undertake the funeral.

While there is obviously limited historical information we can take from this episode, it does highlight the importance of burial rites in people's understanding of what the dead person's journey into the Underworld is like. We can clearly see that the duties of the deceased's remaining relatives – in this case Achilleus – are paramount, and that they must put aside their own private mourning to undertake proper funerary rites. Achilleus cannot undertake this, and Patroklos appears in order to remind him. But there is a disconnect here, between an understanding for the well-being of the dead and for the real-world idea that death causes a tangible and material loss to the living person. I can only really conclude, apropos of my own experiences with death, that in each of these beliefs there is a certain amount of needing to keep up a social ritual in order to continue functioning in an appropriate way following a death.

The duties of the surviving relatives did not stop after the initial funerary rites had been conducted. They were required to visit and tend the gravesite regularly. Special rites were conducted on the third, ninth, and thirteen days following death, and on monthly and yearly visitations.[49] These visits included offering sacrificial meals and drinks to the dead, although liquid-only offerings appear to be more frequent.[50] Decoration of the grave stele and the giving gifts to the deceased are also common practice.[51] There is relatively little textual and archaeological evidence to indicate what these offerings may have been; the vast majority of literary evidence describing funerary offerings of any kind present clearly atypical circumstances. Orestes, for example, offers a lock of hair at the tomb of Agamemnon,[52] but dedication of hair is more likely to occur *during* funerary rituals than afterwards.[53] Orestes, of course, had not been present at his father's funeral, and mentions this during his dedication. The farce of Alkestis's funeral makes it similarly unsuitable to take any clear evidence from: between the funeral that begins before death and the presence of Thanatos, to the Herakles's comic re-enactment of his labours, and Admetus and Pheres's argument overshadowing Alkestis's death. It is clear, however, that the *sema* is particularly important, and possibly more important than the actual remains of the deceased.[54] While this is certainly true in the case of ordinary citizen, there is sometimes an exception regarding the bodies, or more accurately bones, of local heroes lost or stolen to other places. The Delphic Oracle, for instance, instructed the Spartans to retrieve Orestes's bones in order to win war against the Tegeans.[55]

The on-going ritual activity may be likened to the establishment of a privately administered cult, with the deceased acting as the hero who is tended to by his own nearest relatives. This reinforces the importance of maintaining close familial relationships.[56] Although there was a prevailing belief in the Underworld as a place of residence, it was also felt that the deceased had access to their own tombs and that the *sema* was not simply a monument for posterity but was, in Robert Garland's words, 'a place to which the dead would come not only for material but for intellectual nourishment'.[57] There is a parallel between the relationship of the dead and his tomb and that of gods and heroes have with their own temples or shrines: a god will support and protect those who inhabit the space surrounding his temple or a hero may be considered to play an instrumental role in a battle victory.[58] It may seem to us incongruous to hold such conflicting beliefs, but the dissonance of tombstone access and Underworld residence is relatively minor.

It is clear that the Greeks expended a considerable amount of time, energy, and money on the funerary rites themselves, and this may make it appear as though they had a greater consideration for the body, rather than the *psyche*, of the deceased. Without proper treatment of the body, including proper burial, it was thought that the deceased would not be permitted to enter the Underworld. In effect, maltreatment of the body was directly akin to maltreatment of the *psyche*. It was thought that the way the body was presented in funerary rituals might have also represented how the person appeared in the Underworld. This is where Emily Vermule's notion of the 'double' body in death is most helpful, with one body remaining at the grave and the other being sent into the Underworld. This also accounts for the simultaneous beliefs that the deceased resides permanently in the Underworld but is also never far away from their own tomb.[59] There was also an idea that the dead were granted certain 'powers', and a large part of this may have been a belief that they would be able to locate one another in the Underworld. Although there is only a very small amount of evidence that reinforces this idea, it is likely that the concept would have been widely accepted as an aspect of the ordinary activities undertaken by the dead. Klytaimestra, in the *Agamemnon*, implies that Iphigeneia would be there to greet her father upon his arrival in the Underworld,[60] and Antigone expresses her hope that her mother, father, and brother would be present to meet her upon her own death.[61] Similarly, Admetus implores Alkestis to wait for him in the Underworld once she has died.[62] More generally, Plato's Sokrates discusses the ability of the dead to come into contact with others who have previously died.[63] It is most likely that beliefs like this came about as a way of comforting the living, specifically those who were nearing death due to age or illness. Knowing that one would be greeted in the Underworld by the familiar faces of loved ones who would be able to help them come to terms with their disembodiment and dislocation from living society would provide a greater level of comfort. Meanwhile, surviving relatives could entrust the newly dead to deliver messages to the previously deceased.[64]

Concluding note

While in the Underworld the dead were, apparently, free to participate in a number of activities that they enjoyed in life, including feasting and dining, sexual intercourse, and game playing, although this depends on the period of the depiction, and as Robert Garland notes that 'the principal activities of the Homeric dead appear to be gossip, sententious moralising and self-indulgent regret'.[65] However, the activities of the dead, including eating and drinking, are not as clear, and sex probably does not come into our evidence any earlier than Lucian. Grave offerings in the archaic and classical periods indicate burial with objects that could facilitate the comfort and happiness of the dead person. During the seventh and sixth centuries, board games were a particularly popular gift to the deceased, and these sometimes show images of mourning women on the corners of the board.[66] These games were usually made specifically for inclusion with burial gifts, and this may have invested 'the game board with some particular meaning for the chances and skill of life and death', as Sarah Morris and John Papadopoulos comment.[67] Grave offerings could have also been items which belonged to the deceased in life and which they may want to keep in the afterlife, such as special weaponry.[68] We should not view grave goods as merely a show of wealth.[69] The lavishness of grave goods changed over time and they were more equally distributed in some periods than in others, and this was also changed in the classical period with funerary legislation.[70] These graves goods should be viewed within the context of a wider ritual practice contemporary with specific burials.[71]

Notes

1 Burton, 2005: 32.
2 For instance, at Hdt. *Il.* 5.296, 696; 8.123, 315; 14.518; 16.453, 856; 22.362, 467.
3 For example, both Herakles and Theseus mythically entered the Underworld while alive, and in the cult of Hades as Lord of the Dead in Elis the priest would enter the temple – thereby symbolically entering the Underworld – once per year (see Chapter 2 for discussion of this).
4 Jones, 2010: 18.
5 Garland, 1989; MacDowell, 1963.
6 Oakley and Sinos, 1993: 171; Oakley, 2004: 319. Thus, family involvement, which was such a central feature of pre-classical homicide trials, remained a feature of classical Athenian homicide customs, though they were no longer able to proscribe punishments, relatives of the victim were responsible for the initial indictment being made against the suspected murderer. Indictment was achieved by the issue of a formal accusation by one relative of the victim, who was then required to serve the accused with a judicial summons, in front of witnesses, instructing the accused to appear before the Basileus to answer the charges. The relative who has issued both the warning and summons to the accused was then required to act as prosecutor in trial. By keeping the victim's relatives directly involved in the process of accusation and trial classical homicide laws acted as a limitation to private revenge while still allowing slighted family members to actively participate in the bringing about of justice for their relative. See Lys. 6.12; Ar. *Vespp.* 1041–1042; Pl. *Leg.* 871b-c.

7 While the majority of *katadesmoi* are found buried in graves, sometimes even placed in the hand of the deceased, they have also been found in sanctuaries of divinities who have some association with the Underworld, particularly Demeter. See Ogden, 2008: 139.

8 Or perhaps just because this is Aischylos.

9 Aisch. *Eum.* 115–116.

10 Aisch. *Eum.* 135–136.

11 Johnston, 1999: 75, 85–86.

12 Johnston, 1999: 74–75.

13 Sourvinou-Inwood, 1981; cf. 1995: 100–106.

14 Sourvinou-Inwood, 1981: 16.

15 Sourvinou-Inwood, 1981: 16. Although, Sourvinou-Inwood comments, this conflation is further complicated by the probability of multiple authors, both prior to and post writing, which may have changed elements found within the poems to facilitate their accessibility to the contemporary audience to which they were being presented or performed. See also, 1991: 12–13, 14. Here, Sourvinou-Inwood treats the 'conflation' of ideologies as one religious system with the sole exception of *Odyssey* Book 24. She purposefully takes this approach to view the Homeric 'system' as an artificial structure created by a poet who was simultaneously influenced by older and newer ideological frameworks. However, the other side of this argument may show that population expansion did not directly influence local religious belief, particularly beliefs about death. Ian Morris's article 'Attitudes toward Death in archaic Greece' argues directly against Sourvinou-Inwood's assertion that population expansion and the associated social change directly affected beliefs about death. Morris argues that Sourvinou-Inwood's idea of 'urbanisation' is an inappropriate conceptualisation of social stratification for the Greeks and considers her analogy to Medieval France to be misguided. Morris also takes issue with Sourvinou-Inwood's methodological choices, in particular that her study is based on the system of Piere Airès (also utilised by Sarah Iles Johnston in *Restless Dead*) and the simplicity with which this system renders the complex and changing landscape of death related beliefs. Sourvinou-Inwood, in response, reasserts and refines her methodological study within an appendix of *'Reading' Greek Death*. See Morris, 1989: 302–303.

16 Garland, 1985: 119, 71 n. 19; Sourvinou-Inwood, 1981: 15–39; 1995: 412–444.

17 Hom. *Il.* 23.65–107.

18 Bremmer, 1983: 88–89.

19 Vermeule, 1979: 27.

20 Citations from the tablets refer to Bernabé and Jiménez San Cristóbal; 2008; Edmonds, 2011; Graf and Johnston, 2007. For further discussion see Chapter 5.

21 On the presence of two fountains at the entrance to the netherworld, see Bernabé and Jiménez San Cristóbal; 2008: 29–35; Janko, 1984: 91.

22 Bernabé and Jiménez San Cristóbal, 2008: no. L1; Edmonds, 2011: no. B10; Graf and Johnston, 2007: no. 1.

23 Bernabé and Jiménez San Cristóbal, 2008: no. L2; Edmonds, 2011: no. B1; Graf and Johnston, 2007: no. 2. Graf's reconstruction of the text reads [Μνημοσύ]νης τόδ<ε> ἔ[ργον – . See Graf and Johnston, 2007: 6. Edmonds takes a more cautious approach in his reconstruction, citing [Μνημοσύ]νης τόδε [†επιον†-, translating this as 'This [is the?.. of Memory…') see Edmonds, 2011: 22–23.

24 Graf and Johnston, 2007: nos. 1, 2, 8, 25; in the corresponding order Bernabé and Jiménez San Cristóbal, 2008: nos. L1, L3, L2, L4; Edmonds, 2011: nos. B10, B1, B11, B2.

25 Bernabé and Jiménez San Cristóbal, 2008: L11; Graf and Johnston, 2007: 9.

26 Bernabé and Jiménez San Cristóbal, 2011: 75.

27 Herrero de Jáuregui, 2011: 289.

28 Sourvinou-Inwood, 1981: 18.
29 Vermeule, 1979: 2.
30 Garland, 1985: 122.
31 For an overview of funeral-related legislation in Athens see Garland, 1989: 1–15.
32 This is an amalgamation of the tripartite ritual burial systems presented by Garland and Vermeule. See Garland, 1985: 21; Vermeule, 1979: 19 For a full discussion of each stage of the funerary ritual see Garland, 1985: 21–27; Kurtz and Boardman, 1971: 142–161.
33 Parker, 1983: 35.
34 Garland, 1985: 47.
35 Garland, 1985: 43.
36 *LSS* 115, B106-109. Edited text and translation Robertson, 2010: 262, 66.
37 Stafford, 2000: 6.
38 Sourvinou-Inwood, 1981: 24–25.
39 Sourvinou-Inwood, 1995: 177, cf. 171, 175; see also Jones, 2010: 103.
40 Hom. *Od.* 11.72–73.
41 Stafford, 2000: 6.
42 Hom. *Il.* 18.23–27. Trans. Murray/Wyatt.
43 Hom. *Il.* 23.44–46.
44 Hom. *Il.* 22.414.
45 Hom. *Il.* 24.163–165. Trans. Murray/Wyatt.
46 Guralnick, 1974: 64.
47 Cf. Patroklos' being mourned by Achilleus' mortal horses. Hom. *Il.* 17.426–428, 23.280–284.
48 Hom. *Il.* 23.9.
49 Garland, 1985: 104; Kurtz and Boardman, 1971: 147–148 For instances of these regular visitations occurring in contemporary literature see Soph. *El.* 277; Hdt. 4.26; Isok. 2.46; Plat. *Leg.* 717d-e.
50 Vermeule, 1979: 57–58.
51 Garland, 1985: 15–18, 110.
52 Aisch. *Ag.* 6–7.
53 Cf. to Achilleus' dedication of a lock of hair at the funeral of Patroklos, Hom. *Il.* 23.144–146.
54 Sourvinou-Inwood, 1995: 99, 120, 277.
55 Hdt. 1.67. Cf. Cartledge, 2002: 119–120.
56 Garland, 1985: 120. For similar claims regarding the connection between the deceased hero and his tomb in hero-cults see Dietrich, 1965: 34.
57 Garland, 1985: 119.
58 For a thorough example of this, involving the assistance given to the Athenians and Spartans at various times by Herakles, see Bowden, 2005: 5–9.
59 Vermeule, 1979: 7–8. Vermeule later suggests that the Greeks could imagine a kind of tunnel between the tomb of the deceased and their *psyche*, wherever that might be.
60 Aisch. *Ag.* 1555.
61 Soph. *Ant.* 898–902.
62 Eur. *Alk.* 363–364.
63 Pl. *Ap.* 49.
64 Vermeule, 1979: 49.
65 Garland, 1985: 68.
66 An example of this can be found in Whittaker, 2004: 208, fig. 01.
67 Morris and Papadopoulos, 2004: 235–236; Vermeule, 1979: 80. See also Garland, 1985: 70. Garland disagrees with the suggestion that there is any kind of eschatological connection and contests that the board games appear in graves as an object of entertainment for the deceased in the afterlife.

68 Vermeule, 1979: 56.
69 Morris, 1992: 106.
70 See Garland, 1989.
71 Morris, 1992: 108. An interesting comment on the discovery and analysis of grave goods can be found in the fictional Macaulay, 1979. Macaulay's story is set in the year 4022 where an amateur archaeologist, Howard Carson, working in what used to be the United States, discovers a body entombed in a motel room. Carson catalogues what he sees, imagining it to be a ritualised burial – the television, for instance, which the body faces, is called 'the Great Altar', and the bed the deceased is found on 'the Ceremonial Platform'. This is discussed in the specific context of Athenian grave goods in Morris's *Death-Ritual and Social Structure,* where he says of this: 'grave goods also offer perfect ammunition for mockery of naïve direct interpretations. Macaulay's *Motel of the Mysteries* indulges this, with Howard Carson excavating the Toot'n'c'mon motel in the belief that it is a necropolis, seeing everything from a television to a toilet seat as ritual paraphernalia accompanying a corpse propped up in bed with his remote control. It is easy to laugh, but this kind of direct interpretation *is* the way grave goods are usually treated. And up to a point that makes sense ... but, as I said, this only works up to a point. It is hard to forget the example of the "Orphics", whose next life was distinctive, but whose grave good were conventional' (104–105).

Afterword: Hekate, the missing figure

Hekate's reputation in post-classical literature, and predominantly in scholarship, is that of a malevolent sorceress with strong links to the moon and the Underworld, and this sometimes leads to her being called 'chthonic'. George Warr, for example, comments that 'it is amply established by literary and archaeological evidence that this lunar goddess owed her real dignity to chthonic attributes'.[1] He does not detail this 'ample' evidence. In fact, quite contrary to his statement, he discussed her apportionment of honours in Hesiod's *Theogony* with a specific acknowledgement that her realm of influence does *not* extend to the Underworld. This is indicative of a general tendency to associate Hekate with lunar aspects, which is sometimes (but not always) interpreted as her being 'chthonic'. Karl Kerényi asserts that Hekate is a 'reappearance' of Phoibe, giving her a lunar aspect.[2] But this is a hasty (and erroneous) assumption, as Hekate does not have a strong, verifiable association with the moon until the Roman period. The majority of evidence pointing to this connection has been extrapolated from later information. For example, the connection between Hekate and torches has been read as having a nocturnal, and therefore lunar (and 'chthonic'), subtext, but no such connotation is read into Demeter's well-established association with the torch.[3] J. Rabinowitz conjectures that this 'reverse reading' has been made because the Greek pantheon did not provide a strong, well-established, and developed moon goddess. And, although Luna was central to Roman religion, the Roman's did rely heavily on the Greek pantheon as a template for literature and art.

Fritz Graf has argued that early forms of Hekate were associated with passages through a period of liminality,[4] which would explain her role as a guide for young women through transitionary parts of life. Hekate assists Persephone through a kind of marriage-related rite-of-passage, a liminal period in the Homeric *Hymn to Demeter*. But rather than signifying an Underworld association, her role is as an intermediary between Persephone's stages of maturity. This transitionary aspect informs her role as an intermediary between gods and men, which Jenny Straus Clay believes in one of the key attributes of her unusual appearance in the *Theogony*.[5]

Many scholars now agree on Hekate's non-Greek heritage, placing her origin in western Asia Minor, probably Karia.[6] By the fifth century BCE, at least, cults dedicated to Hekate had been established in Greece and she was being actively worshipped in Aegina, Selinous, and Athens.[7] There appears to be no earlier archaeological evidence from mainland Greece for Hekate worship, but there is evidence for worship in Asia Minor.[8] Hekate must have been known to the Greeks prior to this, and perhaps as early as 700 BCE, as her appearance in the Homeric *Hymn to Demeter*, and Hesiod's *Theogony* and *Catalogue of Women* confirm.

Hesiod introduces Hekate at about the mid-point of the *Theogony*. The passage is forty-one lines in length, and tells the story of Hekate's birth, history, influences, and powers.[9] It details more divine-human interaction than any other section of the poem, and grants Hekate increased power, even though the majority of goddesses have their powers reduced by Zeus.[10] The so-called 'Hymn to Hekate'[11] can be briefly summed up as follows:

411: Hekate is presented as the daughter of Asteria and Perses
412–415: Zeus gives Hekate a share of the earth, sea, and heaven
416–418: People always invoke Hekate in prayers and rituals[12]
418–421: Hekate grants favours to people who honour her
422–425: Zeus allows Hekate to keep her Titanic honours
426–428: Hekate assists in the judgement of men
429–447: Hekate blesses those whom she favours, which specifically include
    kings (430, 434), warriors (431–433), athletes (435–438), cavalrymen (439),
    and fishermen (440–442)
448–449: Hekate is honoured by the Olympian gods even though she is an only
    child[13]
450–452: Hekate is *kourotrophos* (nursemaid) to all living creatures

What is notably missing from this section is any reference to attributes that are prominent in later authors, including any typical Underworld-related characteristics, lunar association, magical traits, mentions of cross-roads, torches, or the triple-guise. While there has been much scholarship arguing that the 'hymn' section does not genuinely belong in the *Theogony*,[14] the authenticity of the passage does not appear to have been disputed in antiquity.[15]

Martin West considers that this passage shows Hesiod's own religious beliefs at work, and he subsequently comments that the hymn 'is a section of extreme interest ... for seldom elsewhere do we find a Greek setting out in so full a statement of his personal beliefs concerning the nature and powers of a god'.[16] He bases this argument on several things, both within the poem and from the wider extant body of Hesiod's work. Hesiod's father came from Aeolian Kyme, and his trading activities would have brought him into contact with Hekate-worshipping cities.[17] Thus, West comments, perhaps Hesiod's father was a devotee of Hekate, perhaps even introducing her worship to Boiotia, and accounting for Hesiod's brother's theophoric name 'Perses', the name that Hesiod gives to Hekate's father.

West goes on to comment that Hesiod's verboseness in this passage – mirrored by his address to the Muses – might suggest that this is a personally important subject matter for him. The idea that the 'hymn' section shows Hesiod writing autobiographically was supported by Elisabeth Stein.[18] The argument that the passage reflects Hesiod's own personal preference for Hekate is not very convincing.[19] The claim relies on two small details from the *Works and Days*, namely that Hesiod's brother was named after Hekate's father and that Hesiod's father was training in areas that had prominent Hekate worship (in which he presumably could have participated). There is no indication that this contact resulted in a devotion to the goddess or that this devotion was passed on to Hesiod himself. Furthermore, theophoric names do not necessarily represent personal devotion to the particular god one is named after.[20] The appeal of Hesiod, or at least his father, being a personal devotee of Hekate is that it nicely explains the anomalous nature of this passage, seemingly inserted into the *Theogony*. It is, perhaps, a rather over-stretched interpretation, given the prevalence of theophoric names in antiquity[21] and the problems with the locations of the family and other major cult sites of the goddess.

In the *Theogony*, Hekate is the second-last Titan born, and the passage praising her comes directly before Zeus's birth. Hesiod tells us that Zeus allowed her to keep the prominent position she held among the gods, despite her Titanic origin. So, both in terms of her position in the text and her position in the cosmogony, Hekate acts as an intermediary between the old Titanic gods and the new Olympic gods. This is the first hint at her role as an intermediary, an attribute that is found in other literary and cultic situations as well. The *Theogony* shows Hekate working closely with other gods – Olympic gods! – in order to bring about success for human worshippers, pointing once again to her role as an intermediary. The scenarios Hesiod provides are her 'collaborations' with Poseidon and Hermes:

> καὶ τοῖς, οἳ γλαυκὴν δυσπέμφελον ἐργάζονται,
> εὔχονται δ' Ἑκάτῃ καὶ ἐρικτύπῳ ἐννοσιγαίῳ,
> ῥηϊδίως ἄγρην κυδρὴ θεὸς ὤπασε πολλήν,
> ῥεῖα δ' ἀφείλετο φαινομένην, ἐθέλουσά γε θυμῷ.
> ἐσθλὴ δ' ἐν σταθμοῖσι σὺν Ἑρμῇ ληΐδ' ἀέξειν·
> βουκολίας δὲ βοῶν τε καὶ αἰπόλια πλατέ' αἰγῶν
> ποίμνας τ' εἰροπόκων ὀΐων, θυμῷ γ' ἐθέλουσα,
> ἐξ ὀλίγων βριάει κἀκ πολλῶν μείονα θῆκεν.

And upon those who work the bright, storm-tossed sea and pray to Hekate and the loud-sounding Earth-shaker, the illustrious goddess easily bestows a big haul of fish, and easily she takes it away once it has been seen, if she so wishes in her spirit. And she is good in the stables at increasing the live-stock together with Hermes; and the herds and droves of cattle, and the broad flocks of goats and the flocks of woolly sheep, if in her spirit she so wishes, from a few she strengthens them and from many she makes them fewer.[22]

This shows how and why Hekate has been given a share of the earth, sky, and sea, the three realms of the world that are visible to mankind.[23] She cannot personally ensure that fishermen will receive a 'great haul', she can only *assist* in ensuring success *if* she is called upon. And success can only happen if Poseidon is also predisposed to providing it, and this predisposition can be enhanced if Hekate is willing to assist the individual in question.[24] She may just as easily take away the fisherman's success, or Poseidon might reject her solicitation if he is not predisposed to offer assistance. This is repeated in her aptitude for ensuring success or failure for cattle herders, in conjunction with Hermes. She alone cannot make fishermen's hauls plentiful, nor a farmer's flock swell in size; she is merely able to favourably influence the god who directly presides over that aspect of the world – here, Poseidon for the sea and Hermes for flocks – if she sees fit to do so. Her ability to influence outcomes, but only in partnership with another god, is mirrored in her capacity to work within the realms of earth, sky, and sea without exercising direct control over any single area.

Through these partnerships, Hekate acts as an intermediary between the gods and people, to ensure the success of their ventures, but only if she is correctly invoked and is amenable. D. West describes this process as Poseidon and Hermes 'aid[ing] the goddess when she answers men's prayers concerning fishing and farming respectively',[25] but Hesiod's text shows that Hekate aids the worshipper, by putting their case to the specialist god. It is not the other god who helps Hekate, and neither is she helping the other god fulfil their function. She is assisting the person in correctly soliciting the most appropriate divinity for their task, and effectively providing a reference for their cause. Similarly, when Hekate gives men in battle νίκη ('victory') and κῦδος ('glory'), she is mediating a function of Zeus, namely the glorification of soldiers.[26]

Hesiod's exposition of Hekate also includes the first extant reference to the *kourotrophos* ('nursemaid').[27] Hesiod says that Hekate was nursemaid to all mortal children:

> θῆκε δέ μιν Κρονίδης κουροτρόφον, οἳ μετ' ἐκείνην
> ὀφθαλμοῖσιν ἴδοντο φάος πολυδερκέος Ἠοῦς.
> οὕτως ἐξ ἀρχῆς κουροτρόφος, αἳ δέ τε τιμαί.

> And the son of Kronos made her the nanny of all mortal children
> Who with their own eyes thereafter behold the light of the sunrise.
> So she was born from the start the nurse of these children and these
> are her honours.[28]

This is a function that Hekate carries with her into the classical period. Sacrifices are made to the goddess as *kourotrophos* at her sanctuary in Erchia, in Attica,[29] where there is also a sacrifice to 'Artemis-Hekate', giving a strange situation in which the owner of a sanctuary is made the epithet of another divinity. There might be a sacrifice to Hekate as *kourotrophos* in Samos, although this equally could be a dedication to Ge.[30] Hekate appears as *kourotrophos* in the 'Orphic' hymns,[31] which shows that this cultic attribute continues from Hesiod throughout the classical period.

Hekate appears in the Homeric *Hymn to Demeter* on three occasions: twice towards the beginning of the poem and once at the end. These appearances can appear intrusive in the narrative, but they help to establish Hekate's role as a goddess who has concerns relating to the transitory life-stages (such as coming of age transitions, or in this case, marriage transition), and as a goddess who can act as an intermediary between places and stages.

In the first occurrence Persephone has just been carried off by Hades, screaming, but two gods – Hekate and Helios – hear the young goddess' cries:

οὐδέ τις ἀθανάτων οὐδὲ θνητῶν ἀνθρώπων
ἤκουσεν φωνῆς, οὐδ' ἀγλαόκαρποι ἐλαῖαι,
εἰ μὴ Περσαίου θυγάτηρ ἀταλὰ φρονέουσα
ἄϊεν ἐξ ἄντρου Ἑκάτη λιπαροκρήδεμνος,
Ἡέλιός τε ἄναξ Ὑπερίονος ἀγλαὸς υἱός,
κούρης κεκλομένης πατέρα Κρονίδην:

But no one heard her voice, none of the immortals or of mortal men, nor yet the olive trees with their resplendent fruit – except that of Persaios' daughter still innocent of heart, Hekate of the glossy veil, heard from her cave, and so did the lord Helios, Hyperionos' resplendent son, was seated apart, away from the gods as the maiden called upon her father, Kronos' son.[32]

More information is added in the second appearance of both gods, which occurs after Demeter has been wandering the earth for nine days looking for her daughter:

ἀλλ' ὅτε δὴ δεκάτη οἱ ἐπήλυθε φαινολὶς Ἠώς
ἤντετό οἱ Ἑκάτη σέλας ἐν χείρεσσιν ἔχουσα,
καί ῥά οἱ ἀγγελέουσα ἔπος φάτο φώνησέν τε:
πότνια Δημήτηρ ὡρηφόρε ἀγλαόδωρε
τίς θεῶν οὐρανίων ἠὲ θνητῶν ἀνθρώπων
ἥρπασε Περσεφόνην καὶ σὸν φίλον ἤκαχε θυμόν;
φωνῆς γὰρ ἤκουσ', ἀτὰρ οὐκ ἴδον ὀφθαλμοῖσιν
ὅς τις ἔην: σοὶ δ' ὦκα λέγω νημερτέα πάντα.
ὣς ἄρ' ἔφη Ἑκάτη: τὴν δ' οὐκ ἠμείβετο μύθῳ
Ῥείης ἠϋκόμου θυγάτηρ, ἀλλ' ὦκα σὺν αὐτῇ
ἤϊξ' αἰθομένας δαΐδας μετὰ χερσὶν ἔχουσα.

But when the tenth bright dawn came upon her, Hekate met her with a light in her hand, and spoke to give her news:

Lady Demeter, bringer of resplendent gifts in season, who of the heavenly gods or of mortal men had seized Persephone and grieved your dear heart? I heard her voice, but I did not see who it was. I am telling you promptly of the whole truth of it.

So spoke Hekate; but lovely haired Rhea's daughter said nothing in answer, but quickly ran to her, with burning torches in her hands.[33]

Hekate tells Demeter that she heard Persephone crying out, but that she did not see what had happened. She swiftly darted away (ἀίσσω), with her torches held high. N.J. Richardson suggests that σέλας ἐν χείρεσσιν ἔχουσα ('holding a torch in her hands')[34] implies that there were two torches, in line with later visual representations of the goddess holding a torch in each hand.[35] The passage does not give new information to either the reader or to Demeter, but it does highlight Hekate's role in Persephone's abduction and eventual return. There are two features in these passages that could hint at a 'chthonic' attribute for Hekate. The first is that she was dwelling in a cave when she heard Persephone's cry for help. Caves were often seen as entrances to the Underworld, and some would have been nekyomanteia – oracles of the dead.[36] Caves represent an unknown quantity for people: they can be difficult to enter and traverse, they can be dark and disorienting, and they are particularly well suited as the locations of transitory passages or rites-of-passage.[37] Entering a cave means crossing a threshold, and this can be imagined as a border between the earth and the Underworld. As the *Hymn* depicts Persephone undergoing the most common rite-of-passage for girls, that is marriage, Hekate's cave-dwelling is appropriate both for Persephone's transition and for Hekate's (upcoming) role within it. Hekate will be instrumental in Persephone's rescue, not in entering the 'cave' of the Underworld, but rather in the young maiden's successful navigation through that 'cave'. In this way, Hekate acts as a kind of 'Persephone-*pompe*', a personal guide for the young goddess.[38] Guiding, as we shall see particularly below, is one of Hekate's more prominent cultic aspects. The second indication of a possible 'chthonic' nature is Helios's part in the hymn and the comparison created by the adjacency of the cave-dwelling Hekate and the sun god. Helios is the only one to actually witness Persephone's abduction, Hekate – as she reports – only hears it. While Hekate seeks Demeter out to tell her what has happened, Helios only offers up his information when directly questioned. Helios, the god who lives in the sky and shines down on the earth, never penetrates the Underworld, He is the antithesis of 'chthonic', and this creates a contrast to Hekate and makes it appear like Hekate is one of the gods associated with the Underworld within the *Hymn*. And, she is certainly aligned to Underworld gods, shown both by the assistance she offers to Demeter and will later offer to Persephone. This contrasts with the way that Helios handles the knowledge that he has gained. Where Hekate, aligned with Demeter and Persephone, seeks to reveal the truth, Helios, aligned with Zeus (and his patriarchal rule), has no need to disclose his own information until asked. David West suggests that the poet specifically included these two divinities to highlight the juxtaposition they create between the mortal world – that is, Helios in the upper sky, and Hekate in the lower world (either the Underworld, or simply in her cave), frame the 'mortalness' of the field Persephone was picking flowers in when she was snatched away.[39]

These two things do not conclusively show that Hekate fulfils a function related to the Underworld in the hymn. Although she dwells in a cave, she does not traverse the path into the Underworld, and there is no indication that her cave is a route into the Underworld. It is Hermes who makes the journey to Hades to retrieve Persephone. Hekate's cave-dwelling shows that she inhabits a liminal space, but this is the metaphorical liminality of being between statuses (for instance, between a girl and a wife), rather than the (meta)physical liminality of being between spaces (that is the earth and the Underworld).[40] Along with this there is no true juxtaposition created between Hekate and Helios, nor between the Underworld and the sky, even though this episode places the two gods together. Hekate's presence, and her presence at Demeter's meeting with Helios, presupposes her role as Persephone's attendant after her recovery from the Underworld, and links to her aspects as a goddess who deals in liminal spaces and transitions. Helios's role presupposes that, being in the sky, he would be well placed to witness the abduction, I do not think that Hesiod selects him specifically for comparison.

Hekate's third appearance in the *Hymn* occurs after Persephone has returned from the Underworld:

τῆσιν δ' ἐγγύθεν ἦλθ' Ἑκάτη λιπαροκρήδεμνος,
πολλὰ δ' ἄρ' ἀμφαγάπησε κόρην Δημήτερος ἁγνῆς·
ἐκ τοῦ οἱ πρόπολος καὶ ὀπάων ἔπλετ' ἄνασσα.

Hekate, she of the glittering veil joined them,
Frequently embraced the daughter of holy Demeter.
Henceforth that lady became her handmaiden and servant.[41]

Here she becomes Persephone's 'preceder' (πρόπολος) and 'follower' (ὀπάων). Both these terms could, taken literally, simply show that she became Persephone's attendant, but their combined use creates a somewhat contradictory picture. This contradiction is unimportant given Hekate's position in Persephone's retinue: she is now guiding and guarding the young goddess as thoroughly as possible – 'from behind' and 'in front' – and so providing all-around protection for the young bride. It may be that this is where Hekate's 'psychopompic' function in the Persephone story originates: when the time comes each year, she guides Persephone down into the Underworld, and when Persephone's time below is complete, she is able to ensure she travels back to earth safely. That is, she leads the young goddess into the Underworld and follows her home from the Underworld, so that she is always with the young goddess during her transitory phase. Both πρόπολος and ὀπάων denote action, indicating a physical journey on which Hekate accompanies the young maiden, in this case her journey home from the Underworld. In a later version of this narrative, told by Kallimachos, Hekate's role in Persephone's *katabasis* is much larger, explicitly stating that she accompanies Persephone into the Underworld.[42] And so Hekate assists Persephone, as she assisted Demeter in the upper world.[43]

Hekate was not worshipped at Eleusis, in any guise,[44] and her only association with the narrative is through the Homeric *Hymn to Demeter*.[45] There are no inscriptions bearing her name and no clearly identifiable temple. Kevin Clinton refutes some of the evidence which is presented in support of Hekate worship at Eleusis, namely that the temple of Artemis Propylaia originally belonged to Hekate.[46] There are two main arguments for this association, namely that Hekate's temple in Athens was probably located at the Propylaia of the Acropolis, and that Hekate's function in the *Hymn* is appropriately rendered in cult by the epithet 'Propylaia'.[47] Neither of these, especially without supplementary inscriptional or archaeological evidence, can satisfactorily explain an original identification of the temple of Artemis Propylaia in Eleusis with Hekate, nor can the later association between Hekate and Artemis. The greatest evidence for Hekate worship at Eleusis is the so-called 'running maiden' pediment statue which was identified as Hekate by C. M. Edwards in 1986.[48] This small statue was originally thought to depict Persephone's rape, in which the 'fleeing maiden' either represented Persephone or one of her attendants, one of the Okeanids, running from Hades. Identification as Hekate was based on the iconographic attributes of the goddess elsewhere, including the well-known namesake bell krater by the Persephone painter depicting the young goddess's return from the Underworld.[49] The image shows Persephone, dressed as a young bride, emerging from a rocky outcrop. Hermes stands beside her, with his wand – associated with his role as *psychopompos* – pointing downwards. Hekate dominates the centre of the image, looking back over her shoulder towards the young goddess, appearing to light the way and carrying a torch in each hand. Demeter stands to the right of the image, awaiting her daughter's return. Edwards argues that the statue represents Hekate leading Persephone up from the Underworld, citing its similarity to the image on this vase.[50] There is no other indication that Hekate was worshipped at Eleusis, but her role in the Homeric *Hymn to Demeter*, which presents something of an aetiology (albeit a reversed aetiology), demonstrates that she does have some importance in the mythic narrative of Persephone's rape and abduction. The wholesale lack of convincing evidence, including any inscription and very limited (and shaky) archaeological evidence, strongly suggests that Hekate was not a feature of the Eleusinian Mysteries, nor any other worship centred in Eleusis.

Hekate was worshipped in the Greek world, although there is not a great amount of evidence for cults dedicated to her. Pausanias mentions several cults of Hekate, and there is some scarce archaeological material. None of these cults point to any aspectually Underworld or death-related form of Hekate. This appears to agree with the early literary evidence of the goddess as not related to the Underworld in any meaningful way. The oldest known statue of Hekate comes from Athens and dates to the sixth century.[51] It is a 20-centimetre tall terracotta votive statuette, depicting the goddess crowned and enthroned. She is identified by an inscription: ΑΙΓΟΝ ΑΝΑΘΕΚΕΝ ΘΕΚΑΤΕΙ ('Aigon dedicates [this] to Hekate'). This small statuette does not tell us much about the goddess's cult, but it does show that people were actively dedicating items to Hekate in Athens at the time. In Athens she was most probably worshipped at the Propylaia, the gateway to the Acropolis, and perhaps near to the temple of the wingless Nike, under the guise of ἐπιπυργιδία.[52] This epithet is formed from an elision of ἐπί and πύργος, meaning 'on the tower'. This is, reportedly, where Alkamenes' infamous triple headed statue was placed, the first to depict the goddess in the triple form, dating from around 430 BCE,[53] although all of our information about the statue comes from Pausanias.[54]

There is limited literary evidence for widespread Athenian worship of Hekate. In perhaps the most famous example of this, Aristophanes, in the 422 BCE production of *Wasps*, has a character, Philokleon, proclaims:

> ὅρα τὸ χρῆμα, τὰ λόγι' ὡς περαίνεται.
> ἠκηκόη γὰρ ὡς Ἀθηναῖοί ποτε
> δικάσοιεν ἐπὶ ταῖς οἰκίαισι τὰς δίκας,
> κἂν τοῖς προθύροις ἐνοικοδομήσοι πᾶς ἀνὴρ
> αὑτῷ δικαστηρίδιον μικρὸν πάνυ,
> ὥσπερ Ἑκάταιον, πανταχοῦ πρὸ τῶν θυρῶν.

> Lo and behold, the prophecies come true. I'd heard that some day the Athenians would judge cases in their very houses, and that every man would build himself and itty bitty law court in his yard; they'd be on doorsteps everywhere, like shrines of Hekate.[55]

It is likely that Alkamenes's three-headed Hekate statue preceded the production, as the Propylaia was finished around a dedicated before the production of the play.[56] This passage appears to say that there was a prevalent habit in Athens of setting up small shrines dedicated to Hekate in front of private houses.[57] Robert von Rudloff suggests that these functioned like Herms,[58] and connected with a 'well-established' aspect of Athenian Hekate as a protector of entranceways, as evidenced by her probable place at the Propylaia.[59] Alkamenes's three-headed Hekate might have preceded this, as the Propylaia was finished around a decade before the production of the play.[60] But Philokleon says that 'some day' (ποτέ) the Athenians would set up such shrines, and that they would be 'similar to' or 'like' (ὥσπερ) the Hekataion, not that they would be little shrines of Hekate or, more importantly, that this was already a widespread practice in Aristophanes's time. There is little evidence for any such statues or shrines prior to the fourth century BCE,[61] and they are certainly not sufficiently widespread to suggest one at each house, or even at the majority of houses. There is only one other literary indication of this, from a fragment of Aischylos that says δέσποιν' Ἑκάτη, τῶν βασιλείων πρόδομος μελάθρων ('Lady Hekate, you who dwell in front of the royal palace').[62] Alan

Sommerstein comments that 'shrines of Hecate were frequently placed outside house doors'[63] implying that this practice has become commonly accepted in Athens, although – as above – there is no evidence for this. What the fragment does show, however, is that there was a commonly accepted idea that Hekate was a goddess who protected entranceways, in some capacity, as early as Aischylos's time, and that this function was important enough to be considered appropriate even for a royal house. This, in part, authenticates the cult of Hekate at the Propylaia of the Acropolis, and cements her established cultic role as a goddess of physical thresholds, such as the entranceway.

There is a sacred precinct of Hekate in Selinus,[64] on Sicily, which is located next to the propylaia of the main sanctuary of Demeter Malophoros.[65] The original site probably dates to the second half of the seventh century BCE, and it was certainly in use by the sixth century. There is no corroborating literary evidence, or descriptions any specific ritual activity, and identification with Hekate is not definite, only probable. The placement of the site, along with the association with the entranceway guardianship, is suggestive of the placement of the Eleusinian temple dedicated to Artemis, which von Rudloff and others have identified as originally being a temple of Hekate.[66]

Pausanias mentions two Corinthian cults in which Hekate was worshiped in some capacity. The first of these is in a small town called Titane where, he says, Helios's brother Titan first lived.[67] In the portico of the temple of Asklepios there was a statue of Hekate, along with statues of Dionysos, Aphrodite, the 'Mother of the Gods', and Tyche ('Good Fortune'). Furthermore, there is an altar of Hekate in the precinct of Apollo Delphinios[68] on Miletus, with a dedication by the three prytaneis, that dates to the sixth century, which is the earliest inscriptional evidence for Hekate worship in the Greek world.[69] However, Constantine Yavis thinks the altar itself may be older than this.[70] The inscription reads:

......
ΕΟΘΡΑΣ...
.ΛΕΩΔΑΜΑΣ
ΟΝΑΞΟ ΠΡΥΤ[Α]
ΝΕΥΟΝΤΕΣ Α-
ΝΕΘΕΣΑΝ ΤΗ-
ΚΑΤΕΙ

the prytaneis Eothras, Leodamas, and Onaxo, as promised, dedicate [this] to Hekate.[71]

In Argos there was a temple of Hekate, located next to the temple of Eileithyia, the goddess of childbirth. This is the only temple of Hekate which we know with reasonable certainty existed in antiquity.[72] According to Pausanias, there were two cult statues here, one made of bronze and the other of stone.[73] We do not know the temple of Hekate or Eileithyia came into use first,[74] and so cannot say whether this was an association made from Hekate to Eileithyia or the other way around. Either way, connection to Eileithyia presupposes Hekate in her function as *kourotrophos*. While there is no evidence that this aspect is represented here, it is the most probable of Hekate's known cult functions. Pausanias tells us that the temple of Eileithyia was dedicated by Helen of Sparta on the occasion of the birth of her daughter, Iphigeneia,[75] who was subsequently adopted by her sister Klytaimestra. And, Hekate has a connection to Iphigeneia through the goddess Artemis. We know very little about the Hekate cult in Argos, beyond the connection with Eileithyia and the (assumed) role as *kourotrophos* which this connection implies.

There might also be a cultic link between the goddess and Aigina, of which Pausanias says:

θεῶν δὲ Αἰγινῆται τιμῶσιν Ἑκάτην μάλιστα καὶ τελετὴν ἄγουσιν ἀνὰ πᾶν ἔτος Ἑκάτης, Ὀρφέα σφίσι τὸν Θρᾷκα καταστήσασθαι τὴν τελετὴν λέγοντες. τοῦ περιβόλου δὲ ἐντὸς ναός ἐστι, ξόανον δὲ ἔργον Μύρωνος, ὁμοίως ἓν πρόσωπόν τε καὶ τὸ λοιπὸν σῶμα.

The goddess the Aiginetans particularly honour is Hekate; they celebrate her mystery every year, saying Orpheus of Thrace established it. Inside the enclosure is a shrine with a wooden idol by Myron: it has only one face and the rest of the body in keeping.[76]

There is no pre-Roman archaeological evidence for a temple of Hekate on the island, and so we cannot be sure if there was earlier cult activity here. By the end of the fifth century BCE, the local goddess, Aphaia, had been absorbed into the functions of Artemis and Athena,[77] and there is no trace of connection to Hekate.

There is some evidence for cultic worship of Hekate in Thrace as early as the sixth century BCE. There is, for example, a fragment of a Pindaric hymn to the city of Abdera which says:

ἐν δὲ μηνὸς
πρῶτον τύχεν ἆμαρ·
ἄγγελλε δὲ φοινικόπεζα λόγον παρθένος
εὐμενὴς Ἑκάτα
τὸν ἐθέλοντα γενέσθαι.

That day fell
on the first of the month,
and Hekate, the maiden with ruddy feet,
was graciously announcing her prophecy
eager for fulfilment.[78]

Theodor Kraus takes this as evidence for cult of the goddess here,[79] as this is the only time Pindar mentions Hekate in his extant works. Therefore, it must indicate that she was an important goddess for the city, since she clearly was not important in Pindar's own religious leanings. In the hymn she predicts a decisive victory for the city at Mount Melamphyllon. As she does not have a strong oracular function elsewhere, this give further evidence to the importance that Hekate plays for Abdera.

The two places which we might expect to find some kind of Hekate cult are in Hesiod's homeland of Boiotia, and Thessaly, which is often associated with her origin. Neither have any identifiable cult presence for the goddess. R. von Rudloff suggests that it might be the connection to ancient portrayals of Thessalian witches,[80] including Medea, which spurs on the connection to Thessaly, rather than any more meaningful link.[81] What early cult activity does show is that there is no confirmable connection to Underworld-related or aspectually 'chthonic'cults of any kind.

Hekate is not only associated with metaphysical liminal space but also, or in fact primarily, with the much more mundane liminal spaces of the world – crossroads, thresholds, doorways, and the like[82] – spaces that represent a 'break' in the organised mortal world.[83] We have already seen this in the Hekate situated on the Propylaia to the Acropolis. The epithet Ἐνοδία ('of the road') is applied to her regularly in both cult and in literature. Although it may be used to describe other divinities, in Hekate's case it can also be used as a substantive name.[84] Specifically of Hekate, it describes the meeting of three roads. Similarly, she is also described with the adjective τριοδῖτις, which relates to dwelling at crossroads, along with other epithets that demonstrate an affinity for guiding over and through liminal points such as προπυλαία, λιμενοσκόπος, πρόδομος, and προθυραία.[85]

Worshipping a divinity in a liminal space comes about through many different concerns. It may be that there is a desire to establish territorial limits, and to seek protection for boundaries, the internal contents or space, liminal points, or the endings and beginnings of such boundaries. It may be symbolic of a transitory period, such as a rite-of-passage, like Persephone's initial travel into the Underworld when she became Hades's wife. Similarly, it might be an ongoing transition, such as Persephone's annual travel into the Underworld to take up residence with her part-time husband.[86] Another concern faced by the mortal in worshipping liminal divinities regards location of 'liminal space' itself, as space which is necessarily separated from its physical surroundings. The physical liminal space – the gateway or doorway, the threshold, crossroad, or frontier – is, by definition, not physically a part of either of the side of it. On this, Sarah Iles Johnston says:

> a threshold is neither inside nor outside of the house, a frontier belongs to neither country, the crossroads are the junction of roads A, B, and C but belong to none of them; liminal places, especially crossroads, offer varied options but not reassuring certainties.[87]

This point, that the liminal does not belong to either of the states that surround it may remind us that Hekate too, according to Hesiod, does not belong to any one sphere of influence, but her honours extend through the earth, the sky, and the waters. She can initiate change throughout the entire world. Theoretically, it would also be possible for Hekate to initiate change on the periphery of any sphere, or on the borders between two or more spheres, and this is where we find the goddess acting at crossroads, and the purpose behind the so-called 'Hekate's dinners'. With the amalgam of Hekate's aspect as a goddess of thresholds and as a goddess who can influence all three earthly spheres it is not only plausible but probable that she would have been seen to have the ability to influence these borderlands. The cave, her mythical dwelling in the Homeric *Hymn to Demeter*, is itself a transitory space between the worlds of the dead and the living. One of the most significant ways in which Hekate is worshiped involves crossroads as a physical manifestation of liminal space, where she is offered 'suppers'.[88]

Although there is a brief connection made between Hekate and the Underworld in the Homeric *Hymn to Demeter*, and particularly in the goddess' cave-dwelling, there is no supplementary evidence for a 'chthonic' aspect or a more meaningful association with the Underworld in cult or literature of the archaic and classical periods. Her strong role as a mediator is reinforced by her position between the Titanic and Olympic gods, and between the gods and people in Hesiod's *Theogony*. Hekate also had a strong association with both physical and metaphysical liminal spaces and thresholds. This may be rendered as the ability to manipulate the workings of the gods on the borders of the three earthly realms.

Hekate's cult presence is small in the archaic and classical periods, and there is very little archaeological evidence for her worship, particularly in any kind of 'chthonic' or Underworld-related contexts. There is no evidence for Hekate worship at Eleusis, even with the evidence of the 'running maiden'. Therefore, Hekate should not be considered an Underworld goddess in the archaic and classical periods, and this is true both in the literature and in her cultic presence.

Notes

1 Warr, 1895: 392.
2 Kerényi, 1974: 36.
3 See Rabinowitz, 1997: 534 n. 32.
4 Graf, 1997: 257–259.
5 Clay, 1989: 27–28.
6 Burkert, 1985: 171; Graf, 1997: 257–259; Johnston, 1994: 21; Kraus, 1960: 55–56; Marquardt, 1981: 250; M. L. West, 1966: 277, contra Farnell, 1896: 505–507. Farnell places her origin in Thrace.
7 Berg, 1974: 130, 34; Miles, 1998b.
8 M. L. West, 1966: 277.
9 Hes. Th. 411–452. For a brief introduction to the previous scholarship on this section see Boedeker, 1983: 79–80.
10 Arthur, 1982: 70; Boedeker, 1983: 89–90.
11 Although the passage is not formally a hymn, it does contain several 'hymnic elements: superlatives, repetitions, a description of the god's τιμή, etc.'. Stoddard, 2004: 7, cf. Griffith, 1983: 52. However, Warr (1895: 390) comments that 'it has too little

consistency to merit the title of a "hymn", which is sometimes bestowed on it. Indeed, it can only be described as an incoherent medley', and 'a strange kind of "contamination"'.

12 Hesiod considers sacrifice to be a regular ritual that includes twice daily libations, and larger offerings wherever possible. This section does not seem to indicate that Hekate requires separate or special offerings from this. On the point that mortals always invoke Hekate, West (1966: 282–283) comments: 'invocations of Hecate were probably not common west of the Aegean at this period; but perhaps Hesiod did not mean "everyone nowadays is invoking Hecate", but rather (paratactically) "a man invokes Hecate and she hears him", i.e. if he invokes her, she hears him'.

13 This suggests a non-Olympian genealogy, as this claim frames the explanation of her retained powers, see Marquardt, 1981: 245.

14 See, for example, Jacoby, 1930: 162–164; Kirk, 1962: 62, 80; Nilsson, 1935: 722; Sellschopp, 1934: 52 n. 83; Warr, 1895: 390–393; Von Wilamowitz-Moellendorff, 1932: 169–172.

15 Warr, 1895: 9, 391. He also argues that the second half of the passage – lines 429–449 – are a later interpolation. This is based on the inclusion of 'stock phrases' which he feels are 'cumbersome' and 'a bad imitation of the Homeric ... it is altogether distinct from the picturesque Hesiodic conceits ... '.

16 M. L. West, 1966: 276–277.

17 M. L. West, 1966: 278, cf. Stoddard, 2004: 8; von Rudloff, 1999; Wachter, 2006: 12.

18 Stein, 1990: 23–24.

19 Cf. Boedeker, 1983: 81. She says: 'arguments explaining Hekate's special status in the poem in terms of Hesiod's belief or family history should be advanced with great caution'.

20 There are two situations in which one might argue that theophoric names do represent personal devotion, both described by R. Parker, and these are when a particular god or goddess assists in the birth of a child (most likely Asklepios, but perhaps Eileithyia), or when an oracular god predicts the safe conception and birth of a child:

> A vivid concrete example can, for once, be quoted. According to a verse inscription of the third century set up at Delphi, Apollo 'heard the prayer' of an anonymous couple and 'granted them an offspring in response' (γενεὰμ μαντεύμασι δῶκεν), requiring a hair-offering in return'; in the eleventh month, after a trouble free pregnancy, the wife gave birth with ease, helped by Lochia, the Fates, and Phoibos, to a thriving (γόνιμος) daughter (with hair already reaching her eyes, and destined to reach her chest in the first year). The parents named the girl Delphois, 'because of the prophecy and in commemoration of Delphi' (μαντείας ἕνεκεμ μνημεῖά τε Δελφῶν).
>
> (Parker, 2000: 63)

There is also the tradition of theophoric names being used as family names, in which each family member is given a different 'version' of the same theophoric name (i.e. the same stem name, with a different suffix). See Loewe, 1936: 16; Parker, 2000: 60–61. However, this is clearly not occurring in the case of Hesiod's brother's theophoric name.

21 Interestingly, the influence of Underworld gods is not generally found in theophoric names, including Persephone, Kore, Hades, Plouton, and lesser divinities like the Erinyes and Eumenides. As such, Parker (2000: 55) concludes: 'it seems to follow that Hekate cannot have had her grimmest aspect in those regions where Hekat- names are common'.

22 Hes. *Th.* 440–447, trans. Most.

23 It is perhaps gilding the lily slightly but I want to point out that the shares she is given are in areas of the *visible* world, decidedly not any part of the world that is

invisible to mankind – that is, she has no share of the Underworld, and likely has no power to influence the Underworld gods in the same way she can supplicate to other gods on behalf of a worshipper (as discussed below).

24 Cf. Marquardt, 1981: 248–249.
25 D. R. West, 1995: 195.
26 Cf. Clay, 1989: 33, 35.
27 Hadzisteliou Price, 1999: 8, 111.
28 Hes. *Th.* 450–452.
29 Toynbee, 1929: 123.
30 Toynbee, 1929: 152.
31 Orph. *Hymn.* 1.8, 12.8.
32 h.Hom. *Dem.* 23–27, trans. West. (with amendments).
33 h.Hom. *Dem.* 51–61, trans. West.
34 h.Hom. *Dem.* 52.
35 Richardson, 1974: 169. For examples of visual representations of the goddess holding a torch in each hand see *LIMC* s.v. Hekate 20, 21, 22, 32, 46, 47, 48, 51, 65, 69, 74.
36 For example, the necromantic rite often involves an imagined *katabasis* into a cave. See Tsagarakis, 2000: 275. For further discussion on nekyomanteia see Chapter 1.
37 Ustinova, 2009: 32.
38 Hermes also plays a significant role in the repatriation of Persephone, and this is discussed in Chapter 6.
39 D. R. West, 1995: 191.
40 Cf. Richardson, 1974: 156. Richardson comments that cave-dwelling and juxtaposition to Helios does not make Hekate a moon-goddess, but he does say that 'her cave and torches may both be due to her "chthonic" associations'. As I have previously mentioned, the torch is associated with other divinities, including Demeter, without having 'chthonic' association, so there is no need to suppose that they do here.
41 h.Hom. *Dem.* 439–441.
42 Kall. *fr.* 466 (Kern). There are several iconographic examples showing Hekate leading Persephone up from the Underworld, for example, an Attic red-figure bell krater, attributed to the Persephone painter from c. 440, Metropolitan Museum of Art, Fletcher Fund 28.57.23; see Foley, 1994: fig. 4, cf. Richardson, 1974: 294–295.
43 Zografou, 2010: 69, cf. Foley, 1994: 131.
44 Clinton, 1979: 45; 1992: 33, 116; Clinton, 1979: 90.
45 This appears an obvious fact to me, as to the anonymous commenter who wrote 'Hecate *cannot* be associated with Eleusis and the mysteries,' in the Joint Library of the Hellenic and Roman Societies' copy of, Clinton 1992: 116 (seen originally 20 March, 2015, sadly now erased), and indeed to Clinton himself, who writes 'the *Hymn* announces that Hekate will be the minister and companion of Persephone (line 434). This is usually interpreted to mean that Hekate played an important role in the cult. Our records, however, contradict this idea. Although we have fairly full documentation with respect to names of deities worshipped at Eleusis and fairly full documentation with respect to titles of priests and priestesses and the deities they served, nowhere over a span of ca. 1,000 years does the name Hekate appear at Eleusis', see Clinton, 1979: 45.
46 Clinton, 1979: 116, cf. von Rudloff, 1999: 37–38. Von Rudloff believes that this temple does indicate Hekate worship at Eleusis.
47 Scholars who have argued this include Edwards, 1986: 316; Kraus, 1960: 63; Richardson, 1974: 295; Von Wilamowitz-Moellendorff, 1932: 167.
48 Edwards, 1986. See plate 19, fig. 4 for artist's reconstruction of the statue. Cf. *LIMC* s.v. Hekate 16.
49 Edwards, 1986: 308, see plate 21, fig. 9 for images of the bell krater.
50 Edwards, 1986: 308.
51 Berlin Antiquarium TC7729.

52 This is related by Pausanias (2.30.2), who says that the Athenians called this image of the goddess Epipyrgidia – 'on the tower'. Cf. Zografou, 2010: 102, 64.

53 Kraus, 1960: 84.

54 Examples of the triple-headed Hekate can be found at *LIMC* s.v. Hekate 115–142.

55 Aristoph. *Wasps*. 799–804, trans. Henderson.

56 Harrison, 1965: 96.

57 Cf. Kraus, 1960: 105.

58 On the similarity of *hekataia* to herms see Johnston, 1994: 220.

59 von Rudloff, 1999: 93.

60 Harrison, 1965: 96.

61 Harrison, 1965: 96.

62 Aisch. fr. 388 (Sommerstein).

63 Sommerstein, 2008: 327.

64 Yavis, 1949: 77; Zuntz, 1971: 98.

65 On the sanctuary of Demeter Malophoros, including dates, see Miles 1998a; Yavis, 1949: 110–115.

66 See n. 58 above, and Clinton's arguments against this categorisation.

67 Paus. 2.11.5.

68 Hekate shares no specific relationship with Asklepios, but interestingly Asklepios' mythic father, Apollo, receives numerous *Hekat*-root epithets in literature, which area also known to be applied to Artemis (e.g. Aisch. *Sup.* 676). These include, primarily, ἕκατος ('far shooting'), ἑκατηβόλος ('far darting') and ἑκηβόλος ('attaining his aim'). There is no convincing etymology for 'Hekate', and so we cannot draw any truly meaningful conclusions from this shared eponym. It may just be a coincidence that the two divinities share names with a common root and connections to Artemis. According to Hesiod's *Theogony*, Apollo's and Hekate's mothers, Leto and Aseria, were sisters, making the two gods cousins. Cf. Marquardt, 1981: 256.

69 Marquardt, 1981: 251.

70 Yavis, 1949: 137.

71 Kawerau and Rehm, 1914: no. 129. Cf. Kraus, 1960: 11, who relates that this alter was in use well into the first century, being rededicated by Pausanias, Son of Metrodor around 78/77.

72 Tomlinson, 1972: 214.

73 Paus. 2.22.7.

74 von Rudloff, 1999: 40.

75 Paus. 2.22.7.

76 Paus. 2.30.2.

77 von Rudloff, 1999: 40.

78 Pind. *Pae.* 2. 75–79. trans. W. H. Race.

79 Kraus, 1960: 65.

80 For example, Aristoph. *Clouds* 749; Plut. *Mor.* 400b, 416f; Plato *Gorgias* 513a; Horace *Epodes* 5.46; Lucan *BC.*6.438; Propertius 1.19; Polyainos 8.43. The first extant connection between Medea and Thessalian witches occurs in Euripides's *Medea* of 431 BCE, although this does not provide a clear enough connection to say that there was certainly a link between Hekate and witches at this time.

81 von Rudloff, 1999: 45.

82 Johnston, 1990: 23.

83 Johnston, 1994: 218 1991: 217–218.

84 Johnston, 1994: 24.

85 Johnston, 1991: 218.

86 For further discussion on this see Chapters 2 and 3.

87 Johnston, 1994: 25.

88 Johnston, 1994: 217.

Appendix 1: Underworld gods on curse tablets[1]

Divinities are included in this list where they are also included in the analysis presented in this book. In some cases (such as 'The holy goddess') that may be speculative and based on an understanding established norms and titling of divinities.

Reference	Location	Date	Gods involved
DTA84	Greece, Attica	Classical/Hellenistic (Faraone, 1991: 27 n. 47)	Hermes
SGD107	Sicily, Selinous; Sanctuary of Demeter Malophoros at Gaggara	450 or earlier (Ferri); c. 475-450 (Jeffery, 1955; and Miller, 1973)	the holy goddess (Demeter)
DTA89	Greece, Attica	4th century (Wünsch, 1897)	Hermes the Binder, Lord Hermes
DT73	Greece, Attica	Classical/Hellenistic (Faraone, 1991: 27 n. 47)	Hermes the Binder
SGD75	Greece, Athens	Classica/Hellenistic (Faraone, 1991: 27 n. 47)	Hermes the Binder, Earth the Binder, Persephone
DTA85	Greece, Attica	Classical/Hellenistic (Faraone, 1991: 27 n. 47)	Hermes
DTA86	Greece, Attica	No later than 4th century BCE (Gager, 1992: 160)	Hermes the Binder
DTA88	Greece, Attica	3rd century (Wünsch, 1897)	Hermes the Binder
DTA98	Greece, Athens, Patissia	3rd century (Wünsch, 1897)	Earth
DTA100	Greece, Attica; a grave near Athens	360-330 BCE (Wünsch, 1897)	Hermes, Earth

(*Continued*)

Reference	Location	Date	Gods involved
DTA107	Greece, Attica	Beginning of the 4th century (Wünsch, 1897)	Hekate of the Underworld, Hermes of the Underworld
DT39	Greece, Achaia, Melos	4th century (Audollent, 1904)	Hermes the Binder
DT50	Greece, Athens	4th century (Audollent, 1904)	Hermes the Binder, Persephone
DT52	Greece, Attica, Menedhi	Later 4th century (Jordan, 1999: 119); 3rd/2nd century (Audollent, 1904)	Hermes of the Underworld
DT67	Greece, Attica	4th century (Audollent, 1904)	Hermes the Binder
DT68	Greece, Attica	4th century (Jordan in Jameson, Jordon, and Kotansky, 1993: 130)	Pherephattei (Persephone), Hermes the Binder, the unhappy dead
DT69	Greece, Attica		Earth, Hermes of the Underworld, Pherephattei (Persephone)
SGD18	Greece, Attica	4th century (Gager, 1992: 200)	Hermes ('the underworldly, the trickster, the binder, Erionios,')
SGD19	Greece, Athens	4th century (Jordan, 1985)	Gods, Hermes of the Underworld, the Trickster, the Binder
SGD20	Greece, Athens; 'House D' in industrial area of Agora	4th century (Young, 1951: 222)	Those below
SGD42	Greece, Athens, Dekeleia	First half of the 4th century (Jordan, 1985)	Hermes the Binder, Earth, Persephone
SGD44	Greece, Athens	Middle of the 4th century (Peek, 1941: 98)	Hermes, Hermes the Binder, Persephone, Hades
SGD64	Karystos, Euboia	4th century (Guarducci, 1978: 248-249)	Hermes the Binder
NGCT9	Greece, Athens, Kerameikos	Earlier than the 4th century (Jordan, 2002)	Hermes Erionios, Persephone, Lethe
NGCT24	Greece, Attica	very early 4th century (Jordan, 1985)	Hermes the Erionos, (Hermes) the Trickster
NGCT82	Italy, Calabria, Tirilolo; cemetery	4th/3rd century (Lazzarini, 1994)	Hermes
DTA79	Greece, Attica	3rd century (Wünsch, 1897)	Hermes

(*Continued*)

(Cont.)

Reference	Location	Date	Gods involved
DTA81	Greece, Attica	3rd century (Wünsch, 1897)	Hermes
DTA87	Greece, Attica	4th century (Wünsch, 1897)	Hermes the Binder
DTA93	Greece, Athens, Patissia	Classical/Hellenistic (Faraone, 1991: 28 n. 59)	Hermes of the Underworld, Hermes the Trickster, Hermes the Binder
DTA94	Greece, Athens, Patissia	3rd century (Wünsch, 1897)	Lord Binder
DTA102	Greece, Attica, Athens	4th century (Wilhelm, 1904)	Gods below, Persephone, Hermes, Hades, Daemons
DTA103	Greece, Athens, Peiraeus	3rd century (Wünsch, 1897)/ 4th century (Wilhelm,, 1904)	Hermes, Persephone
DTA104	Greece, Attica	3rd century (Wünsch, 1897)	Hekate of the Underworld
DTA105	Greece, Attica	3rd century (Wünsch, 1897)	Hekate of the Underworld, Hermes of the Underworld
DTA106	Greece, Attica	3rd century (Wünsch, 1897)	Hekate of the Underworld, Hermes of the Underworld
DTA108	Greece, Attica	3rd century (Wünsch, 1897)	Hekate of the Underworld, Erinyes
DTA109	Greece, Attica	3rd century (Wünsch, 1897)	Praxidikeai, Hermes of the Underworld
DTA120	Greece, Attica	3rd century (Wünsch, 1897)	Hermes
DT72	Greece, Attica	3rd, maybe 4th century (Gager,, 1992: 165)	Hermes the Binder, Earth, Hekate, all the gods, mother of the gods
DT85	Greece, Boiotia	3rd or 2nd century (Faraone, 1991: 13), no later than the Hellenistic period (Dickie, 2000: 576); 2nd or 3rd century CE (Gager, 1992: 87)	(Beloved) Hermes
DT86	Greece, Boiotia	No later than the Hellenistic period (Dickie, 2000: 576)	Hermes and Earth
DT92	Chersonesos, northern shores of the Black Sea; discovered in a grave	3rd century (Audollent, 1904)	Asia (Fate)

(*Continued*)

(Cont.)

Reference	Location	Date	Gods involved
SGD150	Kyrenaika	3rd century (Gallavotti, 1963)	Praxidike
NGCT79	Sicily, Lilybaion; grave	Late 3rd century (Jordan, 1997)	Persephone, (in the presence of the priest-ess of Demeter)

Hermes

Hermes	#	References
Hermes	12	*DTA* 79, 81, 84, 85, 100, 102, 103, 120; *DT* 86; *SGD* 18, 44; *NGCT* 82
Hermes of the Underworld	9	*DTA* 105, 106, 107, 109; *DT* 52, 69, 93; *SGD* 18, 19
Hermes the Trickster	4	*DTA* 93; *SGD* 18, 19; *NGCT* 24
Hermes the Binder	17	*DTA* 73, 87, 89, 93; *DT* 39, 50, 67, 68, 72; *SGD* 18, 19, 42, 44, 64, 75, 86, 88
Lord Binder	1	*DTA* 94
Erionios	3	*SGD* 18; *NGCT* 9, 24
Lord Hermes	1	*DTA* 89

Note

1 Much of this information was compiled together from Eidinow, 2007a: 352–454.

Appendix 2: Underworld-related cults of Demeter

Cults of Demeter χθόνια: an underworld provenance?

Hermione

Pausanias gives, in rapid succession, two origin stories for the cult of Demeter Chthonia in Hermione. First, he relates the 'Hermionian' version: the sanctuary was founded by siblings Klymenos and Chthonia, children of Phoroneus. He quickly moves on to the second, 'Argive' version. In this, Demeter travelled to the Argolis and was entertained by two local men. But a third man, Kolontas, did not receive the goddess into his home, and he did not pay due respects to her. His actions received the open disdain of his own daughter, Chthonia. In punishment for his transgression against her, Demeter burned Kolontas to ashes (καταπίμπρημι) in his home. The reverent Chthonia was saved by Demeter and transported to Hermione, where she established a sanctuary for the goddess. The cult of Demeter in Hermione, along with the annual summer festival, was named after one of the two mortal women named 'Chthonia'.[1] On the surface it appears as though Pausanias uses this aetiology to avoid discussing 'chthonic' aspects of the cult, which are implied by both the epithet and the (physical and religious) landscape surrounding the sanctuary. This is at odds with the supplementary evidence from the cult, and – perhaps more crucially – with Pausanias's own extended treatment of the festival and the surrounding landscape. His story cannot escape the Underworld aspects of the cult. It is noteworthy that, whichever of Pausanias's aetiologies we choose to accept, the cult is founded by a female. While there are some cases of women founding cults elsewhere,[2] in this case there is a strong connection between the founder and the form of the cult. As we shall see, the cult has a distinct Underworld quality which is embodied by the name of the founder, and perhaps feeds into the eschatological notion behind the possible mystery rites being performed here. The sanctuary of Demeter Chthonia is unquestionably the primary sanctuary of the area and it is singled out by Pausanias as being λόγου μάλιστα ἄξιον ('most worthy of mention').[3]

Pausanias is our most thorough source for the cult and festival, and in this section I will detail his discussion of the cult and, primarily, the festival. He reports that the temple façade included statues of priestesses, and that there were seats inside the temple for the elderly women involved in the unusual festival sacrifice. It is common for goddesses to have priestesses as attendants.[4] Pausanias does not record a cult statue, but he does say that the main object of devotion was unknown. It is unlikely that this is a cult statue, as he says αὐτὸ δὲ ὃ σέβουσιν, 'that thing [neuter] that they worship', which would constitute a strange way for him to refer to a statue. Pausanias remarks that the form of the 'thing' was kept secret by the elderly priestesses of the cult.[5] He spends most of his discussion on the summer-time 'Chthonia' festival. This included a procession that appears to have been open to all. It was led by priests and magistrates, who were followed by citizen men and women. Within the procession was a group of children dressed in white and wearing wreaths of woven hyacinths (or irises), which the locals called κοσμοσάνδαλον, which were inscribed with 'AI',[6] the letters of mourning and an exclamation of grief. The procession itself was followed by a group of men who led four untamed cows, bound together by ropes. One at a time, the cows were unbound and allowed to rush into the temple, where four elderly women were waiting, and they were locked inside. Whichever of the women was able to would catch the cow and slit its throat with a sickle. Each cow was, in turn, let into the temple and the elderly women would sacrifice it, with each cow required to fall onto the same side of the women as the first had done.[7]

The ritual is clearly subversive. The animals are killed by elderly women.[8] Sacrifices are performed in secret, with a sickle, inside the darkened and closed off recesses of the temple, and the animals must behave uniformly in death. Although secrecy is not unusual, sickles are not found anywhere else in connection to a sacrificial slaughter,[9] so this is clearly meant to represent a deviation from commonly accepted practices. Pausanias describes the sacrifices itself with the term κατεργάζομαι twice,[10] which usually means 'work upon' or 'cultivate'.[11] Pausanias only uses the term on three other occasions in *Descriptions of Greece*, each time discussing a particularly brutal killing,[12] and it is not used to describe sacrifice anywhere else in the extant corpus of Greek sources. This shows that the sacrifice was viewed (at least by Pausanias) as being particularly brutal, emphasising the violence inherent in the killing much more than σφάζω ('slay' or 'slaughter'), or the more standard term for sacrifices θύω ('offer sacrifices' or 'offer by burning'). Although Pausanias also refers to this sacrifice as θυσία,[13] his emphasis on the brutality of the ritual reinforces its status as transgressive in relation to other kinds of sacrifices (in his own work and elsewhere). As I discuss in chapter 1, while there is no such thing as a 'normal' ancient Greek ritual there is ritual vocabulary and grammar that are used to build actions and meanings in ritual practice. That this particular ritual is made of so many rare or otherwise unattested elements means it would have been sufficiently 'unusual' to be subversive of what an ancient audience might normally consider 'usual'.

Next, Pausanias moves from the festival to the landscape surrounding the sanctuary of Demeter Chthonia. There are some Underworld-related cult features in the landscape surrounding the sanctuary. Opposite Demeter Chthonia's sanctuary is a temple dedicated to Klymenos, whom Pausanias calls βασιλέα ὑπὸ γῆν ('king under the ground'), and he tells us that Klymenos is a ἐπίκλησις ('surname') for the Underworld King.[14] In other words, Klymenos is a proxy for Hades. This feature alone reinforces the links between Demeter Chthonia, the Underworld, and the foundation of the cult in several prominent ways. Chthonia is Klymenos's sister, as Demeter is Hades's sister. Hades is also Demeter's son-in-law, and Klymenos is described as the husband of Demeter Chthonia's daughter-figure. As Hades's bride can be alternatively called Persephone or Kore, so Klymenos's bride is also called Persephone in some sources and Kore in others. I will discuss this in more detail below.

Behind the sanctuary of Demeter Chthonia there are three χωρία ('places'), each surrounded by a stone wall. These are named after Klymenos, Plouton, and the Archerousian lake (τὸ μὲν Κλυμένου, τὸ δὲ Πλούτωνος, τὸ τρίτον δὲ αὐτῶν λίμνην 'Αχερουσίαν).[15] In Klymenos's place there is a large chasm in the earth, which is reportedly where Herakles dragged Kerberos up from the Underworld. This unprecedentedly easy access pushes the Hermionian landscape into a liminal space between the mortal world and the Underworld.

There are no fewer than seven other temples dedicated to Demeter, Demeter and Kore, or Demeter and Persephone in the urban and extra-urban landscape of the city,[16] but Pausanias's singling out of the sanctuary of Demeter Chthonia, along with the Underworldly cultic context of the surrounding area, shows that this is an important – if not the important – cult in Hermione.[17]

Aelian's short account focuses on the cult's sacrifice, and centres on the testimony of 'Aristokles':

> Τὴν Δήμητρα Ἑρμιονεῖς σέβουσι, καὶ θύουσιν αὐτῇ μεγαλοπρεπῶς τε καὶ σοβαρῶς, καὶ τὴν ἑορτὴν Χθόνια καλοῦσι. μεγίστας γοῦν ἀκούω βοῦς ὑπὸ τῆς ἱερείας τῆς Δήμητρος ἄγεσθαί τε πρὸς τὸν βωμὸν ἐκ τῆς ἀγέλης καὶ θύειν ἑαυτὰς παρέχειν. καὶ οἷς λέγω μάρτυς Ἀριστοκλῆς, ὅς πού φησι
> Δάματερ πολύκαρπε, σὺ κὴν Σικελοῖσιν ἐναργὴς
> καὶ παρ' Ἐρεχθείδαις. ἐν δέ τι τοῦτο μέγα
> κρίνετ' ἐν Ἑρμιονεῦσι· τὸν ἐξ ἀγέλης γὰρ ἀφειδῆ
> ταῦρον, ὃν οὐ<κ> αἴρουσ' ἀνέρες οὐδὲ δέκα,
> τοῦτον γραῦς στείχουσα μόνα μόνον οὔατος ἕλκει
> τόνδ' ἐπὶ βωμόν, ὃ δ' ὡς ματέρι παῖς ἕπεται.
> σὸν τόδε, Δάματερ, σὸν τὸ σθένος· ἴλαος εἴης,
> καὶ πάντως θάλλοι κλᾶρος ἐν Ἑρμιόνῃ.

The people of Hermione honour Demeter and sacrifice to her in an impressive and exciting style, and they call her festival the Chthonia. I have heard that the largest cattle allow themselves to be led by the priestess from the herd to the altar of Demeter to be sacrificed. I call as my witness to this Aristokles, who says somewhere:

Demeter, goddess of many fruits, you manifest yourself both to the people of Sicily and to the sons of Erechtheus. But among the Hermionians, *this* is judged a great thing: an old woman, all by herself, leads by the ear, from the herd to the altar, a wondrous bull that not even ten men could lift up; he follows her as a child follows its mother. Yours, Demeter, yours is the power. Be propitious to us and grant that every farm in Hermione may thrive exceedingly.[18]

The story we get from Aelian then is not at all like the subversive, violent, hidden sacrifice of Pausanias. And it is internally contradictory, pointing to a conflation of several sources.[19] Aelian tells that 'the largest cattle' are sacrificed, and that they apparently willing submit to the sacrifice. But, Aelian's mysterious source, Aristokles, tells us that a single bull is sacrificed – although he agrees on the peaceful submission of the sacrificial animal. There are some hints of Pausanias's very detailed narrative too, including notably the elderly woman (though not only one), but leading out the subversive, violent, and hidden nature of Pausanias's sacrifice. Aelian is sketchy about introducing Aristokles, providing no concrete detail about the man nor where he hears about Aristokles's testimony. It might be that Aristokles was the author of a treatise *On the Sacred Rites of Hermione* (περὶ τῶν Ἑρμιόνης ἱερῶν), quoted by a commentator of Theocritus.[20]

Demeter Chthonia is briefly mentioned in Euripides's *Herakles*, of around 416 BCE, although it provides no further context to Pausanias's account. In this episode, Herakles and his father, Amphitryon, are discussing the hero's descent into the Underworld, and the capture of the three-headed beast, Kerberos.[21] Amphitryon asks whether his son left the beast with Eurystheos and Herakles replies that χθονίας νιν ἄλσος 'Ερμιών τ' ἔχει πόλις ('the grove of the chthonian goddess and the city of Hermione have him now').[22] Both Euripides and Pausanias situate Kerberos's capture in the grove behind the temple of Demeter Chthonia in Hermione. Strabo does not connect the association between Hermione and the Underworld with Herakles's final labour, but he does say that Hermionians are never buried with coins, as they do not need to pay Charon because there is a direct link between the city and the Underworld.[23] There is little reason to think that this does not share some common heritage with Pausanias's and Euripides's accounts. Thus, Euripides's version of Kerberos's capture and the close connection between Hermione and the Underworld can serve to geographically contextualise Pausanias and Strabo's later comments.

The sixth-century BCE poet Lasos, who was from Hermione,[24] gives some further information in a fragment that is probably from a hymn written in honour of Demeter.

Δάματρα μέλπω Κόραν τε Κλυμένοι' ἄλοχον
μελιβόαν[25] ὕμνον ἀναγνέων
Αἰολίδ' ἂμ βαρύβομον ἁρμονίαν

I sing Demeter and Kore, wife of Klymenos,
Raising the honey-voiced hymn
In the deep-sounding Aeolian harmony.[26]

Athenaeus quotes the passage twice,[27] and he describes it as a portion of a hymn dedicated to Hermionian Demeter[28] that may have been performed at the Chthonia festival.[29] The Klymenos described by Pausanias fits the profile of this earlier characterisation of the hero, and Kore's husband. This forges a more meaningful link between Demeter Chthonia and Klymenos in Hermione, particularly if this hymn was written for or performed at the festival. The link between Klymenos/Hades, Demeter, and Persephone/Kore is supported both by elements of the festival and later Hellenistic and early Imperial inscriptions from the site, which are dedicated jointly to the trio.[30]

A late third- or early second-century BCE inscription[31] contains an agreement between Hermione and Asine regarding the arrival of πρεσβευταί ('ambassadors') to perform sacrifice at the Chthonia festival. This probably refers to the city of that name founded around 700 BCE on the west Messenian Gulf by refugees from the Argolid Asine.[32] The opening lines of the inscription specifically mention a cow, and this could refer to Asine providing one of the special sacrificial animals for the cult's festival.[33] By this time, the Chthonia festival had clearly become a draw for foreigners, and the inscription specifically mentions renewal of συγγένεια ('kinship') and φιλία ('friendship'),[34] and a specific provision for ambassadors to be treated with ξένια ('hospitality').[35]

There is a possibility that the Chthonia festival included some kind of programme of mystery rites. The inclusion of Mysteries in the cult may account for both the strong foreign interest (or local solicitation of such interest) in the cult and for the growth in the popularity of the Chthonia festival during the Hellenistic period.[36] The most notable evidence for this is the local Argolic version of Persephone's abduction, and its association with the cult of Demeter Chthonia. This includes pseudo-Apollodoros's claim that the Hermionians alerted Demeter to Persephone's abduction,[37] which is corroborated by Pausanias's earlier account of local Argives assisting Demeter's search for her missing daughter.[38] Pausanias's narrative of the cult's establishment, in which Kolontas is burned alive while his daughter, Chthonia, is saved, presents a kind of inversed attempted immortalisation of Demophoon in the Homeric *Hymn to Demeter.*[39] Most obviously Kolontas's fiery death, contrasted with Demophoon's nightly 'burning', illustrates Demeter's complex approach to fertility and barrenness, life and death. Furthermore, Chthonia's quasi-immortalisation in both the name of the festival and the goddess's cultic epithet echoes Demophoon's similarly quasi-immortalisation through the establishment of annual rites in his honour. The sanctuary at Hermione is topographically suitable for a re-enactment of Demeter's search for Persephone, something like the sacred drama that might have been performed during initiatory rituals at Eleusis.[40] The 'place' of Plouton might have served a function similar to the

Eleusinian Ploutonian,[41] although this was not considered to be the place where Hades had abducted Persephone[42] and was not thought of as a passage between the Underworld and the mortal world.

Further to this, and more substantially, are several fourth- and third-century BCE name-lists[43] from the area, which could represent lists of initiates. The lists contain the names of individuals, either alone or followed by a patronymic or matronymic name. These have been identified as men and women who have undergone initiation into the Mysteries of Demeter.[44] One of the lists includes the line ἔτους ἕκτου· Κλινοσώ,[45] indicating that these could be individuals who were initiated in the sixth year of service of Klinoso, the eponymous priest of Demeter. All together the lists contain around five hundred names – a fairly considerable number for Hermione alone to have provided to the cult as initiates. On the other hand we might expect to find the *ethnikon* included in the name lists if they were foreigners,[46] and this is not a feature of the extant lists.

The mystic aspect of the cult is emphasised[47] in a third-century BCE fragment written by Philikos of Korkyra,[48] which may be the beginning of a *Hymn to Demeter*.[49]

τῇ χθονίῃ μυστικὰ Δήμητρί
τὲ καὶ Φερσεφόνῃ καὶ
Κλυμένῳ τὰ δῶρα.

Both the mystic rites belonging to Demeter Chthonia
and the gifts of Persephone and Klymenos.[50]

The fragment expresses a strong connection between Demeter Chthonia, Klymenos, and the daughter-goddess (who is here Persephone, rather than Kore) providing a bridge between Lasos's earlier and Pausanias's later accounts. The inclusion of a goddess who is explicitly Persephone in a cult context is rare, and that may give weight to the hymn being a literary, rather than a cultic, version of the narrative.

While the section I have quoted above validates the Hermionian cult landscape, there is little in the remainder of the quite substantial fragment which indicates that the hymn refers to Hermione, either to the cult of Demeter Chthonia or to the cultic landscape more generally.[51] There might be a connection between the fragment's contents and Attica which is referenced along with demes Eleusis and Halious.[52] Although there might not be a conclusive link to either Attica or Hermione, the remainder of the fragment certainly suggests Eleusinian-style cult activity.[53] Corroborating the connection to the Eleusinian Mysteries – or at least to the mythic allusions to Eleusis – Iambe appears towards the end of the fragment.[54] Christopher Brown's analysis of the highly fragmentary opening section reveals that there may be references to Persephone, Hades, Demeter's search for her missing daughter, and barrenness being cast across the earth – all elements which would fit into an Eleusinian or Hermionian context. The next part of the fragment is much better preserved,[55] and directly references an episode in the narrative of

Demeter's establishment of the Eleusinian Mysteries, where she is propitiated to (apparently by other goddesses) in response to rendering the earth barren. So, while the fragment itself does not add much (confirmable) evidence to the Hermionian cult, the reference to 'Persephone and Klymenos' as a pair is significant. It illustrates the level of (mythic) acceptance of Klymenos as a Hades-substitute, particularly when coupled with the notion of the god as synonymous with the 'king under the ground'.

The Hermionian cult of Demeter Chthonia is fleshed out by Pausanias, and his account gives a sense of the relationship of the sacred landscape to the Underworld, even if he does not emphasise the connection. This is confirmed by supplementary epigraphic and literary evidence. Although there is no other evidence for the form of the festival Pausanias has clearly gone to great lengths to emphasise the transgressive nature of the festival and, in particular, its sacrifice. The brief mention of the sacrifice in Aelian confirms this. Pausanias also reports that Plouton descended into the Underworld after Kore's abduction at nearby Lerna,[56] and that there were Demetrian Mysteries performed there. He mentions a grave of unhewn stones in Hermione as which Demetrian Mysteries were performed,[57] although this ritual is not directly connected to the discussion of the Chthonia festival or cult. It does show that there were Demetrian Mystery rites performed at Hermione, and these may be connected to the cult of Demeter Chthonia by supplementary evidence of mystic rites being performed.

The procession and festival of Demeter Chthonia evoke some elements of Persephone's abduction narrative. For instance, the hyacinth garlands worn by processing children pick up Persephone's act of picking flowers – hyacinths are twice mentioned in the Homeric *Hymn to Demeter*.[58] The first is immediately before Persephone's abduction, and the hyacinth is included in a list of flowers being picked by the maiden goddess and the Okeanids. There is an established trope of girls being abducted while picking flowers,[59] and Persephone is arguably the most famous of these. So, the hyacinth-like quality of the Hermionians' κοσμοσάνδαλον evokes the flower picking scene of Persephone's abduction. The pre-abduction state of purity is represented in the simple fact that only children wore the hyacinths in the cult. Further, pseudo-Apollodoros tells us that it was the Hermionians who initially told Demeter that Plouton had snatched Persephone away, after which Demeter travelled from Hermione to Eleusis.[60] Persephone features in some of the supplementary evidence for the cult of Demeter Chthonia, particularly in her role as wife of the King of the Underworld (whether that is Hades or, in the Hermionian context, Klymenos).

Pausanias's narrative of the cult's establishment, in which Kolontas is burned alive while Chthonia is saved, presents a kind of inversion of Demeter's immortalisation of Demophoon in the Homeric *Hymn to Demeter*.[61]

Sparta

The locals of the cult of Demeter Chthonia in Sparta believed (again, according to Pausanias) that their cult had been passed on to them παραδόντος σφίσιν

'Ορφέως ('under the influence of Orpheus').[62] Pausanias says that he personally believes that the cult was based on the Hermionian cult, but he does not say any more. It may seem strange for Demeter to be given prominence in the Spartan pantheon, particularly given that the Spartiates did not have a personal relationship with the land, and were not involved in its cultivation,[63] which was chiefly left to the *perioikoi* and helots.[64] Pausanias mentions that the Spartans also had a cult dedicated to Demeter Eleusinia,[65] a temple of Kore Soteira,[66] and there were several other sanctuaries dedicated to Demeter and Kore within Lakonia.[67] There may have also been an Eleusinia-type festival with games, and a fifth-century inscription mentions several chariot racing victories by a Spartan named Damonon at the *Eleuhunia*,[68] which is probably a Spartan vocalisation of 'Eleusinia'.[69] It is most likely that the inscription refers to a local Lakonian Eleusinia, rather than the Attic festival, because of a lack of evidence for Damonon succeeding in other universal festivals.[70] Unambiguous references to Demeter and Kore as the focus of Eleusinian-style cult here do not start until the third century.[71] If the *Eleuhunia* was related to the Attic cult, then there is a precedent for local replication of inter-*polis* cults, meaning it is not implausible for the Spartan cult of Demeter Chthonia to have been copied from Hermione. Similarly, the connection to Orpheus gives the cult an Underworld precedence and could be the local instantiation of a route into (or out of) the Underworld, if it was thought that this was related to Orpheus's attempted rescue of Eurydike. For a divinity whom the local inhabitants (that is, the Spartiates) supposedly had no affinity for, it seems they have dedicated more temples, sanctuaries, and festivals than required to her and her daughter.[72] Their very existence, however, refutes this fact. It means that Spartiates did, indeed, have a connection to and need for Demeter and Persephone. Not least because they too would starve if the harvest failed.

Worship of Eleusinian Demeter has obvious agricultural connotations, and we might suppose that a single city had no need for two strong agrarian cults dedicated to the same goddess. It is therefore probable that the cult dedicated to Demeter Chthonia worshipped the goddess in an Underworld guise, especially when we take both the connection to Orpheus and the possible connection to the Hermionian cult into account. Following this, we now have evidence for two possible cults of Demeter in an Underworld guise without overarching agrarian overtones, which are only vaguely connected by location: Hermione and Sparta.

Kallatis

Another probable cult of Demeter Chthonia exists in the Doric colony of Kallatis on the Black Sea, which had been founded by the end of the sixth century BCE.[73] Epigraphic evidence here suggests that several cults, including a cult dedicated to Demeter Chthonia, were faithfully replicated from the city's metropolis, Megara.[74] Two specific inscriptions, from the fourth and first centuries BCE, mention Demeter Chthonia.[75] The earlier inscription refers to a group of private θοινάται ('banqueters') honouring the goddess.[76]

Pherai

Demeter Chthonia is referenced in one of the so-called 'Orphic' gold tablets, found in Pherai,[77] and dates from the late fourth or early third century BCE.[78] Unlike many other 'Orphic' tablets, this example does not narrate the deceased's journey into or through the Underworld, but Demeter Chthonia's presence indicates that it retains a strong eschatological nuance. The text is short in comparison to some other tablets:

πέμπε με πρὸς μυστῶ<ν> θιάσους· ἔχω ὄργια []
Δήμητρος χθονίας τέλη καὶ Μητρὸς ὀρεί[ας

Send me to the *thaisoi* of the initiates; I possess the tokens []
The rites [or offices] of Demeter Chthonia and of the Mountain Mother.[79]

While the gold tablets represent an initiatory based cult,[80] this does not indicate conflation between the so-called 'Orphic' (or 'Bakchic') cult of the god tablets more generally and the possible 'mystery' cult of Demeter Chthonia at Hermione. Indeed, this text appears to indicate that, overall, the tablets might not have been used by a homogenous group of like-thinkers or believers, but rather a wider phenomenon divorced from any kind of strict 'Orphism'.[81] This does not indicate that the tablets – particularly those whose texts diverge most significantly from the main body of texts – were made externally to one another. As Robert Parker and Maria Stamatopoulou comment, regarding the Pherai tablet, 'it belongs to the same genre as [the other tablets] even if all the words in it are different'.[82] Mystery-type elements in the cults of Demeter Chthonia, in Hermione or elsewhere, could have influenced the choice of Demeter Chthonia as the divinity invoked in this tablet, but that there is no mention of either Kore or Klymenos, along with the presence of Meter Oreia ('Mountain Mother') make the connection untenable. There is no evidence for a fixed cult of Demeter Chthonia and Meter Oreia, and therefore this tablet cannot bear relationship to such a cult.

Other 'chthonic' cults of demeter: rape, grief, and (in)fertility

Mythic traditions outside the Homeric *Hymn to Demeter* present a more complex picture of Demeter's reaction to Persephone's abduction. Pausanias offers several different accounts which share common elements. The main crossovers occur in the traditions associated with Phigalia[83] and Thelpousa. Phigalia is predominantly a cult of agrarian plenty and poverty and which I will not discuss here.

Thelpousa

Pausanias subtly links the Phigalian cult to another Arkadian cult of Demeter, in Thelpousa, by commenting that anyone who was 'learned in tradition, would understand' why Μέλαιναν ('Black') Demeter from Phigalia was originally represented as being half-horse. This also accounts for the connection made between the Phegalian cult and horses in their response from Delphi. Pausanias's report here is similar to that from Phigalia, except Demeter rebuffs Poseidon's advances by disguising herself as a mare. In response, the god transformed himself into a stallion and then raped her. Initially angry, Demeter set her anger and grief aside, following which she bathed in the river Ladon. This is why she receives two cult epithets from the locals, Erinys and Lousia: Fury and Bather.[84] The former reinforces the association between Demeter and (the) Eriny(e)s. This may hint at the ancient nature of this cult, which could extend back to early archaic or Mycenaean times.[85] There were reportedly two statues in the temple at Thelpousa, one representing each guise. Erinys was the larger of the two,[86] and stood with a torch in her right hand and a *kiste* in her left.[87] Torches are frequently associated with Demeter in various places throughout the Greek world, and used in many non-'chthonic' settings,[88] such as at Eleusis. Although the torch could indicate a nocturnal setting, it does not, in itself, indicate a 'chthonic' aspect to the cult. Similarly, the *kiste* is associated with revelation during the Eleusinian initiation rites. Thus, there is no particularly Underworld-related connotation in Pausanias' reported representation of Demeter Erinys, and many of the 'chthonic' or malefic attributes of the Erinyes are potentially interpolations of later source material, such as Aischylos' influential description of the goddesses in the *Eumenides*.

The horse only plays a significant role in the Thelpousan tradition, although its brief inclusion in the Phigalian version demonstrates a connection between the two local traditions. In Thelpousa, Demeter and Poseidon's forced union, with both in the form of horses, produces both the horse Arion and a daughter, whose name cannot be unknown by uninitiated.[89] Pausanias, following the Arkadian tradition, calls her Despoina ('the Mistress'), and comments that she was the most worshipped divinity in the region.[90] A daughter of Demeter, with a descriptive pseudonym, whose true identity is hidden to the uninitiated, is a familiar trope. Pausanias clearly differentiates Despoina and Kore (who he unequivocally equates with Persephone by way of Homeric revelation) but he does not give Despoina a divine name.[91]

There is also a sanctuary of Demeter Eleusinia in Thelpousa, located on the other side of the city but also on the river Ladon.[92] If this cult was connected in some way to the cults of Demeter Erinys and Lousia, this would show an increased likelihood of a 'chthonic' or Underworld-related function for these latter cults. The strong possibility of this connection is emphasised by the shared iconographical attributes of a typical Eleusinian Demeter and Demeter Erinys – the torch and *kiste*. Rather than being directly connected the cults probably were complementary to one another. Eleusinian Demeter has obvious agricultural and mystery-related overtimes, as association with Eleusis would occur whether there was a formal connection between the two cults or not. Meanwhile, Demeter Erinys has a clear 'chthonic' connotation, because of her connection with (the) Eriny(e)s, traditional Underworld-dweller(s), who were strongly associated with cursing in archaic literature. Any connection would also depend on the dates of the cults' establishments, with the cult of Demeter Eleusinia probably not having been established before the fourth century.[93]

Myrrhinous

Pausanias reports an altar dedicated to Demeter Anesidora ('sender up of gifts'), located in a temple in Myrrhinous, in Attica.[94] The connection between the Underworld and fecundity is explicitly suggested by the act of seed burying, which occurs, for instance, in the Homeric *Hymn to Demeter*,[95] and is suggested by the epithet 'Anesidora'. Pausanias does not detail the temple nor the cult attached to it, but mentions several other statues located there, including Zeus Ktesios, Tithrone Athena, 'first-born' Kore, and the Semnai Theai. The close connection with Kore is unsurprising and tells us little about the nature of the cult – Demeter and Kore are found together in several different contexts. That she is 'first-born' could be a reference to Demeter's second daughter, Despoina, whom she gives birth to while searching for Persephone, who is in the Underworld. This would obviously give the cult a stronger connection to any Underworld aspects, which are evoked by 'Anesidora'. The connection to Zeus Ztesios (as god of grain), and Kore, coupled with the 'upward' motion implied by gifts being sent up, means this form of Demeter should be read with a strict agrarian function.

Akragas

A sanctuary in Akragas, on Sicily, has been identified as a 'Sanctuary of Chthonian Divinities'[96] and could have included an archaic cult of Demeter and Persephone.[97] There are three small shrines here, each with an altar and 'circular constructions'.[98] One of these small shrines forms a part of a series of three structures, or intended structures, one of which may have been a peripteral temple. It appears that, within the temple dedicated to Demeter and Persephone/Kore, each of the goddesses had an individual altar.[99] Within the wider sanctuary there are two distinct altar types present,[100] and what appears to be a sacrificial pit,[101] indicating the possibility for sacrificial rituals dedicated to both Olympian and 'chthonian' divinities. H. Berve and G. Gruben suggest that the large number of altars at the sanctuary indicated that Hades and Hekate were worshipped at the site, alongside Demeter and Persephone.[102]

The general area contained four such temples, three of which are now ruins and one that was transformed into a 'Temple of the Dioskouroi' in the nineteenth century. Material finds here indicate that the sanctuary was active in the archaic period, but there is a general lack of information. Identification as a sanctuary dedicated to Demeter and Persephone/Kore is not confirmed, but there are similarities to the temple of Demeter and Persephone in Kyrene.[103]

Syracuse

Hesychios of Alexandria connected Syracusian Demeter and Persephone to the cult of Demeter Chthonia by giving the goddesses the epithet 'Hermione'.[104] This may be because of Hermionian membership in the colonisation of the Corinthian colony of Syracuse.[105]

Mytilene

The sanctuary dedicated to Demeter on Mytilene may have included some form of worship or sacrifice to the goddess in a 'chthonic' form. The sanctuary itself displays no evidence of overt Underworld related practices, but the large number of piglet remains could indicate a Thesmophoria or Thesmophoria-like festival.[106] D. Ruscillo claims that the presence of a hearth altar in the sanctuary is 'fitting for the worship of chthonic deities, such as Demeter and Persephone', and a similar altar was found in the so-called 'Sanctuary of Chthonian Divinities' in Akragas,[107] which may have been a sanctuary of Demeter and Persephone. Nonetheless, this alone does not indicate that the Mytilenean sanctuary should be considered a cult dedicated to Demeter in a chthonic guise. It appears that there are multiple altars here, possibly dedicated to Demeter and Persephone (or Kore) separately, as in Akragas or Eleusis. One of the altars has yielded almost no animal remains.[108] There is a sacrificial ash pit adjacent to the other altar and it appears that victims were burnt inside it, as almost all its contents are burned and calcined piglet remains,[109] some of which appear to have only been a few days old at sacrifice. There are some remains that indicate prenatal victims, which would show sacrifice of pregnant sows, a practice commonly categorised as 'chthonic'.[110] Further to this, the remains of entire piglet skeletons show that holocaustic sacrifice took place here.[111] While we must be wary of ascribing a 'chthonic' label based entirely on circumstantial ritual practices, a practice which often yields unreliable results, the combination of pregnant sacrifice and holocaustic sacrificial practices may indicate dedication to a 'chthonic' Demeter.

Notes

1   Though Demeter is given the epithet 'Chthonia' elsewhere, in some later literature and in several other cults. Some of these will be discussed in more detail below, but they include cults of Demeter Chthonia in Sparta (supposedly after the Hermionian cult, or Orpheus, see Paus. 3.14.5–7), in the Doric colony of Kallatis (Paus. 1.43.5–6; *IScM III* 40, 48A) and on a so-called Orphic gold tablet from Pherai (see Chapter 6 and Bernabé and Jiménez San Cristóbal, 2008: L13a; Edmonds, 2011: D5; Graf and Johnston, 2013: 28 Pherai 2; Parker and Stamatopoulou, 2004: 6).
2   Dewald, 1981: 110–112; Lyons, 1997: 164, 69–70.
3   Paus. 2.35.4.
4   Lyons, 1997: 115.
5   Paus. 2.35.8.
6   The petals of the ὑάκινθος were, reportedly, permanently inscribed with 'AI' or 'AIAI' by Apollo, in mourning for either Hyakinthos or Aias, as the flowers were said to have sprung up from the earth from the blood of the fallen hero. Our source for this narrative

is Ovid (*Meta.* 13.382–398), so Pausanias's idea about the inscribing of petals could, in fact, stem from this story rather than anything significant at Hermione.

7　A similar account of the sacrifice is given by Aelian, which will be discussed below. See initially Breglia, 1997: 56–57; Johnston, 2012: 222–2; Prauscello, 2013: 83–84.

8　On the abnormality of women performing sacrifices see Dillon, 2002: 115–116, 245–246. On elderly women indication 'a ritual in opposition to the normal rules' see Bremmer, 1987: 199.

9　Johnston, 2012: 217.

10　Paus. 2.35.7.

11　For example, Hdt 5.24; Soph. *El.* 1022; Thuc. 4.65; Xen. *Mem.* 2.5.11; Arispho. *Ec.* 247.

12　Paus. 3.15.5, 4.25.10, 8.4.10; see Detienne, 1989: 141; Johnston, 2012: 217–218.

13　Paus. 2.35.4.

14　Paus. 2.35.9–10.

15　Paus. 2.35.10.

16　Cf. Cole, 1994: 206; Prauscello, 2011: 27.

17　Cf. Perlman, 2000: 164.

18　Aelian, *On Animals* 11.4. Text, following A. Gronovius (1744) and J.G. Schneider (1784), and translation Johnston, 2012: 223.

19　Breglia, 1997: 56–57; Prauscello, 2013: 84.

20　schol. Theoc. 15.64; cf. Page et al., 1981: 31–31; Prauscello, 2013: 85.

21　Although Euripides does not mention Kerberos by name.

22　Eur. *Her.* 615. Kovaks's Loeb edition and Barlow's Aris and Philips edition both translate this as 'Demeter's grove', with reference to the Underworld being the home of Hades and Persephone (*Her.* 608, cf. 1104). See Barlow, 1996: 151; Kovaks, 1998: 336–37, cf. Bond, 1981: 219.

23　Strab. 8.6.12.

24　Prauscello, 2011: 20.

25　L. Prauscello's article shows that this could read Μελίβοια, rather than μελιβόαν, and would therefore refer to Kore as a cult epithet. Linguistically and metrically the epithet would fit and would show the cultic importance of cattle tending (through μέλω/μέλομαι) rather than honey (though μέλι). See Prauscello, 2011: 19–27.

26　Lasos. *Fr.* 702 *PMG* (Page) = Athen. 14.624 e. Cf. Johnston, 2012: 215; Prauscello, 2011: 21, 2013: 77; Privitera, 1965: 21. One might note the absence of the sigma in this section, and s-suppression (in a lipogrammatic sense) is common of Lasos, see Porter, 2007: 1–21, and particularly 11–13 on this fragment.

27　Athen. 10.455c-d; 14.642e-f.

28　Athen. 10.455 c (ὁ εἰς τὴν Δήμητρα δὲ τὴν ἐν Ἑρμιόνι ποιηθεὶς τῶι Λάσωι ὕμνος), 14.625 e (Λᾶσος ὁ Ἑρμιονεὺς ἐν τῶι εἰς τὴν <ἐν> Ἑρμιόνι Δήμητρα ὕμνωι).

29　Prauscello, 2013: 89 and n. 77.

30　*IG* IV 686–91, 727, cf. 715.

31　*IG* IV 679.

32　Perlman, 2000: 163 and n. 30; Sfameni Gasparro, 1986: 219–220; cf. Paus. 2.36.4–5; 4.34.9–12.

33　Cf. Perlman, 2000: 163 n. 31.

34　*IG* IV 679.7–8.

35　*IG* IV 679.21.

36　See Perlman, 2000: 164, cf. Breglia, 1997: 62–64; Parker and Stamatopoulou, 2004: 12; Sfameni Gasparro, 1986: 220–221.

37　[Apollod.] *Bibl.* 1.5.1.

38　Paus. 1.14.2.

39　Perlman, 2000: 165.

40 Perlman, 2000: 166. For arguments for and against the sacred drama being included in the Eleusinian Mysteries see Richardson, 1974: 20–30.
41 Mylonas, 1961: 146–149.
42 Mylonas, 1961: 148–149. This is despite the suggestion at Orphic *Hymn* 11.12.
43 *IG* IV 728, 730–735; *SEG* XI 382.
44 Boeckh *CIG* 1207, 1211; cf. Perlman, 2000: 165.
45 *IG* IV 731.11.
46 Perlman, 2000: 166.
47 Prauscello, 2011: 22.
48 Brown, 1990: 174.
49 Giuseppetti, 2012: 117.
50 *SH* 676.
51 Brown, 1990: 175–176.
52 Attica: line 58; Eleusis: 36; Halimous: 54; cf. Brown, 1990: 176.
53 Giuseppetti, 2012: 118, 21.
54 *SH* 680; the section of text leading up to and including the Iambe passage is given in Brown, 1990: 177.
55 This section of the text is given at Brown, 1990: 183.
56 Paus. 2.36.7.
57 Paus. 2.34.10.
58 h.Hom. *Dem.* 7, 427.
59 Richardson, 1974: 140–142, with a catalogue of references.
60 [Apollod.] *Bibl.* 1.5.1.
61 Perlman, 2000: 165.
62 Paus. 3.14.5.
63 Cartledge, 2002: 162; Parker, 1988: 99.
64 Parker, 1988: 99.
65 Paus. 3.2.5–7.
66 Paus. 3.13.2.
67 For example, a *megaron* of Demeter in Kainepolis (Paus. 3.26.9), a shrine of Demeter in Gythion (Paus. 3.21.8), and a shrine of Demeter in Aigilia (Paus. 4.17.1),
68 *IG* V^1 213.
69 Buck, 1955: 26; Parker, 1988: 101. For arguments against this being a cult dedicated to the indigenous Lakonian Eleuthia/Elusia (as a local variant of the childbirth goddess Eileithyia), see Parker, 1988: 101–102.
70 Parker, 1988: 101. Also see the entry in Hesychios, s.v. Ἐλευσίνια· ἀγὼν θυμελικὸς ἀγόμενος Δήμητρι παρὰ Λάκωσιν.
71 Parker supposes that the first is a dedication by Kymbadeia (*SEG* 11.677b) which is tentatively dated by Cook to the third century. See Parker, 1988: 102 n. 35.
72 Although it does not necessarily follow that the Spartiates would not have provided finance and support for religious institutions primarily of interest to the *perioikoi* and helots.
73 Avram, 1999: 9–11, 2006: 67.
74 Paus. 1.43.5–6. See Avram, 1999: 91–95, 342–344
75 *IScM* III 40 (first century) and 48A (fourth century) in Avram, 1999: 312–314, 42–46, cf. Parker and Stamatopoulou, 2004: 12; Prauscello, 2013: 79.
76 *IScM* III 40. cf. Avram, 1999: 313; Johnston, 2012: 214 n. 5.
77 The tablet is Edmonds, 2011: D5/Graf and Johnston, 2013: 28 Pherai 2/Bernabé and Jiménez San Cristóbal, 2008: L13a. It was originally published in Parker and Stamatopoulou, 2004; cf. Ferrari and Prauscello, 2007.
78 Discussion of P. H. Parsons in Parker and Stamatopoulou, 2004: 5–6.
79 Text: Parker and Stamatopoulou, 2004: 6; trans. Johnston.

80 F. Graf believes so, commenting that 'the deceased persons who were carrying the Gold Tablets had been initiated into a mystery cult' (Graf and Johnston, 2013: 140). Two of the tablets, including this one, specifically mention initiates, the other is Edmonds, 2011: B10/Graf and Johnston, 2013: 1 Hipponion/Bernabé and Jiménez San Cristóbal, 2008: L1.

81 Along with this, there is also the fact that none of the tablets so far uncovered have been Attic in origin, which 'Orpheus-initiators' are well attested as active in Attica. See Parker and Stamatopoulou, 2004: 23, 24.

82 Parker and Stamatopoulou, 2004: 25.

83 See Paus. 8.42.

84 Paus. 8.25.4.

85 This supposition is based on the presence of Erinys on three Linear B tablets, V52, Fp(1)1, and Fh390. See Bendall, 2007: 125; Boëlle, 2004: 169; Davies and Duhoux, 1988: 197; Johnston, 1999: 250; Murray, 1979: 107–08; Ventris and Chadwick, 1973: 305–307.

86 Paus. 8.25.6., cf. Jost, 1985: 63.

87 Dietrich, 1962: 129.

88 Some scholars have been quick to add a nocturnal element to cults when the image of the torch is present, for example Bookidis and Stroud, 1997: 2. In relation to the cult of Demeter and Kore on the Akrokorinthian hill in Corinth conclude that the cult probably involved nocturnal rites because of the surrounding mythic story (provided by later sources Diodorus Siculus and Plutarch).

89 Paus 8.25.5., cf. Dietrich, 1962: 130.

90 Paus. 8.37.9: ταύτην μάλιστα θεῶν σέβουσιν οἱ Ἀρκάδες τὴν Δέσποιναν ('The Arcadians worship Despoina more than any other god').

91 Paus. 8.37.10.

92 Paus. 8.25.2.

93 Bowden, 2007: 73.

94 Paus. 1.31.4.

95 h.Hom. *Dem.* 307–308.

96 Hinz 1998: 79; Holloway 1971: 81.

97 Berve and Gruben, 1963: 434; Yavis, 1949: 71.

98 Holloway, 1991: 80.

99 Yavis, 1949: 75 This occurred at other sanctuaries dedicated to the pair as well, for example, at Eleusis. See Clinton, 1974: 82.

100 Both hollow rectangular and ceremonial altars have been found at the sanctuary. See Yavis, 1949: 71–74.

101 Yavis, 1949: 131. This is the altar A11/12 in Hinz 1998: 80 There is some evidence that Greek's might have dug out sacrificial pits for Underworld divinities. Odysseus digs such a pit with his dagger to sacrifice into (Hom. *Od.* 11.25–29, 11.31; cf. 10.517–520), and there is also evidence that this was practiced in connection to Hittite Underworld gods as well, see Chapter 6 and cf. Collins, 2002: 225–228.

102 Berve and Gruben, 1963: 434.

103 White and Renyolds, 2012: 176.

104 Hesychios *s.v.* Ἑρμιόνη· καὶ ἡ Δημήτρη καὶ ἡ Κόρη ἐν Συρακούσαις.

105 Jameson et al., 1993: 69.

106 Ruscillo, 2013: 182–85.

107 Ruscillo, 2013: 185.

108 Ruscillo, 2013: 186.

109 Ruscillo, 2013: 187.

110 Bremmer, 2005.

111 Ruscillo 2013: 188.

Bibliography

Agamben, Giorgio and Monica Ferrando (2014), *The Unspeakable Girl: The Myth and Mystery of Kore*, ed. Julia Wyman, trans. Leland de la Durantaye (London: Seagull Books).

Albinus, Lars (2000), *The House of Hades: Studies in Ancient Greek Eschatology* (Aarhus: Aarhus University Press).

Aleshire, Sara B. (1994), 'Towards a Definition of "State cult" for Ancient Athens', in Robin Hägg (ed.), *Ancient Greek Cult Practice from the Epigraphical Evidence* (Stockholm: Paul Åströms Förlag), 9–16.

Alexiou, Margaret, Dimitrios Yatromanolakis and Panagiotis Roilos (2002), *The Ritual Lament in Greek Tradition* (2nd edn., Lanham: Rowman and Littlefield Publishers).

Atherton, Catherine (2002), 'Introduction', in Catherine Atherton (ed.), *Monsters and Monstrosity in Greek and Roman Culture* (Bari: Levante Editori), VII–XXXIV.

Audollent, Auguste (1904), *Defixionum Tabellae: Quotquot Innotuerunt Tam in Graecis Orientis Quam in Totius Occidentis Partibus Praeter Atticas in Corpore Inscriptionum Atticarum Editas* (Frankfurt: Minerva GmbH).

Avagianou, Aphrodite (1991), *Sacred Marriage in the Rituals of Greek Religion* (Bern: Peter Lang).

Avram, Alexandru (1999), *Inscriptions Grecques Et Latines De Scythie Mineure, III. Callatis Et Son Territorie* (Bucharest: Editura Enciclopedia).

Avram, Alexandru (2006), 'The Territories of Istros and Kallatis', in Pia Guldager Bilde and Vladimir F. Stolba (eds.), *Surveying the Greek Chora: The Black Sea Region in a Comparative Perspective* (Aarhus: Aarhus University Press), 59–80.

Barlow, Shirley A. (1996), *Euripides' Heracles with Introduction, Translation, and Commentary* (Wiltshire: Aris and Phillips).

Baudy, Gerhard (1997), 'Hermes', in Hubert Cancik and Helmuth Schneider (eds.), *Der Neue Pauly*, 5 vols. (Stuttgard: Verlag J.B. Metzler), 426–431.

Beaulieu, Marie-Claire (2008), 'The Sea as a Two-Way Passage between Life and Death in Greek Mythology', PhD (University of Texas at Austin).

Beaulieu, Marie-Claire (2016), *The Sea in the Greek Imagination* (Philadelphia: PENN/ University of Pennsylvania Press), 265.

Beaumont, Lesley A. (2012), *Childhood in Ancient Athens: Iconography and Social History* (London: Routledge).

Beazley, J. D. (1942), *Attic Red-Figure Vase Painters* (Oxford: Clarendon Press).

Becker, Andrew Sprague (1990), 'The Shield of Achilles and the Poetics of Homeric Description', *American Journal of Philology*, 111 (2), 139–153.

Beekes, Robert S. P. (1998), 'Hades and Elysion', in H. Jay Jasonoff, Craig Melchert and Lisi Oliver (eds.), *Mír Curad: Studies in Honour of Calvert Watkins* (Innsbruck: Institut für Sprachwissenschaft der Universität Innsbruck), 17–28.

Beekes, Robert SP (2010), *Etymological Dictionary of Greek*, 2 vols. (Leiden: Brill).

Bendall, Lisa Maria (2007), *Economics of Religion in the Mycenaean World: Resources Dedicated to Religion in the Mycenaean Palace Economy* (Oxford: Oxford University School of Archaeology).

Bernabé, Alberto (2002), 'La Toile De Pénélope: A-t-il Existé Un Mythe Orphique Sur Dionysos Et Les Titans?', *Revue De L'histoire Des Religions*, 219 (4), 401–433.

Bernabé, Alberto (2011), 'Are the 'orphic' Gold Leaves Orphic?', in Radcliffe G. Edmonds (ed.), *The 'Orphic' Gold Tablets and Greek Religion: Further along the Path* (Cambridge: Cambridge University Press), 68–101.

Bernabé, Alberto and Ana Isabel Jiménez San Cristóbal (2008), *Instructions for the Netherworld: The Orphic Gold Tablets*, trans. Michael Chase (Leiden: Brill), xii, 379 p.

Berve, Helmut and Gottfried Gruben (1963), *Greek Temples, Theatres, and Shrines* (London: Thames and Hudson).

Bianchi, Ugo (1976), *The Greek Mysteries* (Leiden: Brill).

Bierl, Anton (1994), 'Apollo in Greek Tragedy: Orestes and the God of Initiation', in Jon Solomon (ed.), *Apollo: Origins and Influences* (Tuscon: The University of Arizona Press), 81–96.

Bluck, R. S. (1961), *Plato's Meno* (Cambridge: Cambridge University Press).

Boëlle, Cécile (2004), *PO-TI-NI-JA: L'éLément Féminin Dans La Religion Mycénienne (D'après Les Archives En Linéaire B)* (Paris: De Boccard).

Bond, Godfrey W. (1981), *Euripides Heracles: With Introduction and Commentary* (Oxford: Clarendon Press).

Bonnechere, Pierre (2003), 'Trophonius of Lebadea: Mystery Aspects of an Oracular Cult in Boeotia', in Michael B. Cosmopolous (ed.), *Greek Mysteries: The Archaeology and Ritual of Ancient Greek Secret Cult* (London: Routledge), 169–192.

Bookidis, Nancy and Ronald S. Stroud (1997), *The Sanctuary of Demeter and Kore: Topography and Architecture* (Corinth: Results of Excavations Conducted by The American School of Classical Studies at Athens, XVIII.3; Princeton: The American School of Classical Studies at Athens).

Bowden, Hugh (2005), 'Herakles, Herodotos and the Persian Wars', in Hugh Bowden and Louis Rawlings (eds.), *Herakles and Hercules: Exploring a Graeco-Roman Divinity* (Swansea: The Classical Press of Wales), 1–14.

Bowden, Hugh (2007), 'Cults of Demeter Eleusinia and the Transmission of Religious Ideas', *Mediterranean Historical Review*, 22 (1), 71–83.

Bowden, Hugh (2010), *Mystery Cults in the Ancient World* (London: Thames and Hudson).

Boyer, Pascal (2002), *Religion Explained: The Human Instincts that Fashion Gods, Spirits and Ancestors* (London: Vintage Books).

Breglia, L (1997), 'Falce Di Demetra, Falce per Demetra', in N. Parise (ed.), *Bernhard Laum: Origine Della Moneta E Teoria Del Sacrifico. Atti dell'Incontro Di Studio, Roma 1995* (Rome: Istituto italiano di numismatica), 43–69.

Bremmer, Jan N. (1983), 'Scapegoat Rituals in Ancient Greece', *Harvard Studies in Classical Philology*, 87, 299–320.

Bremmer, Jan N. (1987), 'The Old Women of Ancient Greece', in Josine Blok and Peter Mason (eds.), *Sexual Asymmetry: Studies in Ancient Society* (Amsterdam: J.C. Gieben), 191–216.

Bremmer, Jan N. (1994), *Greek Religion* (Oxford: Oxford University Press).

Bremmer, Jan N. (2002), *The Rise and Fall of the Afterlife* (London: Routledge).

Bremmer, Jan N. (2005), 'The Sacrifice of Pregnant Animals', in Robin Hägg and Brita Alroth (eds.), *Greek Sacrificial Ritual, Olympian and Chthonian* (Stockholm: Paul Åströms Förlag), 155–165.

Bremmer, Jan N. (2007a), 'Myth and Ritual in Greek Human Sacrifice: Lykanon, Polyxena and the Case of the Rhodian Criminal', in Jan Bremmer (ed.), *The Strange World of Human Sacrifice* (Leuven: Peeters), 55–79.

Bremmer, Jan N. (2007b), 'Ritual', in Sarah Illes Johnston (ed.), *Ancient Religions* (Cambridge, MA: The Belknap Press of Harvard University Press), 32–44.

Bremmer, Jan N. (2010a), 'Introduction', in Jan Bremmer and Andrew Erskine (eds.), *The Gods of Ancient Greece: Identities and Transformations* (Edinburgh: Edinburgh University Press), 1–18.

Bremmer, Jan N. (2010b), 'Manteis, Magic, Mysteries and Mythography: Mess Margins of Polis Religion', *Kernos*, 23, 13–35.

Bremmer, Jan N. (2012), 'Demeter in Megara', in Attilio Mastrocinque and Concetta Giuffrè Scibona (eds.), *Demeter, Isis, Vesta, and Cybele: Studies in Greek and Roman Religion in Honour of Giulia Sfameni Gasparro* (Stuttgart: Franz Steiner Verlag), 25–37.

Bremmer, Jan N. (2013), 'Divinities in the Orphic Gold Leaves: Euklês, Eubouleus, Brimo, Kybele, Kore and Persephone', *Zeitschrift Für Papyrologie Und Epigraphik*, 187, 35–48.

Bremmer, Jan N. (2014), *Initiation into the Mysteries of the Ancient World* (Berlin: De Gruyter).

Brisson, Luc (1985), 'Les Théogonies Orphiques Et Le Papyrus De Derveni', *Revue De L'histoire Des Religions*, 202 (Journal Article), 389–420.

Brisson, Luc (1992), 'Le Corps 'dionysiaque'. L'anthropogonie décrite dans le Commentaire sur le Phédon de Platon (1. par. 3-6) attribué à Olympiodore est-elle orphique?', Σοφίης Μαιήτορες, *"Chercheurs de sagesse"*. *Hommage à Jean Pépin* (Paris: Institut d'Études Augustiniennes), 483–499.

Brisson, Luc (1995), *Orphée Et l'Orphisme Dans l'Antiquité Gréco-romaine* (Aldershot: Variorum).

Brown, Christopher G. (1990), 'Honouring the Goddess: Philicus' Hymn to Demeter', *Aegyptus*, 70 (1/2), 173–189.

Brumfield, Allaire Chandor (1981), *The Attic Festivals of Demeter and Their Relation to the Agricultural Year* (New York: Arno Press).

Buck, C. D. (1955), *The Greek Dialects* (Bristol: Bristol Classical Press).

Burkert, Walter (1985), *Greek Religion* (trans. John Raffan, Cambridge, Mass.: Harvard University Press).

Burkert, Walter (1987), *Ancient Mystery Cults* (Cambridge, MA: Harvard University Press).

Burkert, Walter (2001), *Savage Energies: Lessons of Myth and Ritual in Ancient Greece* (trans. Peter Bing, Chicago: Chicago University Press).

Burkert, Walter (2005), 'Hesiod in Context: Abstraction an Divinities in an Aegean-Eastern Koiné', in Emma Stafford and Judith Herrin (eds.), *Personification in the Greek World: From Antiquity to Byzantium* (Aldershot: Ashgate), 3–20.

Burkert, Walter (2011), 'Hades: Cornucopiae, Fertility and Death', Anne Mackay (ed.), *ASCS 32* (www.ascs.org.au/news/ascs32/Burton.pdf).

Burkert, Walter (2018), 'Worshipping Hades: Myth and Cult in Elis and Triphylia', *Archiv Für Religionsgeschichte*, 20 (1), 211–227.

Burton, Diana (2005), 'The Gender of Death', in Emma Stafford and Judith Herrin (eds.), *Personifications in the Greek World: From Antiquity to Byzantium* (Aldershot: Ashgate), 45–68.

Butler, Judith (2000), *Antigone's Claim: Kinship between Life and Death* (New York: Columbia University Press).

Calame, Claude (1996), *Thésée Et L'imaginaire Athénien. Légende Et Culte En Grèce Antique* (Lausanne: Payot).

Calame, Claude (1999), 'Indigenous and Modern Perspectives on Tribal Initiation Rites: Education according to Plato', in M. W. Padilla (ed.), *Rites of Passage in Ancient Greece: Literature, Religion, Society* (London: Associated University Presses), 278–317.

Calame, Claude (2008), 'Les Lamelles Funéraires D'or: Textes Pseudo-orphiques Et Pratiques Rituelles', *Kernos*, 21.

Calame, Claude (2009), *Greek Mythology: Poetics, Pragmatics and Fiction* (trans. Janet Lloyd, Cambridge: Cambridge University Press).

Carey, Chris (1995), 'Rape and Adultery in Athenian Law', *The Classical Quarterly*, 45 (2), 407–417.

Cartledge, Paul (2002), *Sparta and Lakonia: A Regional History 1300-362 BC* (London: Routledge).

Caskey, John L. and Sotirios I. Dakaris (1962), 'The Dark Palace of Hades', *Archaeology*, 51 (2), 85–93.

Christensen, Lisbeth Bredhold (2009), '"Cult" in the Study of Religion and Archaeology', in Jesper Tae Jensen et al. (ed.), *Aspects of Ancient Greek Cult: Context, Ritual and Iconography* (Aarhus: Aarhus University Press), 13–28.

Clarke, Michael (1999), *Flesh and Spirit in the Songs of Homer: A Study of Words and Myths* (Oxford: Clarendon Press).

Clay, Jenny Strauss (1984), 'The Hecate of the Theogony', *Greek, Roman, and Byzantine Studies*, 25, 27–38.

Clay, Jenny Strauss (1989), *The Politics of Olympus: Form and Meaning in the Major Homeric Hymns* (Bristol: Bristol Classical Press).

Clinton, Kevin (1974), *The Sacred Officials of the Eleusinian Mysteries* (Philadelphia: The American Philosophical Society).

Clinton, Kevin (1979), 'IG I2 5, the Eleusinia and the Eleusinians', *The American Journal of Philology*, 100 (1), 1–12.

Clinton, Kevin (1986), 'The Author of the Homeric Hymn to Demeter', *Opuscula Atheniensia*, 16, 43–49.

Clinton, Kevin (1992), *Myth and Cult. The Iconography of the Eleusinian Mysteries* (Stockholm: Paul Åströms Förlag).

Clinton, Kevin (1993), 'The Sanctuary of Demeter and Kore at Eleusis', in N. Marinatos and R. Hägg (eds.), *Greek Sanctuaries: New Approaches* (London: Routledge).

Cohen, David (1993), 'Consent and Sexual Relations in Classical Athens', in Angeliki E. Laiou (ed.), *Consent and Coercion to Sex and Marriage in Ancient and Medieval Societies* (Washington, DC: Dumbarton Oaks), 5–16.

Cole, Susan Guettel (1994), 'Demeter in the Ancient Greek City and Its Countryside', in Susan E. Alcock and Robin Osborne (eds.), *Placing the Gods: Sanctuaries and Sacred Space in Ancient Greece* (Oxford: Clarendon Press), 199–216.

Coleman, John E. and Katherine Abramovitz (1986), 'Excavations at Pylos in Elis', *Hesperia Supplements*, 21, i–244.

Collins, Billie Jean (2002), 'Necromancy, Fertility and the Dark Earth: The Use of Ritual Pits in Hittite Cult', in Paul Mirecki and Marvin Meyer (eds.), *Magic and Ritual in the Ancient World* (Leiden: Brill), 224–241.

Cook, Arthur Bernard (1914), *Zeus: A Study in Ancient Religion*, 1 vol. (Cambridge: Cambridge University Press).

Corbett, P. E. (1970), 'Greek Temples and Greek Worshippers: The Literary and Archaeological Evidence', *Bulletin of the Institute of Classical Studies*, 17 (1), 149–158.

Dakaris, Sotirios I. (1973), 'The Oracle of the Dead on the Acheron', in Evi Melas (ed.), *Temples and Sanctuaries of Ancient Greece: A Companion Guide* (London: Thames and Hudson), 139–150.

Davies, A. M. E. and Y. E. Duhoux (1988), *Linear B: A Survey* (Louvain-La-Neuve: Peeters).

Detienne, Marcel (1989), 'The Violence of Wellborn Ladies: Women in the Thesmophoria', in Marcel Detienne and Jean-Pierre Vernant (eds.), *The Cuisine of Sacrifice among the Greeks* (Chicago: University of Chicago Press), 129–147.

Deubner, L. (1966), *Attische Feste*, 2 vols. (Berlin: Akademie-Verlag).

Dewald, Carolyn (1981), 'Women and Culture in Herodotus' Histories', in Helene P. Foley (ed.), *Reflections of Women in Antiquity* (New York: Gordon and Breach), 91–125.

Dietrich, Albrecht (1893), *Nekyia: Beiträge Zur Erklärung Der Neuentdeckten Petrusapokalypse* (Leipzig: Druck und Verlag Von B.G. Teubner).

Dietrich, Bernard C. (1962), 'Demeter, Erinys, Artemis', *Hermes: Zeitschrift Für Klassische Philologie*, 90, 129–148.

Dietrich, Bernard C. (1965), *Death, Fate and the Gods: The Development of a Religious Idea in Greek Popular Belief and in Homer* (London: The Athlone Press).

Dillon, Matthew P. J. (2002), *Girls and Women in Classical Greek Religion* (London: Routledge).

Dowden, Ken (1989), *Death and the Maiden: Girls' Initiation Rites in Greek Mythology* (London: Routledge).

Edmonds, Radcliffe G. (1999), 'Tearing Apart the Zagreus Myth: A Few Disparaging Remarks on Orphism and Original Sin', *Classical Antiquity*, 18 (1), 35–73.

Edmonds, Radcliffe G. (2004), *Myths of the Underworld Journey: Plato, Aristophanes, and the 'orphic' Gold Tablets* (Cambridge: Cambridge University Press).

Edmonds, Radcliffe G. (2011), 'The 'orphic' Gold Tablets: Text and Translations, with Critical Apparatus and Tables', in Radcliffe G. Edmonds (ed.), *The 'orphic' Gold Tablets and Greek Religion: Further along the Path* (Cambridge: Cambridge University Press), 15–50.

Edmonds, Radcliffe G. (2013), *Redefining Ancient Orphism: A Study in Greek Religion* (Cambridge: Cambridge University Press).

Eidinow, Esther (2007a), *Oracles, Curses, and Risk among the Ancient Greeks* (Oxford: Oxford University Press).

Eidinow, Esther (2007b), 'Why the Athenians Began to Curse', in Robin Osborne (ed.), *Debating the Athenian Cultural Revolution: Art, Literature, Philosophy, and Politics 430-380 BC* (Cambridge: Cambridge University Press), 44–71.

Eidinow, Esther (2011), 'Networks and Narratives: A Model for Ancient Greek Religion*', *Kernos*, 24, 9–38.

Fairbanks, Arthur (1907), *Athenian Lekythoi: With Outline Drawing in Glaze Varnish on a White Ground* (New York: MacMillan).

Faraone, Christopher A. (1991), 'The Agonistic Context of Early Greek Binding Spells', in Christopher A. Faraone (ed.), *Magika Hiera: Ancient Greek Magic and Religion* (Oxford: Oxford University Press), 3–32.

Faraone, Christopher A. (1999), 'Curses and Social Control in the Law Courts of Classical Athens', *Dike*, 2, 99–121.

Farnell, Lewis Richard (1907), *The Cults of the Greek States*, III vols. (Oxford: Clarendon Press).

Ferrari, Franco and Lucia Prauscello (2007), 'Demeter Chthonia and the Mountain Mother in a New Gold Tablet from Magoula Mati', *Zeitschrift Für Papyrologie Und Epigraphik*, 162, 193–202.

Ferrari, Gloria (2003), 'What Kind of Rite of Passage Was the Ancient Greek Wedding?', in David B Dodd and Christopher A. Faraone (eds.), *Initiation in Ancient Greek Rituals and Narratives: New Critical Perspectives* (London: Routledge), 27–42.

Foley, Helene P. (1994), *The Homeric Hymn to Demeter: Translation, Commentary, and Interpretive Essays*, ed. Helene P. Foley (Princeton: Princeton University Press), 28–64.

Frazer, J. G. (1912), *The Golden Bough* (3rd edn., 5.1, London: McMillan and Co).

Friend, J. L. (2009), 'The Athenian Ephebeia in the Lycurgan Period: 334/3-332.1 B.C', PhD (The University of Texas at Austin).

Furley, William D. (1996), *Andokides and the Herms: A Study of Crisis in Fifth-century Athenian Religion* (London: Institute of Classical Studies).

Gager, John H. (1992), *Curse Tablets and Binding Spells from the Ancient World* (Oxford: Oxford University Press).

Gantz, Timothy (1993), *Early Greek Myth: A Guide to Literary and Artistic Sources* (vol. 2, Baltimore: Johns Hopkins University Press), xxi, 873p.

Garland, Robert (1981), 'The Causation of Death in the Iliad: A Theological and Biological Investigation', *Bulletin of the Institute of Classical Studies*, 28 (1), 43–60.

Garland, Robert (1985), *The Greek Way of Death* (London: Duckworth).

Garland, Robert (1989), 'The Well-Ordered Corpse: An Investigation into the Motives behind Greek Funerary Legislation', *Bulletin of the Institute of Classical Studies*, 36 (1), 1–15.

Georgoudi, Stella (2010), 'Sacrificing to the Gods: Ancient Evidence and Modern Interpretations', in Jan Bremmer and Andrew Erskine (eds.), *The Gods of Ancient Greece: Identities and Transformations* (Edinburgh: Edinburgh University Press), 92–105.

Giuseppetti, Massimo (2012), 'Two Poets for a Goddess: Callimachus' and Philicus' Hymns to Demeter', in M. A. Harder, R. F. Regtuit and G. C. Wakker (eds.), *Gods and Religion in Hellensitic Poetry* (Leuvern: Peeters), 103–129.

Given, John (2009), 'When Gods Don't Appear: Divine Absence and Human Agency in Aristophanes', *Classical World*, 109 (2), 107–128.

Gould, John (1985), 'On Making Sense of Greek Religion', in P. E. Easterling and J. V. Muir (eds.), *Greek Religion and Society* (Cambridge: Cambridge University Press), 1–33.

Grace, Sam (2013), 'Patron Saint of Grad Students', *Sam Grace Talks to Imaginary Anthropologists*.

Graf, Fritz (1974), *Eleusis Und Die Orphische Dichtung Athens in Vorhellenistischer Zeit* (Berlin: Walter de Gruyter).

Graf, Fritz (1985). *Nordionische Kulte: Religionsgeschichtliche Und Epigraphische Untersuchungen Zu Den Kulten von Chios, Erythrai, Klazomenai Und Phokaia*. Vol. 21. Bibliotheca Helvetica Romana. Rom: Schweizerisches Institut in Rom.

Graf, Fritz (1997), *Magic in the Ancient World, Trans. F. Phillip* (Cambridge, MA: Harvard University Press).

Graf, Fritz (2003a), 'Initiation: A Concept with A Troubled History', in David B. Dodd and Christopher A. Farone (eds.), *Initiation in Ancient Greek Rituals and Narratives: New Critical Perspectives* (London: Routledge), 3–24.

Graf, Fritz (2003b), 'Initiation: A Concept with A Troubled History', in David B. Dodd and Christopher A. Farone (eds.), *Initiation in Ancient Greek Rituals and Narratives: New Critical Rerspectives* (London: Routledge), 3–24.

Graf, Fritz and Sarah Illes Johnston (2007), *Ritual Texts for the Afterlife: Orpheus and the Bacchic Gold Tablets* (1st edn., Abingdon: Routledge).

Graf, Fritz and Sarah Illes Johnston (2013), *Ritual Texts for the Afterlife: Orpheus and the Bacchic Gold Tablets* (2nd edn., Abingdon: Routledge).

Greco, Emanuele (2006), 'Greek Colonisation in Sourthern Italy: A Methodological Essay', in Gocha R. Tsetskhladze (ed.), *Greek Colonisation: An Account of Greek Colonies and Other Settlements Overseas* (vol. 1, Leiden: Brill), 169–200.

Griffin, Jasper (1980), *Homer on Life and Death* (Oxford: Clarendon Press).

Guralnick, Eleanor (1974), 'The Chrysapha Relief and Its Connections with Egyptian Art', *The Journal of Egyptian Archaeology*, 60, 175–188.

Hadzisteliou Price, T. (1978), *Kourotrophos: Cutls and Representations of the Greek Nursing Deities* (Leiden: E.J Brill).

Hägg, Robin and Brita Alroth (eds.) (2005), *Greek Sacrificial Ritual, Olympian and Chthonian: Proceedings of the Sixth International Seminar on Ancient Greek Cult, Göteborg University, 25-27 April 1997* (Stockholm: Paul Åströms Förlag), 99–112.

Hall, Jonathan M. (2001), *Hellenicity: Between Ethnicity and Culture* (Chicago: The University of Chicago Press).

Ham, Greta (1999), 'The Choes and Anthesteria Reconsidered: Male Maturation Rites and the Peloponnesian Wars', in Mark W. Padilla (ed.), *Rites of Passage in Ancient Greece: Literature, Religion, Society* (Toronto: Associated University Presses), 201–218.

Hamilton, Richard (1992), *Choes and Anthesteria: Athenian Iconography and Ritual* (Ann Arbor: The University of Michigan Press).

Harris, Edward M. (2013), *The Rule of Law in Action in Democratic Athens* (Oxford: Oxford University Press).

Harris, Edward M. (2015), '"Yes" and "No" in Women's Desire', in Mark Masterson, Nancy Sorkin Rabinowitz and James Robson (eds.), *Sex in Antiquity: Exploring Gender and Sexuality in the Ancient World* (London: Routledge), 298–314.

Harrison, Jane Ellen (1903), *Prolegomena to the Study of Greek Religion* (3rd edn., Cambridge: Cambridge University Press).

Harrison, Jane Ellen (1908), 'Helios-Hades', *The Classical Review*, 22 (1), 12–16.

Harrison, Jane Ellen (1912), *Themis: A Study of the Social Origins of Greek Religion* (Cambridge: Cambridge University Press).

Headlam, Walter and CES Headlam (1909), *The Plays of Aeschylus* (London: George Bell and Sons).

Held, George F. (1983), 'Antigone's Dual Motivation for the Double Burial', *Hermes*, 111 (2), 190–201.

Henrichs, Albert (1991), 'Namenlosigkeit Und Euphemismus: Zur Ambivalenz Der Chthonischen Mächte Im Attischen Drama', in Annette Harder and Heinz Hofmann (eds.), *Fragmenta Dramatica: Beiträge Zur Interpretation Der Griechischen Tragiker-fragmente Und Ihrer Wirkungsgeschichte* (Göttingen: Vanderhoek and Ruprecht), 161–201.

Henrichs, Albert (2010), 'What Is a Greek God?', in Jan Bremmer and Andrew Erskine (eds.), *The Gods of Ancient Greece: Identities and Transformations* (Edinburgh: Edinburgh University Press), 19–39.

Herrero de Jáuregui, Miguel (2011), 'Dialogues of Immortality from the Iliad to the Gold Leaves', in Radcliffe G. Edmonds (ed.), *The 'Orphic' Gold Tablets and Greek Religion: Further along the Path* (Cambridge: Cambridge University Press), 15–50.

Hinz, Valentina (1998), *Der Kult Von Demeter Und Kore Auf Sizilien Und in Der Magna Graecia* (Wiesbaden: Dr. Ludwig Reichert Verlag).

Holloway, R. Ross (1971), 'Archaeological News from South Italy and Sicily', *American Journal of Archaeology*, 75 (1), 75–81.

Holloway, R. Ross (1991), *The Archaeology of Ancient Sicily* (London: Routledge).

Hulton, A. O. (1962), 'Euripides and the Iphigenia Legend', *Mnemosyne*, 15 (4), 364–368.

Huxley, G. L. (1969), *Greek Epic Poetry from Eumelos to Panyassis* (London: Faber).

Innes, Alison and Darrin Sunstrum (2016), 'Mythological Tour of the Solar System 9: Pluto/Hades', *mythTake*.

Ionescu, Christine (2007), *Plato's Meno: An Interpretation* (Plymouth: Lexington Books).

Jameson, Michael H., David R. Jordan and Roy D. Kotansky (1993), *A Lex Sacra from Selinous* (Durham: Greek, Roman and Byzantine Monographs).

Janakieva, Svetlana (2005), 'Noces Prolongées Dans l'Hadès: d'Evadné Aux Veuves Thraces', *Revue De L'histoire Des Religions*, 222, 5–23.

Janda, Michael (2000), *Eleusis: Das Indogermanische Erbe Der Mysterien* (Innsbruck: Institut für Sprachwissenchaft der Universität Innsbruck).

Janko, R. (1984), 'Forgetfulness in the Golden Tablets of Memory', *The Classical Quarterly*, 34 (1), 89–100.

Japan Today, Lifestyle (2014), 'Solo Wedding Service for Single Women Who Want to Be Brides for a Day'.

Jenkins, Ian (1983), 'Is There Life after Marriage? A Study of the Abduction Motif in Vase Paintings of the Athenian Wedding Ceremony', *Bulletin of the Institute of Classical Studies*, 30, 137–145.

Johnston, Sarah Iles (1990), *Hekate Soteira: A Study of Hekate's Roles in the Chaldean Oracles and Related Literature* (American Classical Studies, 21; Atlanta, GA.: Scholars Press).

Johnston, Sarah Iles (1991), 'Crossroads', *Zeitschrift für Papyrologie und Epigraphik*, 88, 217–224.

Johnston, Sarah Iles (1994), 'Penelope and the Erinyes: Odyssey 20.61-82', *Helios*, 21 (2), 137–159.

Johnston, Sarah Iles (1999), *Restless Dead: Encounters between the Living and the Dead in Ancient Greece* (Berkeley: University of California Press).

Johnston, Sarah Iles (2003), '"initiation' in Myth, 'initiation' in Practices: The Homeric Hymn to Hermes and Its Performative Context', in David B. Dodd and Christopher A. Faraone (eds.), *Initiation in Ancient Greek Rituals and Narratives: New Critical Perspectives* (London: Routledge), 155–180.

Johnston, Sarah Iles (2012), 'Demeter in Hermione: Sacrifice and Ritual Polyvalence', *Arethusa*, 45 (2), 211–241.

Johnston, Sarah Iles (2013), 'Demeter, Myths, and the Polyvalence of Festivals', *History of Religions*, 52 (4), 370–401.

Jones, Christopher (2010), *New Heroes in Antiquity: From Achilles to Antinoos* (Cambridge, Mass.: Harvard University Press).

Jordan, David R. (1985), 'A Survey of the Greek Defixiones Not Included in the Special Corpora', *Greek, Roman, and Byzantine Studies*, 26, 151–197.

Jordan, David R. (1997), 'An Address to a Ghost at Olbia', *Mnemosyne*, 50 (2), 212–219.

Jost, Madeleine (1985), *Sanctuaires Et Cultes d'Arcadie* (Etudes péloponnésiennes/Ecole Française d'Athènes; Paris: J. Vrin) 592 P., 64 P. Of Plates.

Kearns, Emily (2010), *Ancient Greek Religion: A Sourcebook* (Chicheser: Wiley-Blackwell).

Keller, Mara Lynn (1988), 'The Eleusinian Mysteries of Demeter and Persephone: Fertility, Sexuality, and Rebirth', *Journal of Feminist Studies in Religion*, 4 (1), 27–54.

Kindt, Julia (2009), 'Polis Religion – A Critical Appreciation', *Kernos*, 22, 9–34.

Kindt, Julia (2012), *Rethinking Greek Religion* (Cambridge: Cambridge University Press).

Kovaks, David (1998), *Euripides III: Suppliant Women. Electra. Heracles* (Loeb Classical Library, Cambridge: Cambridge University Press).

Kurtz, Donna Carol (1975), *Athenian White Lekythoi: Patterns and Painters* (Oxford: Clarendon Press).

Kurtz, Donna Carol and John Boardman (1971), *Greek Burial Customs* (London: Thames and Hudson).

Larson, Jennifer (2007), *Ancient Greek Cults: A Guide* (New York: Routledge).

Larson, Jennifer (2016), *Understanding Greek Religion: A Cognitive Approach* (London: Routledge).

Lebessi, Angeliki (2010), 'Hermes as Master of Lions at the Syme Sanctuary, Crete', *British School at Athens Studies*, 18 (Cretan Offerings: Studies in Honour of Peter Warren), 195–202.

Leitao, David D (2003), 'Adolescent Hair-Growing and Hair-Cutting Rituals in Ancient Greece: A Sociological Approach', in David B. Dodd and Christopher A. Faraone (eds.), *Initiation in Ancient Greek Rituals and Narratives: New Critical Perspectives* (London: Routledge), 109–129.

Lincoln, Bruce (2003), 'The Initiatory Paradigm in Anthropology, Folklore, and History of Religions', in David B. Dodd and Christopher A. Farone (eds.), *Initiation in Ancient Greek Rituals and Narratives: New Critical Perspectives* (London: Routledge), 241–254.

Linforth, Ivan (1941), *The Arts of Orpheus* (Berkeley: Arno Press).

Lloyd, G. E. R. (1962), 'Right and Left in Greek Philosophy', *The Journal of Hellenic Studies*, 82, 56–66.

Loraux, Nicole (1987), *Tragic Ways of Killing a Woman* (Cambridge, Mass.: Harvard University Press).

Lowell, Robert (1978), *The 'oresteia' of Aeschylus* (London: Faber and Faber).

Lyons, Deborah (1997), *Gender and Immortality: Heroines in Ancient Greek Myth and Cult* (Princeton: Princeton University Press).

Ma, John (2008), 'The Return of the Black Hunter', *The Cambridge Classical Journal*, 54, 188–208.

Macaulay, David (1979), *Motel of the Mysteries* (Boston: Houghton Mifflin).

MacDowell, Douglas M (1963), *Athenian Homicide Law in the Age of the Orators* (Manchester: Manchester University Press).

Mackin Roberts, Ellie (2018), 'Girls Playing Persephone (In Marriage and Death)', *Mnemosyne*, 71 (2), 209–228. (Published under Ellie Mackin).

Mackin Roberts, Ellie (2019), 'Weaving for Athena: The Arrhephoroi, Panathenaia, and Mundane Acts as Religious Devotion', *Journal for Hellenic Religion*, 12, 61–84.

Mair, Jonathan (2012), 'Cultures of Belief', *Anthropological Theory*, 12 (4), 448–466.

Margon, Joseph S. (1972), 'The Second Burial of Polyneices', *The Classical Journal*, 68, 39–49.

Marinatos, Nanno (2003), 'Striding across Boundaries: Hermes and Aphrodite as Gods of Initiation', in David B. Dodd and Christopher A. Farone (eds.), *Initiation in Ancient Greek Rituals and Narratives: New Critical Perspectives* (New York: Routledge), 130–152.

McInerney, Jeremy (1999), *The Folds of Parnassos: Land and Ethnicity in Ancient Phokis* (Austin: University of Texas Press).

Mikalson, Jon D. (2010), *Ancient Greek Religion*, (vol. 2 Chichester: Wiley-Blackwell).

Mikalson, Jon D. (1991), *Honor Thy Gods: Popular Religion in Greek Tragedy* (Chapel Hill: The University of North Carolina Press).

Morford, Mark P. O., Robert J. Lenardon and Michael Sham (2011), *Classical Mythology* (International 9th edn., Oxford: Oxford University Press).

Morgan, Catherine (1993), 'The Origins of pan-Hellenism', in Nanno Marinatos and Robin Hägg (eds.), *Greek Sanctuaries: New Approaches* (London: Routledge), 18–44.

Morris, Ian (1989), 'Attitudes toward Death in Archaic Greece', *Classical Antiquity*, 8 (2), 296–320.

Morris, Ian (1992), *Death-Ritual and Social Structure in Classical Antiquity* (Cambridge: Cambridge University Press).

Morris, Sarah P. and John K. Papadopoulos (2004), 'Of Granaries and Games: Egyptian Stowaways in an Athenian Chest', *Hesperia Supplements*, 33 (ΧΑΡΙΣ: Essays in Honor of Sara A. Immerwahr), 225–242.

Morrison, James V. (1999), '"homeric Darkness: Patterns and Manipulation of Death Scenes in the 'Iliad'"', *Hermes: Zeitschrift Für Klassische Philologie*, 127, 129–144.

Murray, Caroline Mary (1979), 'Mycenaean Religion: The Evidence of the Linear B Tablets', PhD (Cambridge University Press).

Mylonas, George E. (1961), *Eleusis and the Eleusinian Mysteries* (Princeton: Princeton University Press).

Nilsen, Don L. F. and Alleen Pace Nilsen (2009), 'Naming Tropes and Schemes in J.K. Rowling's Harry Potter Books', *The English Journal*, 98 (6), 60–68.

Nilsson, Martin P. (1906), *Griechische Feste Von Religiöser Bedeutung: Mit Ausschluss Der Attischen* (Leipzig: Druck und Verlag von B.G. Teubner).

Nilsson, Martin P. (1935), 'Die Eleusinische Gottheiten', *Archiv Für Religionswissenschaft*, 32, 99–141.

Nilsson, Martin P. (1967), *Geschichte Der Griechischen Religion* (3rd edn.; Munich: C.H Beck'sche Verlagbuchhandlung).

Nock, A. D. (1986), 'The Cult of Heroes (1944)', in Z. Stewart (ed.), *Essays on Religion and the Ancient World* (Oxford: Clarendon Press), 575–602.

Oakley, John H. (2004), *Picturing Death in Classical Athens: The Evidence of the White Lekythoi* (Cambridge: Cambridge University Press).

Oakley, John H. and Rebecca H. Sinos (1993), *The Wedding in Ancient Athens* (Madison: The University of Wisconsin Press).

Ober, Josiah (2003), 'Postscript: Culture, Thin Coherence, and the Persistence of Politics', in Carol Dougherty and Leslie Kurke (eds.), *The Cultures Within Ancient Greek Culture* (Cambridge: Cambridge University Press), 237–256.

Ober, Josiah (2005), 'Culture, Thin Coherence, and the Persistence of the Polis', in *Athenian Legacies: Essays on the Politics of Going on Together* (Princeton: Princeton University Press), 69–91.

Ogden, Daniel (2001), *Greek and Roman Necromancy* (Princeton: Princeton University Press).

Ogden, Daniel (2008), *Night's Black Agents: Witches, Wizards and the Dead in the Ancient World* (London: Hambledon Continuum).

Øistein Endsjø, D. (2002), 'To Lock up Eleusis. A Question of Liminal Space', in S. Des Bouvrie (ed.), *Myth and Symbol 1: Symbolic Phenomena in Ancient Greek Culture* (Bergen: The Norwegian Institute at Athens), 233–258.

Omitowoju, Rosanna (2002), *Rape and the Politics of Consent in Classical Athens* (Cambridge: Cambridge University Press).

Padilla, Mark W. (1999), 'Introduction', in Mark W. Padilla (ed.), *Rites of Passage in Ancient Greece: Literature, Religion, Society* (Toronto: Associated University Press), 15–23.

Page, D. L., R. D. Dawe and J. Diggle (eds.) (1981). *Further Greek Epigrams: Epigrams before A.D. 50 from the Greek Anthology and Other Sources, Not Included in 'hellenistic Epigrams' or 'the Garland of Philip'* (Cambridge: Cambridge University Press).

Parke, HW (1977), *Festivals of the Athenians* (London: Thames and Hudson).

Parke, HW and DEW Wormell (1956), *The Delphic Oracle*, vol. 2 (1, Oxford: Blackwell).

Parker, Robert (1983), *Miasma: Pollution and Purification in Early Greek Religion* (Oxford: Clarendon Press).

Parker, Robert (1987), 'Festivals of the Attic Demes', in Tullia Linders and Gullög Nordquist (eds.), *Gifts to the Gods: Proceedings of the Uppsala Symposium 1985* (Uppsala: Acta Universitatis Upsaliensis).

Parker, Robert (1988), 'Demeter, Dionysos and the Spartan Pantheon', in Robin Hägg, Nanno Marinatos and Gullög C. Nordquist (eds.), *Early Greek cult practice: proceedings of the fifth international symposium at the Swedish Institute at Athens, 26-29 June, 1986* (Stockholm: Paul Åströms Förlag), 99–103.

Parker, Robert (1991), 'The Hymn to Demeter and the Homeric Hymns', *Greece & Rome*, 38 (1), 1–17.

Parker, Robert (1998), 'Pleasing Thighs: Reciprocity in Greek Religion', in Christopher Gill, Norman Postlethwait and Richard Seaford (eds.), *Reciprocity in Ancient Greece* (Oxford: Clarendon Press), 105–126.

Parker, Robert (2000), 'Theophoric Names and the History of Greek Religion', *Proceedings of the British Academy*, 104, 53–79.

Parker, Robert (2003), 'Chthonian Gods', in Simon Hornblower and Antony Spawforth (eds.), *The Oxford Classical Dictionary* (3 revised edn., Oxford: Oxford University Press), 329–330.

Parker, Robert (2005a), *Polytheism and Society at Athens* (Oxford: Oxford University Press).

Parker, Robert (2005b), 'ὡς ἥρωι ἐναγίζειν', in Robin Hägg and Brita Alroth (eds.), *Greek Sacrificial Ritual, Olympian and Chthonian* (Stockholm: Paul Åströms Förlag), 37–45.

Parker, Robert (2011), *On Greek Religion* (Ithaca: Cornell University Press).

Parker, Robert and Maria Stamatopoulou (2004), 'A New Funerary Gold Leaf from Pherai', *Αρχαιολογικη Εφημερις*, 143, 1–32.

Pease, Arthur Stanley (1942), 'Some Aspects of Invisibility', *Harvard Studies in Classical Philology*, 53, 1–36.

Peek, Werner (1955), *Griechische Vers-Inschriften* (Berlin: Österreichische Akademie der Wissenschaften).

Penglase, Charles (1994), *Greek Myths and Mesopotamia: Parallels and Influence in the Homeric Hymns and Hesiod* (London: Routledge).

Perlman, Paula (2000), *City and Sanctuary in Ancient Greece: The Theorodokia in the Peloponnese* (Göttingen: Vandenhoeck and Ruprecht).

Pfister, Friedrich (1912), *Der Reliquienkult in Altertum* (Gießen: Verlag von Alfred Töpelmann (vormals J. Ricker)).

Polinskaya, Irene (2010), 'Shared Sanctuaries and the Gods of Others: On the Meaning of 'common' in Herodotus 8.144', in Ralph M. Rosen and Ineke Sluiter (eds.), *Valuing Others in Classical Antiquity* (Leiden: Brill), 43–70.

Polinskaya, Irene (2013), *A Local History of Greek Polytheism: Gods, People, and the Land of Aigina, 800-400 BCE* (Leiden: Brill).

Porter, James I. (2007), 'Lasus of Hermione, Pindar and the Riddle of S', *Classical Quarterly*, 57 (1), 1–21.

Prauscello, Lucia (2011), 'Μελίβοια: The Chthonia of Hermione and Kore's Lost Epithet in Lasus Fr. 702 PMG', *The Classical Quarterly*, 61 (1), 19–27.

Prauscello, Lucia (2013), 'Demeter and Dionysos in the Sixth Century Southern Argolid: Lasos of Hermione, the Cult of Demeter Chthonia and the Origin of Dithyramb', in B. Kowalzig and P. Wilson (eds.), *Dithyramb in Context* (Oxford: Oxford University Press), 76–92.

Preller, Ludwig (1837), *Demeter Und Persephone: Ein Cyclus Mythologischer Untersuchungen* (Gotha: Justus Perthes Verlag).

Price, Simon (1999), *Religions of the Ancient Greeks* (Cambridge: Cambridge University Press).

Privitera, G Aurelio (1965), *Laso Di Ermione* (Rome: Edizione Dell'Ateneo).

Prückner, Helmut (1968), *Die Lokrischen Tonreliefs: Beitrag Zur Kultgeschichte Von Lokroi Epizephyrioi* (Mainz am Rhein: Verlag Philipp von Zabern).

Pulleyn, Simon (1997), *Prayer in Greek Religion* (Oxford: Clarendon Press).

Quagliati, Q. (1908), 'Rilievi Votivi Arcaici in Terracotta Di Lokroi Epizephyrioi', *Ausonia*, 3, 136–234.

Redfield, James M. (2003a), 'Initiations and Initiatory Experience', in David B. Dodd and Christopher A. Farone (eds.), *Initiation in Ancient Greek Rituals and Narratives: New Critical Perspectives* (London: Routledge), 255–259.

Redfield, James M. (2003b), *The Locrian Maidens: Love and Death in Greek Italy* (Princeton: Princeton University Press).

Rehm, Rush (1994), *Marriage to Death: The Conflation of Wedding and Funeral Rituals in Greek Tragedy* (Princeton: Princeton University Press).

Richardson, NJ (1974), *The Homeric Hymn to Demeter* (Oxford: Clarendon Press).

Richter, GMA (1949), *Archaic Greek Art against Its Historical Background* (New York: Oxford University Press).

Riess, Werner (2012), *Performing Interpersonal Violence: Court, Curse, and Comedy in Fourth-Century BCE Athens* (Berlin: De Gruyter).

Riley, Michael W. (2005), *Plato's Cratylus: Argument, Form, and Structure* (Amsterdam: Rodopi).

Robertson, Noel (1993), 'Athens' Festival of the New Wine', *Harvard Studies in Classical Philology*, 95, 197–250.

Robertson, Noel (2010), *Religion and Reconciliation in Greek Cities: The Sacred Laws of Selinus and Cyrene* (Oxford: Oxford University Press).

Rose, H. J. (1936), 'The Ancient Grief: A Study in Pindar, Fr. 133 (Bergk)', in Cyril Bailey, E.A. Barber, C.M. Bowra, J.D. Denniston and D.L. Page (eds.) *Greek Poetry and Life: Essays Presented to Gilbert Murray* (Oxford: Clarendon Press).

Rose, J. L. (1952), 'The Problem of the Second Burial in Sophocles' Antigone', *The Classical Journal*, 47, 219–221.

Ruscillo, Deborah (2013), 'Thesmophoriazousai: Mytilenean Women and Their Secret Rite', in Gunnel Ekroth and Jenny Wallensten (eds.), *Bones, Behaviour and Belief: The Zooarchaeological Evidence as a Source for Ritual Practice in Ancient Greece and Beyond* (Stockholm: Svenska Institutet i Athen), 181–196.

Schachter, Albert (1986), *Cults of Boiotia: 2. Herakles to Poseidon* (Bulletin of the Institute of Classical Studies Supplements, London: University of London, Institute of Classical Studies).

Schachter, Albert (2000), 'Greek Deities: Local and Panhellenic Identities', in Pernille Flensted-Jensen (ed.), *Further Studies in the Ancient Greek Polis* (Stuttgart: Franz Steiner Verlag), 9–18.

Scheurleer, CWL (1932), 'Die Göttin Bendis in Tarent', *Archäologischer Anzeiger*, 47, 314–334.

Schleiser, Renate (1991), 'Olympian versus Chthonian Religion', *Scripta Classica Israelica*, 11, 38–51.

Schleiser, Renate (1997), 'Chthonische Götter', in Hubert Cancik and Helmuth Schneider (eds.) *Der Neue Pauly 2* (Stuttgard: Verlag J.B. Metzler), 1185–1190.

Scott, Michael (2010), *Delphi and Olympia: The Spatial Politics of Panhellenism in the Archaic and Classical Periods* (Cambridge: Cambridge University Press).

Scullion, Scott (1994), 'Olympian and Chthonian', *Classical Antiquity*, 13 (1), 75–119.

Scullion, Scott (2000), 'Heroic and Chthonian Sacrifice: New Evidence from Selinous', *Zeitschrift Für Papyrologie Und Epigraphik*, 132, 163–171.

Scullion, Scott (2008), 'Tragedy and Religion: The Problem of Origins', in Justina Gregory (ed.), *A Companion to Greek Tragedy* (Malden: Blackwell), 23–27.

Sevinç, Nurten (1996), 'A New Sarcophagus of Polyxena from the Salvage Excavations at Gümüşçay', *Studia Troica*, 6 (1996), 251–264.

Sewell, William H. (1999), 'The concept(s) of Culture', in Victoria E. Bonnell and Lynn Hunt (eds.), *Beyond the Cultural Turn: New Directions in the Study of Society and Culture* (Berkeley: University of California Press), 35–61.

Sfameni Gasparro, Giulia (1986), *Misteri E Culti Mistici Di Demetra* (Rome: L'Erma di Bretschneider).

Shapiro, H. A. (1993), *Personifications in Greek Art: The Representation of Abstract Concepts 600-400 B.C* (Akanthus: Verlag für Archäologie).

Shelmerdine, Susan C. (1995), *The Homeric Hymns* (Newburyport: Focus Classical Library).

Siebert, G. (1990), 'Hermes', *LIMC*, 5, 5.1-285-387; 5.2 198–283.

Simon, Erika (1983), *Festivals of Attica: An Archaeological Commentary* (Madison: The University of Wisconsin Press).

Slavitt, David R. (1998), *Aeschylus, 1: The Oresteia* (Philadelphia: University of Pennsylvania Press).

Snodgrass, Anthony (1980), *Archaic Greece: The Age of Experiment* (London: J.M Dent & Sons Ltd.).

Sourvinou-Inwood, Christiane (1973), 'The Young Abductor of the Locrian Pinakes', *Bulletin of the Institute of Classical Studies*, 20, 12–21.

Sourvinou-Inwood, Christiane (1978), 'Persephone and Aphrodite at Locri: A Model for Personality Definitions in Greek Religion', *The Journal of Hellenic Studies*, 98, 101–121.

Sourvinou-Inwood, Christiane (1981), 'To Die and Enter the House of Hades: Homer, before and After', in J. Whaley (ed.), *Mirrors of Mortality: Studies in the Social History of Death* (London: Europa Publishers), 15–39.

Sourvinou-Inwood, Christiane (1991), *'reading' Greek Culture: Texts and Images, Rituals and Myths* (Oxford: Clarendon Press).

Sourvinou-Inwood, Christiane (1995), *'reading' Greek Death: To the End of the Classical Period* (Oxford: Clarendon Press).

Sourvinou-Inwood, Christiane (2000a), 'What Is Polis Religion?', in Richard Buxton (ed.), *Oxford Readings in Greek Religion* (Oxford: Oxford University Press), 1–37.

Sourvinou-Inwood, Christiane (2000b), 'Further Aspects of Polis Religion', in Richard Buxton (ed.), *Oxford Readings in Greek Religion* (Oxford: Oxford University Press), 38–55.

Spivey, Nigel (2018), *The Sarpedon Krater* (Chicago: University of Chicago Press).

Stafford, Emma (2000), *Worshiping Virtues: Personification and the Divine in Ancient Greece* (London: Duckworth and The Classical Press of Wales).

Steiner, G. (1971), 'Die Unterwelts-beschwörung Des Odysseus in Lichte Nethitischer Texte', *Ugarit-Forschungen*.

Stevens, Susan T. (1991), 'Charon's Obol and Other Coins in Ancient Funerary Practice', *Phoenix*, 45 (3), 215–229.

Stewart, Andrew F. (1997), *Art, Desire, and the Body in Ancient Greece* (Cambridge: Cambridge University Press).

Taplin, Oliver (1977), *The Stagecraft of Aeschylus: The Dramatic Use of Exits and Entrances in Greek Tragedy* (Oxford: Clarendon Press).

Thompson, George (1966), *The Oresteia of Aeschylus*, vol. 2 (Amsterdam: Adolf M. Hakkert).

Tsagarakis, Odysseus (2000), *Studies in Odyssey 11* (Stuttgart: Franz Steiner Verlag).

Tzanetou, Angeliki (1999), "almost Dying, Dying Twice: Ritual and Audience in Euripides' "Iphigenia in tauris"', *Illinois Classical Studies*, 24/25, 199–216.

Ustinova, Yulia (2009), *Caves and the Ancient Greek Mind: Descending Underground in the Search for Ultimate Truth* (Oxford: Oxford University Press).

van Gennep, Arnold (1960), *The Rites of Passage*, ed. G. L. Caggee, trans. M. B. Vizedom (London: Routledge).

van Straten, F. T. (1995), *Hiera Kala: Images of Animal Sacrifice in Archaic and Classical Greece* (Leiden: Brill).

Ventris, Michael and John Chadwick (1973), *Documents in Mycenaean Greek* (2nd edn., Cambridge: Cambridge University Press).

Verbanck, Piérard (1989), 'Le Double Culte d'Héraklès: Légende Ou Réalit?', in A. F. Laurens (ed.), *Entre Hommes Et Dieux. Le Convive, Le Héros, Le Prophète* (Paris: Presses Univ. Franche-Comté), 43–65.

Vermeule, Emily (1979), *Aspects of Death in Early Greek Art and Poetry* (Berkeley: University of California Press).

Vernant, Jean-Pierre (1991), 'A "Beautiful death" and the Disfigured Corpse in Homeric Epic', in Froma I. Zeitlin (ed.), *Mortals and Immortals* (Princeton: Princeton University Press), 50–74.

Versnel, Henk S. (1990), 'What's Sauce for the Goose Is Sauce for the Gander: Myth and Ritual, Old and New', in Lowell Edmunds (ed.), *Approaches to Greek Myth* (Baltimore: Johns Hopkins University Press), 25–90.

Versnel, Henk S. (1993), *Inconsistencies in Greek and Roman Religions II: Transition and Reversal in Myth and Ritual* (Leiden: Brill).

Versnel, Henk S. (2011), *Coping with the Gods: Wayward Readings in Greek Theology* (Leiden: Brill).

Vidal-Naquet, Pierre (1986), *The Black-Hunter: Forms of Thought and Forms of Society in the Greek World* (trans. Andrew Szegedy-Maszak, Baltimore: The Johns Hopkins University Press).

von Reden, Sitta and Simon Goldhill (1999), 'Plato and the Performance of Dialogue', in Simon Goldhill and Robin Osborne (eds.), *Performance Culture and Athenian Democracy* (Cambridge andNew York: Cambridge University Press), 257–291.

Von Wilamowitz-Moellendorff, Ulrich (1932), *Der Glaube Der Hellenen*, vol. II (Berlin: Weidmannsche Buchhandlung).

Wachter, Rudolf (2006), *Kratylos*, 51, 139–144.

Weir Smyth, Herbert (1930), *Aeschylus. 2, Agamemnon, Libation Bearers, Eumenides, Fragments* (Loeb Classical Library, Cambridge, Mass.: Harvard University Press).

White, Donald and Joyce Renyolds (2012), *The Sanctuary's Imperial Architectural Development, Conflict with Christianity, and Final Days*, ed. Donald White, The Extramural Eanctuary of Demeter and Persephone at Cyrene, Libya Final Reports (Philadelphia: University of Pennsylvania Museum of Archaeology and Anthropology).

Whittaker, Helène (2004), 'Board Games and Funeral Symbolism in Greek and Roman Contexts', in S. Des Bouvrie (ed.), *Myth and Symbol II: Symbolic Phenomena in Ancient Greek Culture* (Bergen: Paul Åströms Förlag), 279–302.

Wünsch, R (1897), *Defixionum Tabellae Atticae* (Berlin: Georgium Reimerum).

Yavis, Constantine G. (1949), *Greek Altars: Origins and Typology* (Saint Louis: Saint Louis University Press).

Zancani Montuoro, Paola (1955), *Il Rapitore Di Kore Ne Mito Locrese* (Rendiconti Dell'Accademia di Archeologia Lettere e Belle Arti Di Napoli; Napoli: L'Arte Tipographica).

Zuntz, Günther (1971), *Persephone: Three Essays on Religion and Thought in Magna Graecia* (Oxford: Clarendon Press).

Index